THE SPECTACLE OF U.S. SENATE CAMPAIGNS

THE SPECTACLE OF
U.S. SENATE CAMPAIGNS

Kim Fridkin Kahn

and

Patrick J. Kenney

PRINCETON UNIVERSITY PRESS   PRINCETON, NEW JERSEY

Library of Congress Cataloging-in-Publication Data
Kahn, Kim Fridkin.
    The spectacle of U.S. Senate campaigns / Kim Fridkin Kahn and
Patrick J. Kenney.
       p.   cm.
    Includes bibliographical references and index.
    ISBN 0-691-00504-4 (cl. :alk. paper). — ISBN 0-691-00505-2 (pbk.
: alk. paper)
    1. Electioneering—United States. 2. Elections—United States.
3. United States. Congress. Senate—Elections. 4. United States—
Politics and government—1989– I. Kenney, Patrick J. II. Title.
III. Title: Spectacle of US Senate campaigns.
JK2281.K24   1999
324.7′0973—dc21   98-32011

This book has been composed in Times Roman

The paper used in this publication meets the minimum requirements of
ANSI/NISO Z39.48-1992 (R1997) (*Permanence of Paper*)

http://pup.princeton.edu

Printed in the United States of America

10 9 8 7 6 5 4 3 2 1

10 9 8 7 6 5 4 3 2 1
(Pbk.)

For Jim, Jennifer, and Melissa
and
Sally, Jessica, Sean, Michael, and Mary

Contents

List of Figures

List of Tables _____

Acknowledgments

WE DO NOT know exactly when this book began. To be sure, it was long ago. The beginnings are most likely rooted in conversations with Warren E. Miller and a paper we prepared for the Hoover Conference on Senate Elections at Stanford University in November 1991. Warren encouraged us to investigate the general question of how campaigns influence the attitudes and behaviors of voters, and the conference at Stanford piqued our interest in senatorial campaigns. Warren knew full well that it would take years to measure the information generated by a sizable number of campaigns. We were naive, thus wide-eyed, as we embarked on a long journey.

The project was extremely labor intensive. Thousands of newspaper articles needed to be copied and read, hundreds of candidate commercials were content analyzed, and dozens of campaign managers were interviewed. We are grateful to two groups of students who helped us accomplish these tasks over the years. First, there were the graduate students at Arizona State University who, most likely in their view, were unfortunate enough to be assigned to us as research assistants. They worked diligently and thoroughly at gathering data. We are especially grateful to Lisa Marie Centeno, Cooper Drury, Ann Gordon, Mike Morrell, Mark Schafer, and Melanie Taylor. Second, there were the undergraduates who worked with us as part of the Junior Fellows program at ASU and were a tremendous help to us; they were conscientious, innovative, and a joy to work with. Because the National Science Foundation looked favorably on our grant proposal (SBR-9308421), we were able to hire Jerry Duff and Gregg Stelmach as our research assistants for a year. Without their efforts, the massive data collection would never have come to an end. In addition, we secured a series of smaller grants from Arizona State University that helped pay for numerous expenses associated with the project.

Over the years, we presented some of our ideas and portions of our evidence to various meetings of the American Political Science Association, to an impressive array of congressional scholars at Stanford, and to our gracious colleagues at the University of Arizona. On all of these occasions we received helpful suggestions, intriguing questions, and thoughtful criticisms. It was at the Stanford conference that John Ferejohn and Doug Rivers encouraged us to explore the interconnections among the candidates, the news media, and the voters.

Several colleagues read all or part of the manuscript over the last couple of years. We have incorporated a host of their suggestions into this book. We are happy to acknowledge the assistance of friends at Arizona State University: Jack Crittenden, Ken Goldstein, Richard Herrera, Warren E. Miller, Peter McDonough, Chris Nevitt, Lisa Reynolds, and Avital Simhony. We owe a large debt to Warren E. Miller. He read our NSF proposal and every chapter of the manuscript several times. We also sought help across the country. Several scholars virtually dropped whatever they were doing to read the manuscript. These include Richard Fenno, Paul Herrnson, John Hibbing, and Tom Rice. Tom Mann and Gary Jacobson generously provided assistance with our NSF proposal. On more than one occasion we picked up the telephone and asked for methodological advice from Larry Bartels and Doug Rivers.

We are pleased to be associated with Princeton University Press. In the fall of 1997 we were fortunate to meet our editor, Malcolm Litchfield. Malcolm was supportive of our manuscript from the very beginning. He guided us through the publication process with grace and efficiency. He has answered patiently dozens of questions. Back in Arizona, we have our own copy editor, Pat Crittenden, and we do not send any of our work to anyone until she has edited every page. She edited the entire manuscript, some sections more than once, fixing not only errors but making passages more readable.

The book is dedicated to our families. Kim began the project with no children and ends it with two girls, Jennifer and Melissa. Pat began the project with three children, Jessica, Sean, and Michael, and added Mary somewhere along the way. Our respective spouses, Jim and Sally, however, remained the same. For all of their support, patience, and most importantly, encouragement, we are truly grateful. Despite these many debts, we remain responsible for the analyses and interpretations presented in this book.

Part One —————————————

UNDERSTANDING AND MEASURING
CAMPAIGNS

One

The Nature of Political Campaigns

IN THE FALL of 1990, most Americans watched intently and anxiously as George Bush prepared to send the nation to war in the Persian Gulf. The citizens of Minnesota, however, were treated to a political respite in the form of an engaging senatorial campaign between incumbent Republican Rudy Boschwitz and challenger Paul Wellstone. When the campaign began, Boschwitz, first elected in 1978, was well known, well liked, well heeled, and well respected by Minnesotans. By the end of the campaign, Minnesota voters had decided to retire Boschwitz from the U.S. Senate. The turn of events leading to Boschwitz's defeat illustrates the importance of campaigns and how the actions and reactions among the candidates, the media, and the voters determine electoral fortunes.

In mid-September, the senatorial campaign in Minnesota resembled a typical election involving a popular incumbent with plenty of resources facing an unknown challenger. The first polls taken after Wellstone won the Democratic primary on September 11 revealed that Boschwitz led by approximately 20 points. Wellstone had expended his resources to win the primary, and media coverage of the campaign was sparse because press attention was focused on the state's highly competitive gubernatorial campaign.

Boschwitz's first communication with voters, even before he knew who his opponent would be, was a set of ads reminding voters of his family's escape from Nazi Germany, his experience in the Senate, and his service to Minnesota. After the primary, Boschwitz launched a second round of ads that was aimed at telling voters about his positive personal traits, how he is "warm [and] sympathetic," especially on issues such as child care (Alger, 1996). The ads were uniformly positive and there were no mentions of Wellstone.

Wellstone, in the meantime, was laboring in virtual obscurity. The Minneapolis *Star Tribune*, the largest circulating paper in the state, mentioned Wellstone's name in only thirty-eight paragraphs in the entire month of September, including articles describing his victory in the primary election. Wellstone's response was to produce a set of unconventional and critical commercials stressing the size of Boschwitz's campaign war chest (i.e., Boschwitz spent $6.2 million compared to Wellstone's $1.3 million), his links to large money contributors, his unwillingness to debate the issues, and his voting record on issues such as welfare and the environment. The ads were full of negative messages, but they were presented in a "breezy, lighthearted way" (Alger, 1996: 81).

For example, Wellstone's "Faces" advertisement began with a picture of Boschwitz and a Wellstone voice-over saying, "You'll be seeing this face on TV a lot. It belongs to Sen. Rudy Boschwitz who's got 6 million dollars to spend on commercials." A picture of Wellstone is then shown with Wellstone saying, "This is a face you won't be seeing as much on TV. It's my face. I'm Paul Wellstone, and unlike Mr. Boschwitz, I didn't take money from out-of-state special interests." As the picture of Boschwitz reappears, Wellstone says, "So when you get tired of seeing this face, just imagine the face of someone [Boschwitz's face transforming into Wellstone's face] who is better prepared and in a better position to represent your interests." Wellstone then adds, "Not to mention, better looking" (Alger, 1996). The immediate impact of these unusual and effective ads was to frustrate Boschwitz, stimulate voter interest in Wellstone's campaign, and, most important, attract much-needed media attention.

In fact, as early as October 4, the *Star Tribune* ran an article on the first page of the Metro/State section that claimed one of Wellstone's ads was "the zaniest TV ad of Minnesota's political season." On October 11, a headline on the first page of the *Star Tribune's* Metro/State section heralded "TV Ads Generating Recognition, Respect for Paul Wellstone." The article went on to quote extensively from the advertisement and noted that "the commercials are getting so much attention that some of the top Boschwitz aides are upset." The ads became known as "must see" ads for both journalists and citizens alike. Local television stations replayed some of the commercials during their broadcasts, and national news programs commented on Wellstone's unusual approach to political advertising.

Polls began to detect a narrowing of the race. A poll reported in mid-October showed Wellstone had closed the lead to 15 points. Then, in dramatic fashion, a poll reported on the front page of the *Star Tribune* on October 24 that Boschwitz's lead had narrowed to only 3 points. By this time, the media, although still monitoring a negative, competitive, and sordid gubernatorial campaign, began focusing much more attention on the senatorial contest.[1] In the first fifteen days of October, Wellstone's coverage in the *Star Tribune* nearly tripled over that of the entire month of September. And, in the last ten days of the campaign, media attention in the paper tripled once again, with nearly three hundred paragraphs devoted to Wellstone and his "come from behind" campaign. Wellstone's finances improved dramatically with the positive and prevalent media reports. He raised $400,000 in the last week of October, allowing him to run his now popular ads more frequently.

Boschwitz responded by running a series of five attack ads during the final

---

[1] The gubernatorial campaign was fiercely negative and filled with allegations about the challenger's personal conduct during his marriage and divorce. With only a few weeks to go in the campaign, the challenger quit the race when rumors of a protracted extramarital affair surfaced. His replacement went on to defeat the incumbent in an extremely close battle.

two weeks of the campaign. In these ads Boschwitz characterized Wellstone as a "big-spending liberal." The harsh characterization of Wellstone seemed to work. A poll reported in the *Star Tribune* on the Sunday before the election showed Boschwitz had regained the lead by 9 points.

Nevertheless, concerned about the volatility of the polls, Boschwitz blitzed the airwaves with negative advertisements during the final weekend of the campaign. In addition, he attempted a negative and bizarre communication aimed at Jewish voters during this same period. A letter was sent to them stressing that Wellstone, although Jewish, was married to a non-Jew and had "raised his children as non-Jews." On Sunday, November 4, and Monday the 5th, a series of criticisms aimed both at the letter and at Boschwitz's final advertising blitz appeared in local newspapers. Even the respected Walter Mondale, who had played a minor role during the campaign, criticized Boschwitz's tactics in an article appearing in the *Star Tribune* the day before the election. The former vice-president accused Boschwitz of "a relentless, brutal, heavily financed, and in my judgment, untruthful television assault" unheard of in Minnesota history. The next day Wellstone garnered 50 percent of the vote, defeating Boschwitz by two percentage points.

Although it was more dramatic than most, this race illustrates the complex interactions among candidates, the media, and the voters. During the course of the campaign, it appears that Wellstone's and Boschwitz's actions influenced the media's presentation of the campaign and voters' preferences. In addition, the candidates modified their initial strategies based on polling reports and patterns of press coverage. In the end, most people close to the campaign believed that the combination of the candidates' messages and the news media's portrayal of the race had a profound impact on the final vote tally (Alger, 1996).

This example raises questions about the nature and dynamics of political campaigns. What type of candidate messages captivate the interest of typically jaded reporters and normally distracted citizens? What political conditions conspire to lead candidates to attack their opponents? How does the media coverage of the race motivate candidates to alter their campaign strategies? How do the media present the content of the candidates' messages to potential voters? Do the media focus on issues, or candidate traits, or polling numbers? What role does competition play in shaping the content of candidates' messages and the substance of campaign coverage? How do voters react to a stream of negative messages from candidates?

Our goal in this book is to increase the public's understanding of political campaigns by examining the population of U.S. Senate races contested between 1988 and 1992. Senate elections present an optimal setting for the study of campaigns because they provide impressive variance in campaign strategy, campaign spending, media coverage, and voter reactions (Abramowitz and Segal, 1992; Franklin, 1991; Krasno, 1994; Westlye, 1991). Unlike House races, which are usually low-key affairs, and presidential races, which are often hard-fought contests, campaigns for the U.S. Senate vary considerably in their competitiveness.

In our explorations, we examined the details of the candidates' strategies and messages, the content, tone, and bias of the media coverage, and the attitudes and behaviors of potential voters. We discovered that competition is the driving force in American electoral politics. More than anything else, competition shapes, conditions, and colors the behavior of candidates, the reporting of the press, and the citizens' evaluations of competing candidates. Without competition, campaigns are nothing more than self-aggrandizing exercises by incumbents. Their communications with voters are well-rehearsed scripts recounting their successes as legislators. There is little, if any, discussion of public policy. In addition, when competition is scarce, the media look to other political campaigns and events to report to voters. The press simply ignores noncompetitive campaigns. There are few headlines, virtually no front-page articles, and precious little actual reporting about these low-key campaigns. The ultimate losers in these noncompetitive settings are the voters. Citizens witnessing these campaigns are presented with almost no political information, debate, and discussion on which to evaluate candidates before Election Day.

Competitive elections, in contrast, are characterized by political debates, critiques, and discourse over the issues facing the nation and the leadership qualities of those candidates seeking office. Voters are presented with numerous reasons to vote for one candidate over another. These reasons are plentiful in the candidates' advertisements as well as in the local press. Candidates talk about contemporary issues, they take stands on the issues, and they present comparisons with their opponents. The news media dedicate significantly more resources to the coverage of close races. In competitive campaigns, reporters and editors evaluate the candidates' stands on the issues, they critique politicians' careers, and they analyze their political ads.

Most importantly, voters respond to their political environment. The data and analyses presented in this book clearly demonstrate that "campaigns matter." The activities of the candidates and the media make campaigns more or less competitive. Voters' attitudes about politicians are not fixed and beyond the control of candidates. Polls change in response to the events of campaigns. While campaigns for noncompetitive seats may be largely symbolic, voters observing competitive campaigns listen and respond to the rhetoric of the candidates and the reporting by the local press. We show that "voters are not fools." In competitive contests, citizens are knowledgeable about the candidates and understand the central themes of the campaigns. Even more impressively, individuals adjust their decision rules depending on the closeness of the contests. As campaigns become more competitive, voters respond by relying more heavily on sophisticated criteria, such as ideology and issues, when evaluating the opposing candidates.

In the end, we feel confident concluding that competitive campaigns are an essential element of American democracy. They enliven and enrich people's political life. They empower voters with information to make choices about their representatives.

The Importance of Campaigns

In the United States, elections are the cornerstone of our representative democracy. Through elections, voters determine who is to hold political power and for how long. For the better part of two centuries, norms, practice, and tradition have dictated that political campaigns precede elections in the United States.[2] Campaigns enrich the political process in several important ways. They provide a formal period of time when political parties and politicians introduce themselves to potential voters. During campaigns, competing candidates and the political parties they represent have the opportunity to discuss matters of public policy for a sustained period of time. Campaigns also afford candidates an occasion to highlight their personal qualifications for office, such as their leadership ability, integrity, competence, and compassion. Candidates disseminate their messages to large numbers of voters by distributing campaign brochures, delivering speeches, airing advertisements on television and radio, and orchestrating fund-raisers and political rallies. This concentrated and sometimes intense political campaigning has the potential to provide voters with the information necessary to make informed decisions at the ballot box.

Beyond simply introducing candidates to voters, campaigns provide an avenue for widespread political discussion. No other forum produces political discourse that is as readily accessible to millions of American citizens as political campaigns. An extensive and ongoing political dialogue is often regarded as a key component of a healthy and functioning democracy. As John Stuart Mill (1951: 27) explains in his essay "On Liberty": "There must be discussion, to show how experience is to be interpreted. Wrong opinions and practices gradually yield to fact and argument: but facts and arguments, to produce any effect on the mind, must be brought before it. Very few facts are able to tell their own story, without comment to bring out their meaning." In today's political campaigns, the commentary employed by candidates to animate "factual" discussion is pervasive, presented in deftly

---

[2] Campaigns for senatorial elections began after the passage of the Seventeenth Amendment in 1913. This amendment established that U.S. senators would be selected by direct elections rather than chosen by state legislatures.

designed pamphlets, cleverly crafted commercials, and carefully worded speeches. In addition, local and national news media outlets routinely present the "facts of the matter" concerning the campaign in newspaper and magazine articles, during televised news programs, and on the radio.

More broadly still, in his work *Considerations on Representative Government*, Mill (1991: 321) argues that political discussion enlivens a sense of political community among a disparate citizenry.

> It is by political discussion that the manual labourer, whose employment is a routine, and whose way of life brings him in contact with no variety of impressions, circumstances, or ideas, is taught that remote causes, and events which take place far off, have a most sensible effect even on his personal interests; and it is from political discussion, and collective political action, that one whose daily occupations concentrate his interests in a small circle round himself, learns to feel for and with his fellow citizens, and becomes consciously a member of a greater community.

To be sure, empirical research has demonstrated that the style and tone of political discussion during campaigns affect the likelihood that citizens will participate in their political community by voting. If candidates present interesting ideas that pertain directly to topics that are salient to people's lives, then turnout increases (Ragsdale and Rusk, 1995; Caldeira, Patterson, and Markko, 1985). On the other hand, if the outcome of the election is virtually certain, with little engaging discussion between competing candidates, or worse, if the political discussion is harsh, strident, and unduly negative, then voter participation tends to decline (Ansolabehere and Iyengar, 1995; Filer et al., 1993).

Scholars have also demonstrated that campaigns directly influence the amount and type of political discussion in the United States (Kinder and Sanders, 1996; Zaller, 1992; Page, 1978). Recently, for example, Kinder and Sanders (1996) have shown how presidential campaigns can generate or discourage discussion of racial issues in America, easily the most complicated, emotional, poignant, and divisive issue in our nation's history. Kinder and Sanders explain that the 1988 presidential campaign made clear the links between race and crime generating a national discussion by candidates Bush and Dukakis explicitly on crime, and implicitly on race. In 1992, in contrast, there was virtually no debate on these issues. Instead, the attention of the candidates and the media focused squarely on the economy, drifting occasionally toward health care and welfare reform. Kinder and Sanders note that politicians can use campaigns to generate a political dialogue on important policy matters, if they so choose. They are cautiously hopeful that campaigns can provide a forum for producing solutions to even the most intractable problems. They conclude that "democratic politics could be the place where we learn a language of mutual respect and begin to work out our differences" (Kinder and Sanders, 1996: 289).

Finally, campaigns provide connections between citizens and their government, forming the foundations of a representative democracy. James Madison (1964: 119–120) theorized in *Federalist 49* about the tightly woven links between members of the legislature and the represented. He wrote: "The members of the legislative department, on the other hand, are numerous. They are distributed and dwell among the people at large. Their connections of blood, of friendship, and of acquaintance, embrace a great proportion of the most influential part of the society. The nature of their public trust implies a personal weight with the people, and that they are more immediately the confidential guardians of their rights and liberties."

Two hundred years later, Richard Fenno has marshaled evidence wholeheartedly reaffirming Madison's thoughts. Fenno (1996, 1978) has followed closely "the members of the legislative department," representatives and senators, in their political environments and has seen firsthand the important role campaigns play when it comes to connecting the representatives with the represented. He summarizes (1996: 74–75):

> Campaigns help to establish, maintain, and test the connections between politicians and citizens—connections that constitute the very core of a representational relationship. It is through a campaign that a candidate is introduced to the electorate. It is through a campaign that a candidate locates and builds a constituency. It is through the interpretation of a campaign that the winning candidate derives some of the impulses, interests, and instructions that shape his or her subsequent behavior as a legislator. It is through a campaign that a legislator explains his or her legislative activity to the citizenry. And it is through a campaign that a legislator's contract is renewed or rejected. In all these ways, campaigns connect politicians and citizens and make possible the accountability of politicians to citizens that representative government requires. In short, no campaigns, no connections; no connections, no accountability; no accountability, no representative government.

Campaigns are the "heart and soul" of a representative democracy. One is not possible without the other. To explore the nature of campaigns is to broaden our understanding of how representative democracies function and prosper. In a world currently enamored with new and emerging democracies, it is important to examine the role of campaigns in the most enduring representative democracy in the world.

The Nature of Campaigns

Campaigns are a dynamic process where the actions of the candidates, the news media, and the public are indelibly linked. As figure 1.1 indicates, we

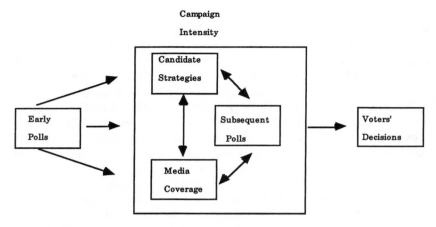

Figure 1.1 The dynamics of political campaigns.

believe that voters' preferences, measured early in the campaign, are the primary catalyst affecting candidate strategies and media coverage at the outset of campaigns. These early polls reflect the relative experience, qualifications, and appeal of the candidates competing in the general election.[3] Furthermore, these polls provide politicians, reporters, editors, and voters with a clear indication of the likely competitiveness of the fall campaign. We argue that early poll results set in motion a series of interactions among candidates, campaign managers, editors, and reporters that inform and shape the attitudes of voters. The interplay of these forces forges a dynamic reciprocal process where poll results, candidate strategies, and media coverage are causally interdependent.

The culmination of the interplay among the candidates, the media, and the polls determines the intensity of the campaign. As the intensity of the campaign changes, so do the quality and quantity of information presented by the candidates and the media. Furthermore, the intensity of the race affects the amount of attention citizens devote to the campaign. By influencing the quality of the political dialogue and people's interest, the intensity of the campaign affects how people make decisions at the ballot box. We turn now to a detailed discussion of the causal interplay among candidates, journalists, and citizens.

[3] The quality of the opponents, and their relative support in preelection polls, are affected by the political characteristics of the state (e.g., the partisan makeup of the state, the size of the pool of potential candidates), the national political climate (e.g., the health of the nation's economy, the popularity of the president), and the characteristics of the incumbent (e.g., the seniority of the senator, the hint of a scandal, the size of the incumbent's victory in the previous election) (Abramowitz and Segal, 1992; Fowler, 1993; Jacobson and Kernell, 1983; Krasno, 1994; Squire, 1989; Stewart, 1989).

Understanding the Candidates' Choice of Campaign Strategy

At the outset of a campaign, candidates, in concert with their campaign managers and political advisers, develop a campaign strategy to ensure their election. Scholars have spent a great deal of time discussing the merits of various strategies for presidential candidates. One classic strategy for candidates is to appear ambiguous on matters of public policy. Shepsle (1972) provides theoretical reasons for such a strategy. He contends that candidates will actually increase their chances of victory if their positions on issues are unclear. His so-called lottery theory argues that candidates have little to gain by offering voters clear positions on issues. Unambiguous issue positions inevitably draw considerable criticism from elements of the media, politicians, interest groups, and opponents. Most important, clearly articulated positions on issues may resonate with only a minority of voters, thereby sending the majority of voters to seek refuge with the opponent.

Although ambiguity on the issues is a popular strategy for many candidates, there is a competing perspective that warns against too much obfuscation. Research and common sense suggest that voters are unlikely to support a candidate whom they know nothing about (Enelow and Hinich, 1981; Bartels, 1986). Nevertheless, since taking a clear position carries the risk of alienating voters with alternative views, candidates need to choose an optimal position on the issues.

The most obvious position for candidates to take is one that mirrors the beliefs of most voters—the celebrated "median voter" position (Downs, 1957). However, locating the "median voter" is easier said than done, even in the era of modern polling techniques. Public opinion may be evenly split on an issue (Page and Shapiro, 1992), or voters may not know where they stand on a particular issue, or worse for candidates, voters may change their position over time (Converse, 1964; Markus and Converse, 1979; Zaller, 1992). Consequently, some scholars believe that candidates should take positions on issues that will generate support from specific party or group-based coalitions (Rabinowitz and MacDonald, 1989; Page, 1978). This argument is based on the premise that candidates are likely to form winning coalitions among like-minded groups holding similar positions on matters of public policy.

Page (1978) has articulated another strategy for candidates to employ when constructing their messages for voters. In his "emphasis allocation theory," Page reasons that candidates need to develop issue priorities around topics with widespread consensus among voters (e.g., clean air and water, an educated society, a growing economy), while purposely avoiding specific positions on issues. He too argues that clear position taking will potentially irritate large segments of the electorate. In addition, the articulation of specific issue stands is too costly for candidates in terms of time and resources. The budgeting of time and resources is important for candidates because money, media coverage, and especially voter attention are at a premium during campaigns.

Explaining Candidate Strategies: The Impact of Competition

Scholars have moved us a long way toward understanding why candidates pursue specific strategies in presidential elections. However, in developing these explanations, scholars have typically assumed that elections are competitive. This assumption is empirically correct in presidential campaigns. Even in the most lopsided presidential elections in this century (i.e., Johnson's defeat of Goldwater in 1964 and Nixon's drubbing of McGovern in 1972), a 10 percent swing by the electorate would have made the race too close to call. Hubert Humphrey's dramatic comeback in 1968 or Reagan's late surge in 1980 are reminders that presidential elections are not over until the ballots are counted. This is not always the case in nonpresidential elections. As discussed above, competition in Senate elections varies significantly. Additional theorizing is needed to account for the development of candidate strategies under differing conditions of competition.

We propose that candidates weigh the results of early polls carefully when developing a campaign strategy. If polls indicate that the outcome is uncertain, then candidates need to create strategies that appeal directly to groups of constituents that have been traditionally supportive of the candidates or the candidates' party. In highly competitive campaigns, candidates may even broaden their appeals to include "swing" voters in the hopes of generating support from as many potential voters as possible. In contrast, when one candidate is leading by a large margin in early polls, then it makes less sense for candidates to develop strategies that focus attention on specific groups. Rather, candidates who are ahead generate messages that appeal broadly to the entire electoral constituency. And, candidates who are hopelessly behind focus attention on generating positive name recognition among prospective voters. An example from two senatorial elections illustrates the point.

In Nebraska, the health of the state's agricultural economy dominates the political scene. The 1988 senatorial election between incumbent David Karnes and former governor Robert Kerrey was no exception: the campaign was fundamentally about farm policy. Both candidates discussed agricultural issues at length and argued their respective views at small-town picnics, in 30-second political advertisements, in press conferences, and at the state fair.

Two years later as the winter wheat was being planted across Kansas, the largest wheat-producing state in the nation, Senator Nancy Kassebaum was seeking a third term in the U.S. Senate. However, agricultural concerns were barely mentioned during Kassebaum's campaign. Instead, the main theme of the senator's reelection campaign was "Kassebaum: A Voice You Can Trust." Her campaign was virtually devoid of any issue discussion, including farm policy. Her opponent, Dick Williams, tried to engage Kassebaum in a policy debate, but ironically not on the subject of agriculture.

The differences in campaign themes for these candidates are best understood by looking at the level of competition in these two contests. The election in Nebraska was much anticipated by Democrats and Republicans alike. An appointed and potentially vulnerable senator was pitted against a popular ex-governor. Resources were plentiful, press coverage was abundant, and, most important, preelection polls showed a horse race. Only 10 points separated the two candidates in September. Not to talk about agriculture would have been a strange strategy indeed. Such a strategy would not have gone unnoticed by the opponent, the press, financial contributors, much less by anxious farmers.

But in Kansas the political setting was different. Nancy Kassebaum, Alf Landon's daughter, had always been popular across the state. Her opponent, Dick Williams, was without resources or campaign skills borne of experience. Williams had actually lost his party's primary, placing second. In a strange turn of events, the winner of the Democratic primary withdrew from the general election campaign and Williams became the Democratic nominee. Early polls revealed that Williams trailed Kassebaum by as many as 70 points. In fact, in the last poll before the election, Williams was behind by an amazing 72 points. Kassebaum, with her lead secure, avoided the potentially controversial and contentious subject of farm policy. The slogan "Kassebaum: A voice you can trust" was based on her experience, her personality, and was inherently believable.

To be sure, scholars of nonpresidential elections have noted that the closeness of the race may be related to the strategies candidates decide to pursue. Westlye (1991) considered such a relationship when he found that the press reported more issue and ideological discussion in "intense" Senate campaigns compared to "low-key" campaigns. Kingdon (1968), examining local and statewide campaigns in Wisconsin in 1962 and 1964, found that candidates offer more specific issue positions in competitive contests than in noncompetitive ones. Goldenberg and Traugott (1984) detected a similar pattern when talking to campaign managers in House elections.[4] Yet, there has been little, if any, discussion about why this relationship exists. What are the characteristics of close races that motivated Karnes and Kerrey to discuss

---

[4] In contrast, Herrnson (1995) finds no difference in the amount of issue emphasis in political advertisements across competitive and noncompetitive House contests in 1992. And Fenno (1978) reports that some House members believe issues should be avoided altogether in competitive races.

agricultural policy? What pressures were lacking in Kassebaum's contest that allowed her to avoid talking about policies that affect wheat farmers?

One answer is that in highly competitive campaigns the number of interested and engaged activists (e.g., interest groups and financial contributors) increases because supporters of both candidates view victory as achievable. As the number of activists increases, so will the number of issues placed on the campaign agenda. Candidates will feel a greater need to address these distinct policy concerns in order to maximize their support at the polls as well as their financial contributions. Consequently, to appeal to these various constituencies, candidates in competitive races will address more issues and take clearer positions on issues than their counterparts in less competitive races.

Robert Dahl (1956: 132) noted the link between competitive elections and pressures brought by various interests in his classic work, *A Preface to Democratic Theory*: "Elections and political competition do not make for government by majorities in any very significant way, but they vastly increase the size, number, and variety of minorities whose preferences must be taken into account by leaders in making public choices."

Today, competing interests that become energized by highly competitive elections are directly represented by political action committees, or PACs, "the electoral arm of an organized interest" (Herrnson, 1995: 104). PACs capture the attention of nearly all politicians because of their ability to distribute money and provide additional campaign services (e.g., polling, campaign ads, issue research, strategic advice) to candidates. In many respects, PACs now perform many of the activities that were traditionally taken on by the political parties (Herrnson, 1995). In close races, PAC assistance may be crucial and instrumental for eventual victory; thus, candidates often reach out to various PACs representing a wide variety of potentially competing interests (e.g., business, labor, ideological). In contrast, when races are not competitive, candidates can be more selective, relying only on PACs with whom they have had established relationships over the years. In competitive races, then, candidates are much more likely to spend considerable time emphasizing issues that appeal to a wide range of interest groups, compared to the narrow set of topics that they may discuss in a low-key contest where neither the media nor the voters are paying close attention.

A second reason competition encourages more issue discussion is that competitive candidates often feel compelled to comment on the issue positions of opponents. Skilled and articulate opponents often force a debate on certain issues and demand responses on questions of public policy. If politicians fail to respond, opponents may accuse candidates of avoiding issues either in advertisements or via the local press. The end result is that the campaign becomes a forum for a wider and more detailed discussion of the issues. On the other hand, if a candidate is leading by a wide margin in the polls, then there is little reason to engage in a dialogue with the opponent on the issues, especially if the issues are controversial.

The pressures to discuss issues in competitive elections are so prevalent that the amount of issue discussion will actually supplant candidates' presentations of noncontroversial topics, such as their own experience and personality traits. Candidates enjoy cultivating a favorable personal image, and voters are skilled at assessing the personal characteristics of candidates since they make similar judgments in their everyday life. For voters, evaluating candidates on personal traits is a useful and efficient decision rule that enables them to manage the complexities of politics more easily (Kinder, 1986; Page, 1978; Popkin, 1991).

Although emphasizing personal traits tends to enhance candidates' standings with voters, candidates in close contests will have less of an opportunity to accentuate their personal qualities. Given limitations on candidate resources and voters' attention, the number of different messages candidates can disseminate is limited (Page, 1978). Therefore, candidates in competitive contests, forced into a discussion of issues, have less time to promote their personal images.

Deciding which themes to emphasize in a campaign is only one element of candidates' campaign strategies. The second component involves candidates' decisions about the tenor of their campaigns. Do candidates discuss their own proposals regarding matters of public policy without attacking their opponents' positions? The answer once again depends on how close the race is. In competitive contests, candidates often need to go beyond extolling their own virtues. In many cases, candidates cannot hope to win if they restrict their campaign messages to detailing their own policy priorities and personal qualities. These candidates cannot win by only convincing voters to support their candidacies; they need to persuade citizens not to support their opponents. Not surprisingly, the need to "go negative" is greater in close contests.

Today, negative campaigning is an important component in all presidential elections (West, 1993; Ansolabehere and Iyengar, 1995). This is not the case in Senate elections (Ansolabehere and Iyengar, 1995; Westlye, 1991). In lopsided contests, there is little reason for the leader to spend time and energy attacking an opponent who has little hope of victory. Likewise, for the candidate who is trailing badly, increasing his or her own name recognition is a top priority long before resources can be used to attack the leader. We look at two elections in Iowa to illustrate the relationship between the closeness of the election and the propensity to run a negative campaign.

In Iowa, in 1988, Republican Tom Tauke attempted to unseat incumbent Democrat Tom Harkin. The campaign was a fierce and bitter ideological battle that was unusually negative and focused on such controversial issues as abortion. Advertisements and political speeches were especially vitriolic. However, four years later, candidates campaigning for Iowa's second Senate seat barely uttered a critical word about each other during the course of the campaign. Senator Charles Grassley and Democrat Jean Lloyd-Jones refrained from attacking each other in their television commercials and as they stumped across the Hawkeye State. Instead, Senator Grassley preferred to emphasize his experience, while State Senator Lloyd-Jones focused on the need to reform the health care system.

Why were negative advertisements blitzing television sets in 1988, but not playing in people's homes during the 1992 campaign? In 1988, the polls in September showed Harkin and Tauke separated by merely 10 points. And the final poll published the last week of the election revealed that Harkin led by only 7 points. In 1992, in contrast, Grassley led by 30 points in September. Late in the campaign, the polls widened further, with Grassley enjoying a 55-point lead over Lloyd-Jones on the eve of the election.

We contend that the closeness of the race directly influences the tone of the campaign, as well as the substance of the candidates' messages. In close elections, candidates will criticize their opponents more frequently, compared to elections where early polling suggests a lopsided race. In addition, in competitive contests, candidates' messages will focus on issues, even at the expense of personal traits. Therefore, voters will witness quite different campaigns in terms of both style and substance, depending on whether polls are predicting a close race.

Explaining Candidate Strategies: The Impact of Media Coverage

Although a strong relationship exists between early polls and candidates' strategies, the behavior of the candidates and the press is also intrinsically linked. As Fenno (1996: 226) explains, "Any discussion of media-candidate relationships must begin without illusion. They need each other, the news media needs stories; the candidates need attention. So they are locked in each other's embrace." Potentially the most significant link in this relationship is the news media's ability, by coverage alone, to influence candidates' chances of acquiring resources.

Press reports about campaigns published early in the election season can increase the candidates' ability to raise money (Goldenberg and Traugott, 1984; Mutz, 1995). Many financial supporters are strategic with their money and are unlikely to support candidates who have little chance of victory (Abramowitz and Segal, 1992; Herrnson, 1995: 109–110; Stewart, 1989). Their main source of information concerning the candidates and the "horse race" is the media. A plethora of news stories about a candidate, especially articles highlighting a candidate's viability, can encourage wealthy donors to contribute generously to a candidate's campaign.[5]

Candidates who garner favorable press attention will be more capable of raising the money necessary to mount a more elaborate and effective campaign. Such campaigns will rely more heavily on television commercials, will hire talented political consultants, and will have the money necessary to conduct a series of tracking polls. Candidates who can wage more expensive campaigns, due in part to early media attention, will be able to generate subsequent news coverage of their campaigns. Well-funded candidates will be regarded by journalists as more viable, thereby enhancing media attention of their campaigns. In addition, since these well-financed candidates will run more aggressive campaigns (e.g., staging campaign events, publicizing favorable poll results, disseminating press releases), newspapers will devote more attention to them in an effort to cover their activities.

The relationship between media reports and the ability of candidates to raise money and establish their viability has been documented extensively in presidential primaries (Aldrich, 1980; Brady and Johnston, 1987; Bartels, 1988; Mutz, 1995). It makes sense that the same sort of relationship exists in Senate elections (Abramowitz and Segal, 1992; Jacobson, 1992; Herrnson, 1995). However, there has been no research investigating the connection between early media coverage and candidate spending in Senate elections.[6]

An example from the 1990 Senate election in Alabama illustrates the close connection between early media coverage, a candidate's ability to raise money, and eventual success in the polls. In 1990 Democratic senator Heflin, known fondly across Alabama as "the judge" because of his tenure as chief justice of the Alabama Supreme Court, was seeking reelection. He won easily. He garnered 61 percent of the vote in his defeat of state senator Bill Cabaniss. Cabaniss's campaign manager, reflecting on the election, lamented that their campaign simply "petered out."

Cabaniss, a wealthy Republican, had enough of his own money to jump-start his campaign. He spent nearly $400,000 in the month of September. For all of Cabaniss's efforts, however, his name appeared in only fourteen paragraphs in the last fifteen days of September in the *Birmingham News*, the largest circulating newspaper in the state. While there was virtually no sub-

[5] Individuals, groups, parties, and PACs contribute money to candidates for many reasons. For a full review, see Herrnson (1985, chapters 5 and 6).

[6] There is a growing literature about the effects of early spending on later spending, and on early spending and eventual success on Election Day (Abramowitz and Segal, 1992; Biersack et al., 1993; Jacobson, 1980; Krasno et al., 1994). And some work exists on how early incumbent spending influences the quality of the challenger (Box-Steffensmeir, 1996; Squire, 1989). However, there is no existing literature on the reciprocal relationship between spending and media coverage in either House or Senate elections.

stantive news coverage about Cabaniss in September, polls reported by the media indicated that Cabaniss trailed the judge by over 30 points.

In the crucial month of October, Cabaniss averaged fewer than five paragraphs a day in the *Birmingham News*. His spending actually decreased in October compared to September. In the first fifteen days of October he spent $283,000, and in the final ten days of the campaign he spent only $177,000. His polling numbers revealed that he trailed by approximately 30 percent throughout the month of October. Without positive media coverage, Cabannis was unable to raise money, and without the money, he was unable to carry his message to voters. Not able to communicate with voters, his chance of defeating Heflin, a long shot from the very beginning, became nil.

All the while, Senator Heflin, who spent nearly $3.5 million on his campaign, reminded voters of his experience and his influence on the Senate's Agricultural Committee. He characterized Cabaniss as a "Grey-Poupon, Gucci-clothed, Mercedes-driving, Jacuzzi-soaking, Perrier-drinking Republican." Cabaniss, with dwindling resources and virtually no free media coverage, could not counterargue the judge. The verdict was a third term for Senator Heflin.

The news media, in addition to influencing the candidates' fund-raising ability, can also affect the substance of the candidates' messages. The media can influence the campaign themes adopted by candidates because candidates recognize the powerful role the media play in campaigns. The press, for instance, can alter the public's agenda by focusing on certain issues and avoiding other topics. (e.g., Iyengar and Kinder, 1987; Krosnick and Kinder, 1990). Candidates, in an attempt to represent the public's interest, try to be responsive to the media's agenda. When issues such as the state of the economy, or the rising costs of health care, or the high incidence of crime receive extensive media attention, they become more salient to citizens. In these situations, candidates feel compelled to discuss these topics because potential voters view these issues as especially pressing.

A Senate election from 1992 illustrates how media coverage influences the main themes candidates choose to emphasize in the campaigns. The Senate race in New Hampshire in 1992 was an open race between Governor Judd Gregg and businessman John Rauh. In New Hampshire, as in many states in 1992, the economy was weak, very weak. Media coverage about the economy in New Hampshire, and across the nation, had spilled off the business pages and onto the front pages in local newspapers long before the fall elections.

Although Republicans from George Bush to Senate and House candidates feared that the stagnant economy would damage their electoral fortunes, Gregg was acutely concerned. During Gregg's four years as governor, the unemployment rate in New Hampshire had tripled. The state had lost 70,000 jobs (*Congressional Quarterly*, 1992: 3348). Media coverage in New Hampshire routinely linked the failing economy with the governor's name, either explicitly or implicitly. Gregg responded by making the economy the main theme in his campaign. He stressed fiscal restraint and tax relief as a way to improve the economy. His strategy was to address this crucial issue head-on. Media coverage about the economy was so prevalent in New Hampshire throughout 1992 that any effort to avoid the issue would have been a strategic mistake.

Thus far we have suggested why the behavior of candidates may be responsive to the closeness of the campaign and the nature of media coverage. We have seen examples of how the closeness of a campaign leads candidates to focus more extensively on policy matters and to adopt a more confrontational tone in their campaign messages. In addition, we discussed how media coverage can influence the candidates' spending patterns as well as the candidates' choice of campaign themes. Candidates, however, are not solitary actors in a political campaign responding to the polls and the press. In some circumstances, the strategies of candidates influence the actions of other campaign participants. We turn now to an examination of how the behavior of candidates and competition can shape news coverage.

Understanding News Treatment of Senate Campaigns

News organizations consider a host of factors when deciding how to cover a political campaign. Two important forces that influence media coverage are the competitiveness of the race and the actions of the candidates. Current theories explaining the operational norms of news organizations, evidence from studies examining campaign coverage, and knowledge about the folkways guiding the behavior of reporters and editors all point to the fact that news coverage of campaigns depends on the closeness of the race and the actions and rhetoric of the candidates.

Explaining Campaign Coverage: The Impact of Competition

News organizations are first and foremost profit-making businesses where economic pressures place a premium on pleasing the audience (Bennett, 1996; Graber, 1989; Sigal, 1973). Given this profit motive, news personnel try to cover political events in ways that will either maintain or enhance their audience. During elections, news personnel pay close attention to the competitive nature of each campaign (e.g., Kahn, 1996; Westlye, 1991; Bartels, 1988; Clarke and Evans, 1983; Goldenberg and Traugott, 1984; Robinson and Sheehan, 1983; Patterson, 1980). Events with uncertain outcomes, whether they are athletic contests, court cases, or political campaigns, are viewed as more dramatic, enthralling, and captivating. Put simply, competitive elections generate more press coverage because these campaigns help news organizations sell more newspapers.

However, news reporting is not solely driven by the profit motive. In addition, journalistic norms influence how reporters and editors cover news events. In particular, reporters and editors share common criteria regarding the "newsworthiness" of a story (Cook, 1996; Davis, 1996; Graber, 1989). Is it timely, is it dramatic, does it contain conflict, is it in some way unusual, is it salient to people's lives, does it involve people who are routinely in the public eye? The reliance on these norms influences coverage of political campaigns. Close elections routinely meet these criteria, while noncompetitive campaigns meet almost none of them. Therefore, journalistic norms, like the news organization's economic orientation, lead to more extensive coverage of competitive campaigns.

One of the most newsworthy Senate campaigns between 1988 and 1992 was the battle in North Carolina between Senator Jesse Helms and Mayor Harvey Gantt of Charlotte. A celebrated conservative white senator was being challenged by a popular liberal black mayor of North Carolina's largest city. The polls from Labor Day to Election Day were always too close to call. News organizations in North Carolina responded by providing heavy coverage of the race. More articles and paragraphs were written about this election by a local newspaper than any other race in the country. Well over two hundred articles appeared in the largest circulating newspaper in North Carolina, the *Raleigh News and Observer*, from early September to Election Day, averaging over three articles per day. Over three thousand paragraphs were printed about these two candidates, averaging over forty paragraphs a day.

There were a number of races between 1988 and 1992 that generated little news attention, such as Grassley and Lloyd-Jones in Iowa in 1992, Thurmond and Cunningham in South Carolina in 1990, and Sasser and Anderson in Tennessee in 1988. These noncompetitive races, which featured entrenched incumbents running against unskilled challengers, were uninteresting to readers and failed to satisfy the standard criteria of newsworthiness. Of all the races contested between 1988 and 1992, the race receiving the least amount of coverage was the 1988 contest between Senator Daniel Patrick Moynihan and attorney Robert McMillan of New York. Early polls suggested that Moynihan was leading by as many as 44 points. Late polls showed him ahead by 50 points. From September 1 to Election Day, the *Daily News* published only seventeen articles about the campaign. There was simply nothing interesting to report about the contest. In addition, polls suggested most voters knew whom they intended to support before the campaign began. Surely, there were thousands of more pressing stories in New York than Moynihan's drubbing of McMillan.

Explaining Campaign Coverage: The Impact of Candidate Strategies

If a political campaign is deemed newsworthy, then editors assign reporters to cover it. Once reporters are on the campaign trail, they rely largely on routine sources to gather news about the political contestants (Bennett, 1996; Clarke and Evans, 1983; Cook, 1996; Sigal, 1973). For example, press releases distributed by the campaigns, political advertisements aired on television and radio, news conferences, and speeches are likely to influence the frequency and content of news coverage. Local reporters often shun more enterprising efforts like initiating interviews with the candidates, engaging in library research to explore a candidate's background, or conducting investigative reports (Clarke and Evans, 1983). Given the journalists' preference for routine sources of news, the behavior of the candidates can have a significant influence on the nature of campaign coverage.

To illustrate the impact of the candidates' choice of strategies on the content of news coverage, we look at two open races contested in Washington in 1988 and 1992. While both races were highly competitive, with late polls showing fewer than 10 points separating the candidates, the eventual winners in both contests emphasized different issues, reflecting their distinct ideological positions. For instance, a main theme of former senator Slade Gorton's 1988 campaign was the need to pass legislation to "crack down" on drug use and drug trafficking. State Senator Patty Murray, in her successful 1992 bid, did not mention drugs as an issue in her major speeches or in her campaign advertisements. The *Seattle Times* coverage of the two campaigns reflects the alternative agendas of the candidates. While approximately the same number of stories was printed about each campaign (seventy-five in the 1988 race and eighty-one in the 1992 race), the drug issue received extensive coverage during Gorton's campaign (forty-eight paragraphs in the *Seattle Times* focused on drugs), and was *never* mentioned in the coverage of Murray's campaign. Since the problem of drugs did not disappear between 1988 and 1992, the difference in news emphasis probably reflects the different agendas advanced by these two candidates.

Candidates, irrespective of the content of their messages, cannot capture the media's attention without spending money. Large amounts of spending will create more campaign activity (e.g., the commissioning of polls to be released to the press, the production of new and innovative advertisements, the staging of political events), which is likely to be covered by reporters. In addition, candidates who can spend more money may be considered more competitive by the press, leading newspapers to cover their campaign messages more extensively.

While candidates' behavior on the campaign trail can influence press patterns, not all candidates are equally adept at generating news coverage. Professional norms of newsmaking as well as organizational routines may lead newspapers to devote more coverage to incumbents, especially compared to challengers. First, traditional standards of news require authoritative figures as sources, and senators are more authoritative than challengers (Cook, 1989). For instance, when a president announces a new initiative in a major speech, journalists will routinely report the incumbent senator's view of the initiative, given the candidate's status as a U.S. senator. Challengers, on the other hand, lack the professional status necessary to make their opinions anything more than electorally expedient. Second, since most news stories emanate from routine processes instigated by the newsmaker, incumbents, who have more resources than challengers, will have an easier time producing news. The perquisites of the office of U.S. senator (e.g., the availability of broadcast recording studios, an office staff capable of routinely writing and distributing press releases) make it easier for incumbents to let reporters know when they are making news.

Senators may also receive more favorable news coverage because the local media depend on them for news about Washington. Reporters' abilities to write compelling stories can be severely limited if they are denied access to local members of the U.S. Senate. This symbiotic relationship may produce more favorable coverage of individual members of Congress. Researchers examining news coverage of U.S. House campaigns have documented that incumbents do receive more favorable coverage than challengers (Clarke and Evans, 1983; Goldenberg and Traugott, 1984).

In summary, we contend that editors and reporters initially use preelection polls to determine whether an upcoming race appears competitive. If the soothsayers promise an uncertain outcome, then news organizations allocate resources to cover the race. Once in the field, reporters rely heavily on the norms of newsworthiness and the folkways of the press to report the actions of the candidates. In most cases, candidates who have the resources to say interesting things in engaging ways draw the lion's share of media attention.

Explaining Voter Preferences: The Impact of Candidate Strategies and Media Coverage

We began by theorizing that the aggregated preferences of voters, measured early in a campaign, shape the behavior of the candidates and the media. Now, it is important to understand how the behavior of candidates and the media alter voter preferences. To be sure, the candidates and the media spend millions and millions of dollars each election cycle attempting to shape and inform voter preferences. And, voter preferences do change in the course of some campaigns. In fact, in more than a quarter of the races in our study (twenty-five out of ninety-seven races), public support changed significantly—by more than eight percentage points—from early September to the end of the campaign.[7]

Several of the Senate races in our study illustrate how the strategies of the candidates can alter the closeness of the race. There is almost uniform agreement that Wellstone's clever commercials in Minnesota in 1990 helped defeat Boschwitz. Likewise, political observers, along with Senator Bill Bradley himself, credit Christine Todd Whitman's efforts to link Democrats (including Bradley) with Governor Jim Florio's unpopular tax increase as an important reason why Bradley's lead slipped from 28 points in September to too close to call in early November. Unlike Boschwitz, however, Bradley held his office.

Beyond their own strategies, candidates and campaign managers believe that media coverage can influence the candidates' standings in the polls. Campaign strategists are well aware that without media coverage even simple name recognition cannot be established (Herrnson, 1995; Jacobson, 1997). Between 1988 and 1992, nearly one-third of the campaign managers of losing candidates mentioned lack of media attention as a reason why their candidates lost the election. The most-cited reason for losing was, not surprisingly, lack of resources, which is indelibly linked to inadequate campaign coverage. Once again, an example illustrates the close link between media coverage, name recognition, and poll standings.

In West Virginia in 1988, Senator Robert C. Byrd's opponent was M. Jay Wolfe. Wolfe's name appeared in only twenty-one paragraphs in the *Daily Progress*, the state's largest circulating newspaper, in the final ten days of the campaign. During the course of the campaign, Senator Byrd's lead in the polls never fell below 40 points. Wolfe, without adequate media attention, was unable to increase public recognition of his name, let alone change voters' preferences about his electability. The National Election Study/Senate Election Study (NES/SES) postelection survey indicated that 50 percent of the folks in West Virginia did not recognize Wolfe's name immediately after the election. In contrast, not one respondent in the survey failed to recognize the name of West Virginia's senior senator.

If the lack of media coverage dooms candidates to low name recognition, intense media coverage can alter poll standings overnight. Campaign insiders, local press pundits, and national observers agree that the media frenzy around one event in the 1992 Hawaii campaign completely damaged the chances of the challenger. Senator Daniel Inouye, a political icon in the Islands, led by 22 points in polls over challenger Rick Reed in September. Reed, in a desperate gamble to discredit one of the most popular political figures in the state's history, released to the local press a tape of a conversation between a woman and a Reed operative suggesting that Senator Inouye

---

[7] The change of 8 points is equivalent to approximately two sampling errors.

had raped the woman some twenty-five years earlier. Intense front-page articles in the *Honolulu Advertiser* and lead-story coverage on all local TV stations immediately questioned the credibility of the story, the woman, and Reed himself. Before the week was out, the press began discrediting and lambasting Reed and his entire campaign strategy. Reed's campaign manager subsequently resigned over the incident. Inouye's lead in the polls jumped from a comfortable 22 points to a staggering 42 points in the course of a week. The NES/SES sample of potential voters in Hawaii revealed that more than 90 percent of respondents recognized Reed's name. While Reed was a household name throughout Hawaii, it was undoubtedly for the wrong reasons.

The literature that explains the reasons behind changing voter preferences during campaigns has experienced somewhat of a rebirth in recent years. The initial research, focusing primarily on presidential elections, found that voters held firm party and candidate preferences during campaigns. Voters decided early in the campaign whom they were going to support. These decisions were based primarily on the party affiliation of the candidate. The campaign simply reinforced this initial preference (Lazarsfeld et al., 1944; Berelson et al., 1954; Campbell et al., 1960; Converse, 1962). However, between the 1950s and the 1990s, the politics of campaigns and elections changed significantly in this country. Today, politicians, campaign managers, financial contributors, campaign consultants, polling experts, and political scientists agree that aggregate vote preferences are more volatile than previously believed, especially in nonpresidential elections.

There are several reasons for the reversal in the belief that campaigns produce only "minimal effects." First and foremost, partisan loyalties have declined since the 1940s and 1950s. Converse (1976) reports that the "steady state period," a time in history when partisan loyalties were at their highest, peaked in the 1950s and early 1960s and ended by 1966. Consequently, voters became more likely to be "candidate centered" when making choices between candidates (Rapaport, 1997; Wattenberg, 1991). Not surprisingly, recent laboratory and survey data show that the formation and stability of voter preferences about candidates as well as issues are susceptible to the following: the amount and type of media coverage (Page, 1996; Bartels, 1993; Page and Shapiro; 1992; Iyengar and Kinder, 1987); publicized discussions among elite politicians (Zaller, 1992); and campaign activities by candidates (Kahn, 1996; Ansolabehere and Iyengar, 1995; Popkin, 1991; West, 1993).

In addition, the early work on campaigns was based solely on presidential elections. The dynamics of congressional elections are quite different. Voters learn a great deal across the time span of a congressional campaign, especially about challengers who begin campaigns virtually unknown. Evidence suggests that voters not only learn names and faces, but also become aware of the issue positions and ideological positions of some candidates (Abramowitz and Segal, 1992; Krasno, 1994; Jacobson, 1997; Westlye, 1991). Studies also indicate that voters weigh the importance of certain criteria much differently in campaigns where information is plentiful compared to campaigns where a dearth of information is available about candidates (Bartels, 1988; Kahn and Kenney, 1997).

In today's campaigns, it is reasonable to assume that individual voter preferences change during the course of a campaign. Most citizens do not hold strong opinions about politics or candidates based on a well-developed belief system (Converse, 1962, 1964; Converse and Markus, 1979; Krosnick, 1990). Thus, candidate preferences are to some degree malleable, especially in the short run. The most significant instrument of change is the campaign itself. The campaign is an intense period when candidates and the media bombard prospective voters with information. To be sure, random fluctuation of candidate preferences occurs in all elections as voters settle into their choices (Finkel, 1993; Converse and Markus, 1979). However, if the campaign information tends to favor one candidate more than another, individual level preferences will change systematically to produce change in aggregate vote preferences.

To understand more fully how citizens make decisions about candidates, it is essential to consider the campaign setting. We theorize that the culmination of the interplay among competing candidates, the media, and the perceived closeness of the race determines the voters' electoral environment. This electoral environment, often called the "intensity" of the campaign, influences how citizens evaluate candidates.[8] When a campaign includes interesting candidates, engaging commercials, and numerous news stories enmeshed in what is considered a close race, voters not only have access to more information, but they are more motivated to process this information. As the intensity of the campaign increases, voters will have more information about the campaign and will have greater opportunity to make more sophisticated decisions about competing candidates.

To date, most scholars have neglected to examine the impact of the electoral climate when examining voting decisions. Nearly all models of electoral choice, from the simplest to the most complex, assume that the decision rules voters employ are unresponsive to variations in the campaign setting.[9] This is especially problematic in nonpresidential elections where campaigns vary dramatically in terms of candidate strategies and media coverage. Re-

---

[8] Previous scholars have used campaign intensity to describe the difference between competitive and noncompetitive elections (Krasno, 1995; Westlye, 1991). We use the term to represent the culmination of the campaign process; to describe the output of the interactions between candidates, the media, and early poll results.

[9] A notable exception is Bartels's (1988) work examining the impact of the context of the campaign on voters' decisions in presidential primaries.

searchers, recognizing this problem, have recently begun to examine the impact of the campaign context on voters' evaluations in senatorial elections. Krasno (1994) demonstrates that voters' recognition and contact with candidates is higher in "hard-fought" races than in "low-key" contests. Westlye (1991) also demonstrates that party defections and ideological and issue voting vary across hard-fought and low-key Senate elections.

These pioneering studies, while underscoring the significance of the campaign setting, have some important limitations. First, prior empirical analyses treat the campaign setting as a dichotomy between hard-fought and low-key races, truncating the variance associated with different types of campaigns. Second, prior work has focused on the impact of campaign intensity on a narrow set of criteria. We attempt to overcome these limitations by measuring campaign intensity as a continuum and by searching more widely for the effects of intensity.

To understand how campaign intensity affects the decision calculi of voters, it is helpful to rely on research in social psychology and public opinion. Social psychologists have determined that most people, most of the time "do not engage in complex computational processes in arriving at judgments" (Otatti and Wyer, 1990: 200). People rarely seek out large amounts of information to aid in the decision-making process; instead, they rely on what social psychologists refer to as "heuristics." These cognitive shortcuts include the reliance on preexisting stereotypes or schemas, established feelings (e.g., positive or negative affect), and recently acquired and easily accessible information (Lupia, 1994; Zaller, 1992).

When campaign intensity is low, voters are likely to depend more heavily on these cognitive shortcuts. In such a setting, where information about the contest is scarce, individuals have little incentive to make complicated judgments about the candidates. Instead, voters will turn to political heuristics or easily accessible cues. For example, people may rely on their stereotypes or schemas about Democrats and Republicans when choosing between candidates (Conover and Feldman, 1989; Feldman and Conover, 1983; Popkin, 1991; Rahn, 1993).

Even though cognitive heuristics are pervasive, people will rely on these shortcuts less frequently when they are making decisions that are salient to their lives. In such situations, individuals will seek out considerable amounts of information, update or even change existing attitudes, and, finally, consider the implications of their decisions (McGuire, 1968). Intense elections may motivate voters to depend less heavily on cognitive cues. Well-produced commercials, highly publicized debates, numerous candidate appearances around the state, and polls showing a close race may capture the attention of normally distracted citizens. In high-intensity campaigns, voters have an incentive to seek and to reflect on detailed information available about candidates. Therefore, voters will be less likely to rely on cognitive shortcuts and more likely to make sophisticated judgments about the competing candidates (Kahn and Kenney, 1997; McGuire, 1968; Westlye, 1991; Wyer, 1974; Zaller, 1992).

We contend, then, that the context of the campaign not only affects the preferences of voters, but can influence how voters arrive at these preferences. An intense campaign may change citizens' views about the political contestants and may lead people to consider a wider range of criteria when drawing distinctions among the candidates.

In this chapter, we have described the nature and consequences of campaigns. It is a dynamic story designed to improve our understanding of the complex set of reciprocal relationships among the three most important actors in campaigns: the candidates, the media, the voters. Aggregated preferences of voters, best captured by polls taken early in the fall, influence the messages presented by candidates and the types of news stories published about the campaign. Candidates continually adjust their strategies in response to updated polling data and the news media's portrayal of the ongoing contest. News organizations, in addition to keeping an eye on the polls, react to the activities of the candidates when informing the electorate about the upcoming election. The interconnections among poll standings, candidate activities, and media coverage determine the intensity of the campaign. And, the intensity of the campaign profoundly affects what voters know about candidates and how they choose between these candidates on Election Day.

Plan of the Book

The next chapter introduces and explains the extensive database that was created to examine the nature and consequences of senatorial campaigns. We discuss in detail the interviews conducted with campaign managers, the content analyses of the candidates' television advertisements, and the content analyses of the media coverage from local newspapers. We also explain how we married the data measuring the campaign environment with the survey data from the National Election Study, in which citizens from each of the fifty states were interviewed about their Senate races.

Chapters 3 and 4 examine the campaign strategies and messages disseminated by candidates. In both chapters we utilize the data from the campaign managers and the thirty-second commercials produced and aired by senatorial candidates. In chapter 3 we begin to see the influence of competition on the behavior of candidates. Candidates react to competitive elections by talking more about issues and less about their personal traits. Polls suggesting that the outcomes of campaigns are uncertain cajole candidates into discussing issues, taking positions on issues, and actually confronting the most controversial issues of our times. The evidence from chapter 3 suggests that candidates cannot be forced into open discussion of public policy by the news media or by their opponents. Only competition pushes them in a direction that they would rather not go.

In chapter 4 we examine decisions by candidates to "go negative." The closeness of the campaign clearly encourages candidates to attack their opponents. We find that as races become more competitive, candidates are more willing to criticize their opponents' issue agendas and their positions on issues. Incumbents are especially affected by the competitiveness of the race. Sitting senators shy away from critical commentary when they lead by large margins in the polls, but attack viciously when the race narrows and victory is uncertain. While the candidates' poll standings clearly influence their likelihood of airing negative commercials, candidates do not consider the strategies of their opponents or the critical nature of campaign coverage when making decisions about negative advertising.

In chapter 5 we shift from examining the behavior of the candidates to examining the performance of the news media. Relying on a content analysis of thousands of newspaper articles, we look at how Senate campaigns are covered by the press. We examine the amount of press attention, the prominence of coverage, the topics discussed, and whether patterns of coverage vary in response to competition, candidate behavior, and biases within newspapers. Predictably, we find that the media elite are persuaded by the actions of the candidates and the closeness of the race. The quantity, quality, and tone of media coverage change dramatically depending upon the candidates' standings in the latest polls and the strategies adopted by candidates. Finally, we isolate a clear bias in the tone of news stories that covaries with the editorial decisions of the newspapers.

In chapter 6 we look more extensively at the correspondence between the candidates' messages and the substance of press coverage. In particular, we look at whether candidates are successful at controlling the content and tone of campaign coverage. In the language of media scholars, we examine the candidates' ability to "set the news media's agenda" and to "frame" coverage of their campaigns. We discover that candidates' abilities to manipulate news coverage vary with the competitiveness of the race, the status of each candidate, and the content of the candidates' messages. In short, challengers are more likely to enjoy a more accurate correspondence between their messages and press coverage, compared to incumbents. Challengers are more successful in gaining coverage for their chosen themes when they discuss specific issues, compared to more ambiguous messages and when races are more competitive.

In chapter 7, we examine the dynamics of competition. Specifically, we look at how the candidates' strategies and the nature of media coverage can change the competitiveness of campaigns. We show that the candidates' standings in the polls vary depending on the challengers' spending patterns and the number of criticisms reported by the press. Challengers who spend money early in the campaign narrow the gap between themselves and incumbents. In addition, races become significantly more competitive when the news media spend a great deal of time criticizing the candidates' policies and personal traits.

In chapters 8 and 9 we examine how the messages produced by the candidates and the news media affect the attitudes and behaviors of individual citizens. The findings from these two chapters are striking. Citizens clearly respond to changes in the campaign climate. When extensive and detailed campaign messages are presented in a competitive setting, ordinary citizens are affected. Citizens are more likely to have contact with campaigns, they are more likely to know the candidates' names, and they are more adept at identifying the main messages of the campaigns. In addition, citizens are more likely to use campaign information to draw conclusions about what they like and dislike about the competing candidates. Furthermore, citizens alter the criteria they use to evaluate candidates depending on the nature of the campaign messages presented. When the messages are more sophisticated, focusing on issues and ideology, voters react by judging the candidates on the basis of these topics and rely less heavily on readily accessible cues such as name recognition or partisanship.

In the book's final chapter, we draw some implications from our findings for the unfulfilled potential of America's campaigns. We find fault with the amount and content of discussion in many senatorial campaigns. When Senate races are not competitive, the campaign dialogue is limited and discussion of the nation's problems and policies is woefully inadequate. When Senate races are more closely contested, issues are discussed more frequently, critical commentary is more plentiful, and citizens respond by becoming more informed and by relying on a more extensive set of criteria when evaluating candidates. Our findings demonstrate that meaningful political conversation among politicians, media elites, and citizens is possible only when elections are competitive.

Two

Measuring the Content and Consequences
of Political Campaigns

IN A REPRESENTATIVE democracy, campaigns are a prescribed period of time for representatives to communicate with the represented. The nature of these communications, how they change, how they are delivered to citizens, how they are mediated, and, ultimately, how they influence voters, is the focus of this study. To understand fully the communication process in campaigns, it is necessary to describe and explain how the actions of the candidates, the news media, and the voters influence one another. In short, we need to determine how the campaign process influences what candidates say, how the media report it, and how the voters react to it.

Coming to grips with the interplay among the candidates, the media, and the voters requires us to measure the behavior of each of these actors during the campaign. We *talked* with campaign managers about the strategies employed by their candidates. We *watched* the candidates' commercials to see what information they presented to voters. We *read* newspapers in each state to discover what the media were reporting during the campaign. Finally, relying on the National Election Study/Senate Election Study (NES/SES), we *learned* how citizens assessed the candidates.

Each of these methods of inquiry has strengths and weaknesses. We believe the confluence of these different approaches yields measurements that provide valid and reliable insights into the behavior of the candidates, the media, and the voters. For example, interviews with campaign managers provide one answer to why candidates choose certain types of campaign messages. In addition, content analyses of the candidates' commercials are important for examining the precise content and tone of the messages. Similarly, content analyses of newspaper articles are essential for determining the nature of the news available to citizens. Finally, interviews with citizens are necessary to ascertain what people are actually learning about the campaign. In the end, this multimethod approach allows us to draw conclusions about the dynamics, content, and consequences of political campaigns.

Why U.S. Senate Elections?

U.S. Senate elections are an ideal laboratory for examining the dynamics of campaigns. These elections vary dramatically in terms of candidate messages and spending strategies. The quality of challengers and the tenure of incumbents are also strikingly different across Senate elections. In addition, the quantity and quality of press attention devoted to Senate elections varies from newspaper to newspaper across states in the same year. And media coverage can vary significantly in the same newspaper across elections in different years. Finally, electoral constituencies vary sharply across states in terms of size, partisan and ideological leanings, and demographic composition.

In addition, and vitally important for testing our theory about the dynamics of campaigns, the level of competition varies sharply from one Senate campaign to another (Abramowitz and Segal, 1992; Westlye, 1991; Franklin, 1991; Krasno, 1994). This variance cannot be found in other federal elections. U.S. House elections are predominantly noncompetitive contests where information about the candidates is scarce, and well-financed incumbents routinely defeat poor-quality challengers (Jacobson, 1997). Presidential races are highly competitive contests characterized by abundant media coverage and equivalent levels of spending by the candidates (Abramson et al., 1995). In our study, we examine the population of Senate races for an entire election cycle. In particular, we look at ninety-seven contested races between 1988 and 1992.[1]

Measuring the Campaign Strategies of Candidates

In our inquiry we are interested in examining the candidates' choice of campaign strategies. In particular, we contend that patterns of press coverage as well as the candidates' standings in the polls can affect the types of campaign messages adopted by candidates. In addition, the candidates' campaign strategies can influence the candidates' popularity and ensuing news coverage. In order to understand the role of the candidates' campaign strategies in campaigns, it is necessary to measure the content and tone of candidates' messages.

Interviewing Campaign Managers

To measure the campaign strategies of candidates, we rely on several sources of information. First, we conducted telephone interviews with the campaign

[1] There were actually 104 Senate races in 1988, 1990, and 1992. However, seven races were eliminated from the analysis. Four races in 1990 were removed because an incumbent was uncontested: Arkansas, Georgia, Mississippi, and Virginia. We also decided to remove the two races in Louisiana because of the state's unique electoral laws. In Louisiana, all candidates enter one race. If one candidate does not capture a majority of the votes, then a runoff is held. Since Louisiana is the only state with this system, we decided to set these elections aside. Finally, we did not examine a special election held in North Dakota on December 4, 1992; this was the only special election held on a unique date during the 1988–1992 election cycle.

managers of the major party candidates running for election to the U.S. Senate in 1988, 1990, and 1992. With ninety-seven contested races, the population of managers consisted of 194 managers (i.e., one for each candidate). These surveys were conducted between November 1991 and June 1993.[2] Interviews were completed with 147 of the 194 campaign managers, yielding a response rate of 76 percent.[3] Of the 47 campaign managers not interviewed, 36 could not be reached and 11 refused to be interviewed.[4]

The interviews averaged twenty-two minutes in length, with the shortest interview ten minutes and the longest forty-five minutes. While the target of the interview was always the campaign manager, in some cases the manager was not available. In these cases, other appropriate staff members were interviewed. Among those interviewed, 125 (85 percent) were campaign managers, eight (5.5 percent) were press secretaries, eight (5.5 percent) were other campaign staff members, and six (4 percent) were the candidates themselves who were also their own campaign managers.

The data represent accurately the population of Senate campaigns in 1988, 1990, and 1992. For example, the sample represents the two parties equally, with 49 percent of the Democratic and 51 percent of the Republican managers interviewed. The completed interviews also draw equally from winning campaigns (53 percent) and losing campaigns (47 percent). Finally, 73 percent of the incumbent/challenger races are included, as are 88 percent of open races.

We were interested in obtaining three general types of information from the managers: (1) the messages disseminated by their campaign, (2) their perceptions of the messages presented by the opponent and the news media, and (3) an assessment of the success or failure of the candidate's message and the opponent's message. To obtain data regarding the content of candidates' messages, we asked the managers to identify general themes as well as specific issue and trait messages.[5] We used an open-ended format where managers were not restricted by closed-ended options to questions (Converse

[2] This project was first conceived in the fall of 1991 during the "Electing the Senate conference" at Stanford University. Initial funding for the campaign manager survey was acquired during the fall of 1991, and interviewing began in November 1991.

[3] The response rate is nearly identical for the three election years: 73 percent for managers of 1988 campaigns, 79 percent for managers of 1990 campaigns, and 72 percent for managers of 1992 campaigns.

[4] In trying to complete the surveys, interviewers called campaign managers up to thirty times, averaging twenty-five call-backs for the respondents who were never reached.

[5] See Appendix A. For ease of interviewing , we developed separate interview schedules based on the status of the candidate and whether the candidate won or lost the election (e.g., winning incumbent, losing candidate in an open race). In Appendix A, we present the interview schedule for incumbents who won reelection.

and Presser, 1986). Interviewers recorded exact responses and allowed candidates to articulate as many as six themes.[6]

We asked a comparable battery of questions to assess the managers' perception of the opponents' campaign strategies and the managers' views regarding media coverage of the campaign. In particular, managers were asked to assess the main themes, policy, and trait themes presented by the opponents as well as to identify the main themes, policy, and trait themes discussed in the news coverage of the race.

To measure managers' assessments and perspectives about the success or failure of their campaign efforts, we asked whether the campaign was successful in presenting their main themes, policy priorities, and trait discussions to voters. Relatedly, we asked managers to explain why they won or lost the election. Finally, we asked them to speculate as to whether their opponents' strategies were successful and why their opponents won or lost. Again, in order not to constrain the managers' responses, these questions were asked in an open-ended format.

We relied on closed-ended scales to tap the managers' assessments of their candidates' talents and the talents of their opponents. For example, we asked managers to rank their candidates' effectiveness as campaigners. We also asked managers to assess the usefulness of various campaign strategies (e.g., personal contact, political advertisements) on a scale ranging from very effective to very ineffective. Finally, closed-ended questions were used to obtain managers' assessments of the ideological positions of their candidates and the candidates' opponents.

The interviews were conducted by fourteen Arizona State University students and one of us, using the ASU Survey Research Lab. Interviewers were trained prior to talking with managers, and interviews were continually monitored. All open-ended comments were coded and categorized by both of us and one graduate assistant.[7]

Content Analyses of Candidates' Advertisements

In addition to the campaign manager interviews, we also systematically examined the candidates' political advertisements to measure how campaign messages were presented to the public. Although campaign managers provided important information about the themes of their campaigns, it was also

---

[6] Based on preliminary interviews, we coded only four responses to the trait questions because managers listed significantly fewer trait themes than issue and main themes.

[7] Reliability checks were conducted to assess the coding of the open-ended comments; intercoder reliability never fell below 95 percent agreement.

important to assess how these strategies were actually represented in the candidates' own campaign communications.

We examined *televised* political advertisements since these commercials are a central component of U.S. Senate campaigns. Herrnson (1995) reports that over 90 percent of Senate campaigns employed television advertising in 1992. Ansolabehere et al. (1993) explain that television advertising represents the biggest single expenditure by Senate candidates, with campaigns allocating more than one-third of their budgets for political advertising. In addition, television advertisements, compared to newspaper advertisements, are considered significantly more effective in swaying voters' opinions and are used much more frequently during statewide and national campaigns (Abramowitz and Segal, 1992; Goldenberg and Traugott, 1984; Jacobson, 1987; Luntz, 1988).

We relied on the Political Commercial Archive at the University of Oklahoma to obtain our sample of political commercials. The archive has the largest collection of U.S. Senate advertisements publicly available. For the 1988–1992 Senate races, the archive has 1,380 commercials for 161 of the 194 candidates, representing 83 percent of the population. The archive does not have ads for some candidates for two reasons: it was unable to acquire ads from a candidate's campaign or from other sources (e.g., local television stations, private collectors), or the candidate did not produce ads because of a lack of resources. For example, there were no ads in the archive for Maria M. Hustace during her 1988 campaign against Senator "Spark" Matsunaga of Hawaii. However, it is unlikely that Hustace ran ads since she was grossly underfunded during her campaign. According to the *Congressional Quarterly*, while Matsunaga had over $600,000 on hand in October 1988, Hustace had only $865 and was $10,000 in debt.

The number of advertisements available for the candidates varied widely since some candidates produced considerably more ads than others. For example, the archive has more than thirty ads aired by Republican Conrad Burns during his competitive bid against Montana senator John Melcher in 1988. In contrast, in the same year, the archive has only one ad for unknown candidate Jasper "Jack" Wyman of Maine. We stratified the sample by candidate and randomly selected four advertisements (if available) for each of the candidates running for the U.S. Senate in 1988, 1990, and 1992. This maximized the number of candidates represented in our political advertisement sample.

Our sample includes 594 ads from 161 candidates. We obtained 266 advertisements for 70 of the 80 incumbents seeking reelection, and 209 advertisements for 58 of the 80 challengers. We sampled 119 advertisements for 33 of the 34 candidates seeking to fill open seats. The sample included 364 ads from GOP candidates and 230 from Democratic candidates. Finally, of the 594 ads, 33 percent aired in 1988, 32 percent in 1990, and 35 percent in 1992.

We were interested in examining several aspects of the candidates' ads to insure an accurate representation of the messages presented by them. We collected data from each commercial about the following: the overall message of the ad; specific discussions of issues, ideology, and traits; and the tone of the ads. In coding the issues in the ads, we measured several dimensions of the policy discussion. First, we coded the candidates' positions on issues, if positions were offered. We also recorded whether they presented plans and programs to improve the current state of local and national affairs. Finally, we were interested in whether the candidates assigned responsibility for the outcomes of particular policies. For instance, a Republican ad might blame the breakdown of the family on Democratic welfare policies. Or candidates might claim responsibility for the success of a program (e.g., day care for children) that they initiated and shepherded through the Senate.

To measure the tone of the ad, we employed several strategies. First, we used a scale where each ad received an overall score that was either positive, negative, or a combination of the two. Second, any negative issue or trait discussion was recorded. As an illustration, assigning blame to a candidate for supporting a failed policy or providing information that highlights the inexperience of a candidate was coded as negative issue and trait mention, respectively. Third, we determined whether the negative message in the ad was a major or minor focus of the commercial.

Three coders were sent to the archive in Oklahoma. Each coder was trained at Arizona State University on a sample of ads. All coders worked separately at the archive. Twenty-five percent of the ads (i.e., 148 ads) were coded by all three to assess reliability. Intercoder reliability among the three coders averaged 80 percent across the ads. (See Appendix B for a copy of the political advertising code sheet.)

Campaign Spending by the Candidates

In addition to assessing the content of the candidates' messages, we examined the level of campaign activity by looking at the candidates' spending patterns.[8] We relied on data available through the Federal Election Commission (FEC) to track candidates' spending during the course of the campaigns. These data allow us to examine how candidates adjust their spending in response to the forces of the campaign. Given the FEC reporting cycles, we examined spending for the following periods: July 1 to August 26; August 27 through September 30; October 1 to October 14; and October 15 through November 23.

---

[8] Spending data have long been used to measure the overall volume of candidate activity (Westlye, 1991; Jacobson, 1980).

The News Media's Coverage of the Campaign

The news media, in allocating resources and deciding how to cover a campaign, consider both the closeness of the race and the actions of the candidates. Furthermore, the substance and tone of news coverage can subsequently influence the candidates' level of support as well as produce changes in the candidates' campaign strategies. Given the central role of the news media in political campaigns, we conducted an extensive content analysis of press coverage in each state holding a Senate election in 1988, 1990, and 1992.

We selected the largest circulating newspaper in each state for analysis simply because more potential voters read these newspapers.[9] In addition, large and small newspapers across the state routinely pick up the same news stories about local campaigns from the wire services.[10] For example, in Minnesota, similar stories about a campaign will appear in newspapers in the Twin Cities, in Duluth, in St. Cloud, in Rochester, or in Moorhead.[11]

Newspapers, instead of television news, were chosen to represent news coverage for substantive and practical reasons. Among the substantive reasons, studies demonstrate that newspapers allocate more resources and more space to their coverage of statewide campaigns, compared with television, thereby producing more comprehensive coverage (Leary, 1977). Westlye (1991: 45) found that, compared with local broadcast news, "newspapers present an amount of information that more closely approximates what campaigns are issuing." In addition, while people rely heavily on television news to keep informed about national politics, they depend on local newspapers for coverage of senatorial and gubernatorial campaigns (Mayer, 1993). Similarly, statewide campaign officials consider newspapers more effective than local television news for communicating with potential voters (Graber, 1993). People also learn more about statewide campaigns from newspapers than from local news broadcasts (Clarke and Fredin, 1978).

Practical considerations also influenced our decision to examine newspapers. Newspapers are routinely saved on microfilm, which makes them easily accessible for analysis. Tapes of local television news, in contrast, are

---

[9] To see whether alternative newspapers from the same state cover Senate campaigns differently, we compared coverage patterns in 1988 in the *Miami Herald* and *Tampa Tribune*, the *Houston Chronicle* and *Dallas Daily News*, the *San Francisco Chronicle* and *Los Angeles Times*, and the *New York Times* and *New York Daily News*. In general, coverage patterns across newspapers were similar in content, amount, placement, and tone.

[10] We were tutored about the folkways of smaller newspapers picking up stories by Mike Connolly. He is the editor of the largest circulating newspaper in St. Paul, Minnesota. We are grateful for his assistance.

[11] See Appendix C for a list of the newspapers examined.

seldom available after a campaign, making a systematic examination of television news more difficult.

News coverage was examined between September 1 and Election Day.[12] We examined every other day from September 1 to October 15 (Monday through Saturday) and every day from October 15 through Election Day. To avoid problems associated with periodicity, we alternated sampling Monday, Wednesday, Friday (i.e., first week), and Tuesday, Thursday, and Saturday (i.e., second week). In addition, every Sunday news coverage was examined for the entire time period.

We examined all articles that mentioned either candidate in the first section, state section, and editorial section of the newspaper. We did not restrict our analysis to campaign-related stories since citizens often acquire information about candidates in stories that are not directly related to the ongoing campaign (e.g., stories detailing a senator's work on legislation relevant to the state). In total, 6,925 articles were coded for the population of Senate elections. Coders examined 2,105 articles for races conducted in 1988, 2,400 articles for the 1990 campaigns, and 2,420 for campaigns in 1992.

In conducting the content analysis of media coverage, we wanted to capture how the media portrayed the race to voters. We also wanted to measure how closely the news coverage mirrored the candidates' messages. We were careful to match the content analysis of the newspapers with the content analysis of the candidates' commercials whenever possible. We coded the amount and substance of issue and trait discussion in the news. The media coverage of the candidates' positions on issues, along with coverage of the candidates' discussion of plans or programs, was also recorded. In addition, we took note whether the papers established responsibility for successful or failed programs, or assigned credit or blame for specific policies.

We spent considerable energy attempting to capture the tone of the coverage. The overall tone of all headlines and articles were scaled as positive, negative, mixed, or neutral. In addition, we recorded the number and source of criticisms. We also measured the content of the criticisms. For example, was the criticism aimed at candidates' character traits or at issue positions?

We measured the sheer amount of coverage given to the candidates, the prominence of coverage (i.e., page location, mention in the headline), the amount and substance of horse-race coverage, and the type of attention given to campaign events such as debates and political advertisements.

The coding of the articles was a labor-intensive enterprise. Coders were trained to copy articles from microfilm, while another group of coders was taught how to content analyze the articles. In all, twenty coders were trained and participated in the media project. Intercoder reliability was assessed re-

---

[12] In those cases where the state's primary election was held after September 1, coding began the day after the primary.

peatedly during the coding process. On average, there was 92 percent agreement across the content codes. See (Appendix D for a copy of the newspaper code sheet.)

Measuring Voter Preferences and Evaluations of Candidates

Voter assessments of candidates needed to be measured at both the aggregate and individual levels during the campaigns. The aggregate-level data are important because the candidates' standings in preelection polls are an important catalyst affecting both the candidates' choice of campaign messages and patterns of news coverage. In addition, poll standings are dynamic and change in response to the actions of the candidates and the press. Beyond measuring aggregate levels of support, it is also important to investigate voters' attitudes and decisions at the individual level. By looking at citizens' impressions of candidates, we can see how the confluence of poll standings, candidate strategies, and media coverage affect the assessments of individual citizens.

Aggregate Vote Preferences

To assess the role of polls in campaigns, we obtained two statewide polls for every race.[13] By examining two different time points during the campaign, we can examine changes in aggregate support for the candidates. One poll for each race, conducted between September 15 and October 1, was obtained to measure support early in the campaign. A second poll assessing support during the last ten days of the campaign was also acquired for every race.

The polling data were taken from two sources. Many of the polls were located by our content analysis of the newspapers. Polls are routinely reported in the largest circulating newspaper in the state. We simply recorded all mentions of polling data in our content analysis. A second source was a political archive known as the "Campaign Hotline." This archive contained a large number of polls reported in newspapers across the nation, along with a small number of polls that were commissioned by candidates.

Individual-Level Voter Evaluations

To study how the intensity of the campaign influences the attitudes and behaviors of potential voters, we relied on the National Election Study (NES).

[13] In the case of Delaware in 1990, polling data were not available. Therefore, we relied on *Congressional Quarterly's* assessment of the race in their preelection issue.

Without the NES, the connection between the campaign participants and the voters could not have been established. During the 1980s, the NES designed the first survey specifically to study Senate elections. As Jonathan Krasno points out, the NES Senate Election Study (SES) is "unique because, like the Senate itself, it includes (roughly) equal numbers of respondents from all fifty states" (Krasno, 1994: 10). National surveys, in contrast, are problematic because most respondents in a nationwide survey are drawn from the largest states, leading to an overrepresentation of competitive Senate contests (Krasno, 1994; Mann and Wolfinger, 1980; Westlye, 1991).

In conducting the NES Senate Election Study, about sixty respondents in each state were randomly selected to be interviewed. The interviews were done by telephone and took place within two months of the 1988, 1990, and 1992 elections. In total, 9,253 interviews were completed, with 3,145 respondents interviewed in 1988, 3,349 in 1990, and 2,759 in 1992. The interviews averaged just over thirty-five minutes in length.

The NES/SES surveys contain numerous questions that measure the forces known to influence the voters' electoral decisions along with questions about the respondents' general awareness of campaigns. For example, some questions focus on a respondent's knowledge, contact, recall, and recognition of candidates. Other questions concentrate on whether respondents were paying attention to the campaign via the media.

The NES/SES also includes a set of questions that measure respondents' ideological placements of Senate candidates, general evaluations of the candidates using feeling thermometers, respondents' issue positions, and questions about respondents' vote decisions. Finally, similar to all NES studies, the interviews included a number of political (e.g., party identification) and demographic questions about the respondents.

The NES/SES contains the most extensive collection of information about voters' perceptions of Senate candidates available. By combining the NES/SES data with information about the closeness of the race, patterns of news coverage, and the content of candidates' messages, we can examine how the intensity of the campaign influences how individuals make decisions about candidates.

Summary

With these rich data sources, we can examine the nature and consequences of political campaigns. We place voters in their unique campaign environment. We examine a significant number of elections across several years. Since the NES/SES has drawn representative samples by states in 1988, 1990, and 1992, we reconstruct, as accurately as possible, the disparate campaign settings where voters experience electoral politics. By doing so, we assess the consequences of campaigns. In other words, we examine how the campaign setting affects voters' thoughts and behaviors.

By assembling the various aspects of campaigns (e.g., candidates' messages, media output, levels of competition), we also examine the nature and dynamics of the campaign process. We peak inside the essential components of campaigns by examining the potential reciprocal relationships among candidates' strategies, media behavior, and competition. We identify how campaigns are constructed and when they might change. For example, we isolate when and how the media report the issue positions of senatorial candidates and whether these decisions are related to the candidates' messages, the level of competition in the race, or both.

To be sure, other scholars have examined the role of political campaigns. However, we believe our data resources and research design give our study some unique strengths. In particular, most earlier research has failed to collect contextual data about the campaign *and* examine a large number of races. For example, Just et al. (1996) and Patterson (1980) collect an impressive amount of information about the citizens' electoral environment, but focus on a single election (the 1992 presidential election and the 1976 presidential election, respectively). Other scholars study a large number of elections but fail to obtain measures assessing the content of the campaign. Krasno (1994), for example, examined voters' reactions to congressional campaigns by looking at the population of U.S. Senate and U.S. House races in 1988; however, he acquired virtually no information about the messages disseminated by the candidates and the news media.

We overcome limitations of prior studies by systematically gathering extensive information about nearly one hundred distinct campaign settings. Marrying voters with their campaign setting affords us the opportunity to examine a host of questions largely unexplored by previous scholars. We turn to several of these questions in the next chapter.

Part Two _____

THE CAMPAIGN STRATEGIES
OF CANDIDATES

Three

In Order To Win

AN EXAMINATION OF CAMPAIGN STRATEGIES

THE MESSAGES produced by candidates running for the U.S. Senate are an amalgam of explanations, criticisms, and promises. Some of the messages are detailed policy prescriptions for the nation's ills; others are simply slogans, perhaps memorable and entertaining. Other messages are aimed at evoking voters' feelings of hope or fear or compassion. For constituents who care to listen, the messages produced by candidates may provide considerable insight into the quality of leadership the candidates promise to provide and the types of governmental programs they are likely to promote.

Countless messages were produced in the ninety-seven Senate races we examined between 1988 and 1992. None was more matter-of-fact than the slogan "Dan Delivers," intended to explain why Senator Daniel Inouye would be a good choice for the people of Hawaii. Few were as detailed as Connie Mack's message regarding the proper ideological direction for Florida and the nation. Not one was more single-minded than Kathy Helling's plea to end abortion in Wyoming. Only a few could be as passionate as Senator Jesse Helms's case against affirmative action in North Carolina, or Phil Gramm's call for lower taxes and smaller government in Texas.

The cost of producing and disseminating these messages is tremendous. Competitive campaigns even in small states can easily exceed a million dollars, while the cost in large states may run into the tens of millions (Herrnson, 1995; Jacobson, 1997). Today, the vast majority of campaign expenditures in Senate elections are used to produce television commercials that convey candidates' messages to potential voters (Herrnson, 1995). Not surprisingly, then, money is the lifeblood of campaigns for the U.S. Senate. Our sample of campaign managers revealed that 65 percent of the losing managers believed that the lack of resources was an important reason why they lost the election. Without money, candidates are unable to produce and disseminate a message; and without an effective message, candidates are unable to raise money. Candidates lacking both money and an engaging message rarely get the opportunity to serve in the U.S. Senate.

In this chapter we examine the strategies candidates employ during their campaigns. All candidates are faced with perplexing decisions about when to spend their money and what messages to send to voters. Thus, two central questions motivate our inquiry. First, how do the competitiveness of the campaign and media attention influence the spending patterns of candidates? Second, how do the closeness of the race and media coverage affect the content of the candidates' messages?

Campaign Spending: The Influence of Polls and Media Coverage

An examination of the spending patterns by candidates in Senate elections between 1988 and 1992 reveals that expenditures change significantly across campaigns. Not surprisingly, spending tends to increase toward the end of the races, when candidates put forth final propaganda campaigns to entice voters to support their candidacies. In fact, incumbents spend, on average, 20 cents per potential voter during the first two weeks of October and 32 cents per potential voter during the final two weeks of the campaign.[1] The increase for challengers is significantly less. They spend, on average, 12 cents per potential voter during the first two weeks of October and 17 cents per potential voter during the final two weeks of the campaign.

However, the average increases in spending belie the fact that the changes in spending from the first two weeks of October to the final two weeks of the campaign can be quite large for many candidates. Senator Claiborne Pell increased his spending a full 75 cents per voter in his bid for reelection against Claudine Schneider in Rhode Island in 1990. Senator Joseph R. Biden increased his spending 67 cents per voter in Delaware between early October and late October in order to defeat M. Jane Brady in 1990. While spending generally increases from early October to early November, twenty-two incumbents and twelve challengers actually decreased their spending across this time period.

What forces explain these changes? Did media coverage of the challenger scare Senator Pell into increasing his spending more than any other senator? Why did some incumbents actually decrease their spending? Did poll results indicate that their lead was safe? Why did expenditures among some challengers decline in the final weeks of the campaigns? Did polls and media coverage convince contributors to withhold donations from these campaigns? While many scholars have examined spending in House and Senate elections, little attention has been given to explain why candidates change their spending strategies during the course of the campaign.[2]

[1] In order to make sensible comparisons of expenditures across populous states and small states (i.e., California and New York versus Wyoming and Idaho), we follow the convention of estimating cost per potential voter.

[2] Scholars have conducted extensive research on where money comes from, how candidates use their money, and its impact on the vote (e.g., Abramowitz and Segal, 1992; Alexander, 1992; Herrnson, 1995; Magleby and Nelson, 1990; Jacobson, 1980).

We know that the ability of candidates to raise money prior to Labor Day, so-called seed money, is affected by the political experience of the candidates and the vulnerability of the incumbents (Krasno, et al., 1994; Stewart, 1989, Squire, 1989). Nonincumbents who have held prior elective office (e.g., House, state legislature) have an easier time securing resources compared to inexperienced candidates. In addition, challengers facing an incumbent who is embroiled in a scandal or experiencing low levels of public support are likely to have an easier time raising money than challengers facing popular incumbents.

For example, in Kansas in 1992, the inexperienced Gloria O'Dell, unable to find financial help during the late summer, spent only $68,000 in September in her attempt to unseat Senator Bob Dole. This translated into less than 4 cents per voter. This was not enough money to increase her name recognition, let alone make a case against one of the most powerful men in the U.S. Senate. In contrast, in Oregon in 1992, Congressman Les AuCoin, having spent several years in the U.S. House, was able to spend $334,000 in September in an attempt to unseat Senator Bob Packwood.

Unlike the trials and tribulations of challengers, incumbents raise money largely in response to the levels of spending of their challengers (Krasno et al. 1994; Stewart, 1989; Jacobson, 1980). For example, Senator Dole spent virtually nothing in September of 1992, realizing full well that O'Dell was not raising enough money to threaten his reelection. On the other hand, Senator Packwood, fearing that AuCoin might unseat him, spent over $1.2 million in the month of September alone.

Although seed money is determined by the background characteristics of candidates, candidate spending during the final weeks of the campaign is a function of how the campaign is unfolding. Specifically, a candidate's ability to raise and spend money during the last few weeks of a campaign is related, in large part, to poll reports and media coverage during the intervening weeks between Labor Day and mid-October. Polls, especially those reported early in the campaign, have a direct effect on how much money candidates are able to raise and spend during the final weeks of the campaign. Put simply, polls that reveal a competitive race provide hope for financial contributors who are supporting the trailing candidate and an incentive for the backers of the leading candidate. Likewise, media coverage during the early days of a campaign helps promulgate the view that certain candidates are interesting and viable, which in turn encourages financial contributors to provide more resources (Mutz, 1995). These resources allow candidates to disseminate their messages more broadly and more often. We turn now to the development of a research design that will allow us to examine the dynamics of campaign spending in Senate elections.

Examining the Dynamics of Spending

To examine whether the closeness of the race and media coverage influence campaign spending, we need to know when candidates spend their money, when polls are reported, and when news articles about the campaign are published. In particular, we need to make sure that poll standings and media coverage precede changes in candidate spending. By establishing the time sequence of events, we can examine the causal relationship among competition, news coverage, and expenditures.

Thanks to the Federal Election Commission (FEC), we can locate the amount of money spent by candidates between October 15 and November 23. This time period represents nicely the candidates' final efforts to convince voters that they should be sent to Washington. In order to assess the change in candidate spending during the campaign, we use candidates' spending totals from the prior FEC reporting period—October 1 to October 14. Candidate spending for two discrete time points allows us to examine how expenditures change across the time period.

To analyze the impact of polls and media coverage on changes in campaign spending, we located measures preceding the spending data from October 15 to November 23. Polls were available for every race between September 16 and October 1.[3] To measure media coverage we relied on the content analysis described in chapter 2. We can establish time order for the media coverage because the date of each newspaper article was recorded. In this analysis we examine coverage from October 1 to October 14.[4] We examine total coverage for both candidates in order to capture the total amount of media attention given to the race.[5]

To be sure, there are other forces that may influence changes in candidates' campaign expenditures besides polling numbers and the amount of media coverage. As mentioned earlier, the campaign spending of the chal-

---

[3] To measure how close the race was, we coded the percentage difference between the two candidates in the polls. For example, if 52 percent of citizens preferred one candidate, while 42 percent preferred the second candidate, then the race was given a score of 10 percent (i.e., $52 - 42 = 10$). The mean percentage difference between the two candidates in the polls between September 16 and October 1 was 27.5 points, with a standard deviation of 17.2 points. The difference between the candidates ranged from 0 to a whopping 72 points.

[4] The unit of measurement is paragraphs because the length of paragraphs is virtually the same across newspapers. The mean number of paragraphs about the candidates from October 1 to October 14 was 121.9 with a standard deviation of 108.6.

[5] We did attempt to analyze the amount of coverage for challengers and incumbents separately. However, the correlation between these two measures is .75, making analyses of the separate candidates difficult due to problems of multicollinearity. The strength of the correlation is not surprising. Although incumbents receive more coverage than challengers, on average, when coverage of the incumbent goes up, coverage of the challenger also goes up, resulting in classic covariation.

lenger influences an incumbent's expenditures (Abramowitz and Segal, 1992; Herrnson, 1995; Jacobson, 1980). Incumbents typically react aggressively to the amount of spending by challengers. Challengers, on the other hand, rarely have the luxury of reacting to the incumbents' spending. They generally spend every cent they raise, irrespective of what the incumbents are spending (Krasno and Green, 1988; Jacobson, 1980).

Furthermore, the characteristics of the candidates may affect changes in spending. Even though these characteristics are associated with the likelihood of acquiring seed money (Biersack et al., 1993; Squire, 1989; Stewart, 1989; Jacobson, 1980), it is possible that some candidate characteristics may be related to changes in spending. For instance, the prior elective experience of nonincumbent candidates may be related to their ability to establish an effective campaign fund-raising organization.[6] A candidate with an experienced organization may be more likely to raise money late in the campaign compared to a candidate experiencing the complexities of an electoral bid for the first time.

For incumbents, years in the Senate represent the experience a senator can draw upon to raise money during the final days of a campaign. In addition, measures of incumbent vulnerability, such as a scandal or a weak performance in the election six years prior, may be related to the candidate's ability to raise money late in the campaign (Abramowitz, 1988; Welch and Hibbing, 1997).[7] When incumbents appear vulnerable, they may have a difficult time raising the large sums of money needed during the last weeks of a campaign to stave off credible challengers. Likewise, this same vulnerability may spur on the fund-raising efforts of challengers.

Finally, the size of a state's population is directly related to spending in Senate races (Lee and Oppenheimer, 1997; Squire, 1989). Ostensibly, candidates should have an easier time acquiring money for the final weeks of a campaign in a larger state compared to a smaller state. Larger states simply have more potential financial donors.

The data used to examine changes in spending for incumbents/open winners and challengers/open losers are analyzed in two different ways.[8] First,

[6] The quality of the challenger is measured by using prior elective experience and establishing a 9-point scale. Following prior work by Squire and Smith (1996) and Squire (1989, 1992) we ranked nonincumbents accordingly: 1 = no prior elective experience; 2 = no prior elective experience, but high name recognition due to celebrity status in the state; 3 = local electoral experience; 4 = state legislator; 5 = state legislative leader; 6 = mayor of a major city; 7 = first-term statewide office holder or U.S. House member; 8 = multiple-term statewide office holder or U.S. House member; 9 = governor.

[7] An incumbent's seniority was measured by years in the Senate. Scandal was captured by following Abramowitz's (1988) notion of identifying special circumstances as reported by *CQ's* October "Election Preview." Finally, the incumbent's winning percentage from the prior election was used to capture weak performance in that election.

[8] All ninety-seven races were included in the analysis. There is one analysis for incumbents

Ordinary Least Squares Analysis (OLS) was used to calculate the parameter estimates for the model. The findings for the incumbents are presented in table 3.1. In addition, the data were analyzed with Two Stage Least Squares Analysis (2SLS) in order to correct for any autocorrelation that may impede on the unbiasedness of the parameter estimates (Johnston, 1972; Markus, 1979).[9] These findings are presented side by side with the OLS findings in table 3.1. The two sets of findings are juxtaposed so that readers can compare them directly. We conducted the same analysis for the challengers, and those findings are displayed in table 3.2.

We turn first to a presentation of the findings for the incumbents. There are five variables that influence change in incumbent spending in both the OLS and 2SLS analyses.[10] Two of the variables measure elements of the cam-

---

and winners of open seats, and another analysis for challengers and losers of open seats. To simplify the presentation of the findings, we refer to the incumbent/open winners category as incumbents. Likewise, we refer to the challenger/open loser category as challengers.

Some scholars have conducted a separate analysis of open seats (Abramowitz, 1988). However, in the 1988–1992 period, there were only seventeen campaigns for open seats. Seventeen cases are too small to conduct multivariate analyses without creating complications associated with small sample sizes. In all of the analyses in this book, we initially include a binary variable to assess whether the race involves an incumbent or two candidates competing for an open seat. When the open-race variable is statistically significant ($p < .10$), it is included in the final analysis. When the open-race variable fails to reach statistical significance, we report the finding in a footnote and the variable is removed from the final analysis. In the analyses reported in tables 3.1 and 3.2, the open variable failed to reach statistical significance ($p < .10$).

[9] The inclusion of a lagged dependent variable, although important to render our analysis dynamic, may cause enough autocorrelation with the dependent variable to bias the estimators. This is especially true when the amount of time between the dependent variable and the lagged variable is short, as in our analysis. Although there exist several techniques that can be used to correct this problem, we opted for 2SLS. In this case it is necessary to "purge" the estimator of the covariation that may exist between the dependent variable and the lagged dependent variable that is due to the serially dependent error terms. What is needed is a surrogate variable for the lagged variable that is correlated with the lagged variable but uncorrelated with the dependent variable. Once this "instrumental" variable is found, it can be substituted into the equation to predict the dependent variable.

To develop an instrumental or surrogate variable we estimated the lagged spending with all the variables in the original model, plus some temporally determined variables. These temporally determined variables serve as exogenous variables because we can establish time order in each instance. The exogenous variables in the model included incumbent and challenger spending for the month of September, media coverage for that month, and the "Cook Report," a prediction published in May about the likely competitiveness of the upcoming general election.

An estimate for the first-stage equation for incumbent/winners spending in early October produced an R-square of .53. The following variables were statistically significant at the $p < .10$ level: incumbent and challenger spending in September, the quality of the challenger, the size of the state. An estimate for the first-stage equation for challengers/losers yielded an R-square of .51. The following variables were statistically significant at the $p < .10$ level: quality of the challenger, challenger/loser spending in September, and the type of race (i.e., incumbent vs. open race).

[10] When we are examining a relatively small number of cases, we report statistical significance at

TABLE 3.1
Explaining Changes in Incumbent Spending

	OLS Unstandardized Coefficients (standard errors)		2SLS Unstandardized Coefficients (standard errors)	
Competition	−5988.15	(2845.77)[b]	−6308.62	(2764.81)[a]
Media coverage	603.83	(365.47)[b]	176.20	(395.41)
Challenger spending	.29	(.12)[a]	.21	(.13)[b]
Challenger quality	−22788.30	(15346.57)[c]	−38245.70	(16327.29)[b]
Scandal	11168.73	(103613.34)	16605.84	(100559.13)
Seniority	10595.33	(4678.45)[a]	7032.37	(4795.99)[c]
Last vote	−2749.91	(4342.90)	−3054.49	(4218.93)
Incumbent spending (lag)	.11	(.09)	.65	(.25)[b]
Population size	605467.22	(94383.64)[a]	312715.57	(156499.78)[b]
Constant	−3022220.21	(671435.46)[a]	−224509.34	(1015670.68)[a]
N	97		97	
R^2	.65		.63[d]	

Notes: The dependent variable is incumbent spending (measured in dollars) from October 15 to November 23. *Competition* is measured from poll results taken September 16 to October 1. Competition ranges from 0 (0 points separating candidates in preelection polls) to 72 (72 points separating candidates). *Media coverage* is the number of paragraphs about the race from October 1 to October 14. *Challenger spending* is measured in dollars and is taken from October 1 to October 14. *Challenger quality* is the scale 1–9 and is described in note 6. *Scandal* is a binary variable and described in note 7. *Seniority* is measured by number of years in U.S. Senate. *Last vote* is the incumbent's percentage of the two-party vote in the previous election. *Incumbent spending* (lagged) is measured in dollars and taken from October 1 to October 14. *Population size* is the log (base 10) of the voting age population of the state.
[a] $p < .01$
[b] $p < .05$
[c] $p < .10$
[d] An R^2 derived from the second-stage equation should be interpreted with caution (Bartels, 1991). The p-values are based on one-sided tests because the hypotheses are directional.

paign: polls from late September and challenger spending. Two additional variables assess characteristics of the candidates: the quality of the challenger, and the seniority of the incumbent. Finally, the size of the state influences changes in incumbent spending.[11]

three levels: $p < .10$, $p < .05$, $p < .01$. In chapters 8 and 9 we examine thousands of voters from the NES/SES survey and we report statistical significance at two levels: $p < .05$ and $p < .01$.

[11] In the earlier discussion in this chapter, we control for the population of the state by dividing spending by population. In the OLS and 2SLS, we control for population size by including population as an independent variable in the regression equations.

TABLE 3.2
Explaining Changes in Challenger Spending

	OLS		2SLS	
	Unstandardized Coefficients (standard errors)		Unstandardized Coefficients (standard errors)	
Competition	− 7840.16	(2761.04)[a]	− 10368.00	(2730.63)[b]
Media coverage	482.69	(354.59)	− 277.93	(413.31)
Incumbent spending	.05	(.09)	− .02	(.10)
Challenger quality	− 11789.53	(14889.63)	− 50729.95	(17977.33)[a]
Scandal	157707.32	(100528.23)	240792.98	(105970.04)[b]
Seniority	2115.46	(4539.15)	3783.16	(4599.46)
Last vote	− 3787.68	(4213.59)	− 1528.37	(4592.45)
Challenger spending (lag)	.69	(.12)[a]	1.51	(.28)[a]
Population size	201050.49	(91573.35)[b]	73917.04	(98944.52)
Constant	− 679398.76	(651443.34)	111127.31	(688179.66)
N	97		97	
R^2	.65		.65[c]	

Notes: The dependent variable is challenger spending (measured in dollars) from October 15 to November 23. *Competition* is measured from poll results taken September 16 to October 1. Competition ranges from 0 (0 points separating candidates in preelection polls) to 72 (72 points separating candidates). *Media coverage* is the number of paragraphs about the race from October 1 to October 14. *Incumbent spending* is measured in dollars and is taken from October 1 to October 14. *Challenger quality* is the scale 1–9 and is described in note 6. *Open* is a binary variables where 1 = incumbent race; 0 = open race. *Scandal* is a binary variable and is described in note 7. *Seniority* is measured by number of years in U.S. Senate. *Last vote* is the incumbent's percentage of the two-party vote in the previous election. *Challenger spending* (lagged) is measured in dollars and taken from October 1 to October 14. *Population size* is the log (base 10) of the voting age population of the state.

[a]$p < .01$

[b]$p < .05$

[c]An R^2 derived from the second-stage equation should be interpreted with caution (Bartels, 1991). The p-values are based on one-sided tests because the hypotheses are directional.

In accordance with much prior work (Krasno et al., 1994; Jacobson, 1990; Green and Krasno, 1988, 1990; Jacobson, 1980), incumbents react to the spending of challengers. An examination of the OLS unstandardized coefficient reveals that for every dollar that challengers spend between October 1 to October 14, incumbents react by increasing their spending by 29 cents, on average, during the final days of the campaign.[12]

In addition to carefully monitoring the spending of the challengers, incumbents react aggressively to poll results by changing their spending. To illus-

---

[12] The coefficient from the 2SLS analysis is strikingly similar, .21 compared to .29.

trate, we turn again to the OLS parameter estimates. A one-point change in the closeness of the race yields a change, on average, of $5,988.15 in incumbent spending. That is, incumbents who see their lead widening reduce their spending. Incumbents who see their lead narrowing increase their spending. As an example, the average change in polls separating the candidates between late September and late October was 8 percentage points. In the typical race, then, incumbents altered their spending, on average, by $47,913 between the middle of October and Election Day.[13]

The seniority of the senator and the quality of the challenger also influence the changes in spending patterns for incumbents. In the case of seniority, senior senators are able to alter spending more readily than junior senators. These senators are experienced campaigners and have reliable sources of cash, enabling them to increase their spending faster than inexperienced senators.

Conversely, the negative sign for the quality of the challenger suggests that the better the opponent, the more difficult it is for the incumbent to increase spending. Undoubtedly, quality challengers are competing for some of the same financial resources that incumbents are attempting to secure. Quality challengers may discourage contributors from generously giving money to the incumbents because these challengers appear viable. These findings suggest that high-quality challengers can actually inhibit the incumbents' abilities to finance their own campaigns.[14]

The OLS and 2SLS findings for the challengers are presented in table 3.2. Only polls measuring the level of competition in late September and early spending by challengers influence changes in spending across both analyses.[15] The effect of competition is stronger for the challengers when compared to incumbents. The impact of competition on changes in spending for challengers is $7,840 in the OLS analysis compared to $5,988 for incumbents; and $10,368 in the 2SLS analysis, compared to $6,308 for incumbents. To illustrate further the differences between challengers and incumbents, we again look at the average change in poll standings between late September and late October in the OLS models. With an average change of 8 percent in

[13] The 2SLS coefficient is again similar to the size of the OLS coefficient.

[14] The number of paragraphs about the race in early October influences the change in incumbent spending in the OLS analysis but not in the 2SLS analysis. This inconsistency requires us to pause before asserting that actions by the press alter incumbents' spending. It is true that the signs of the coefficients are both in the hypothesized direction, suggesting that more coverage leads to increased spending. However, the size of the media coefficient is significantly smaller in the 2SLS analysis.

[15] The quality of the challenger, the seniority of the senator, and the size of the state affect changes in challenger spending in the 2SLS model, but fail to reach statistical significance ($p <$ .10) in the OLS model. As in the incumbent models, we are hesitant to claim that these variables are key explanations for changes in challenger spending.

the polls, incumbents altered their spending, on average, by $47,913. In the same situation, challengers changed their spending, on average, by $62,720.

Although there is a strong relationship between competition and spending for both sets of candidates, we believe the reasons underlying these relationships are quite different. In the case of incumbents, they are monitoring the polling data in order to adjust their spending accordingly (Krasno et al. 1994; Jacobson, 1980). If threatened, they increase spending; if safe, some actually relent in their expenditures. In the case of challengers, the polls are providing clues to contributors about the likelihood of success. If the polls reveal a close race, then receipts increase and spending increases. If the polls suggest that the challenger does not have a credible chance of winning, then expenditures diminish.

These findings inform and complement prior work on the dynamics of campaigns. They complement Bartels's (1988) work on presidential primaries by substantiating a strong relationship between levels of competition in a campaign and candidate strategies. Bartels (1988) also found that early polling data, along with actual results from early primary elections, dramatically affect candidates' abilities to spend in future primary elections.

In addition, these findings help inform and illuminate the research by Krasno et al. (1994) regarding fund-raising by challengers in House elections. These scholars find that receipts from one FEC reporting period are best explained by examining receipts from the previous FEC reporting period. That is, if receipts are down in one period, then they are likely to decrease further in the next period. They speculate that this relationship is, to a large extent, the result of dampened expectations about the likelihood of a challenger's success. Krasno et al. (1994 :472) conclude: "A disappointing FEC report could poison future fundraising by convincing potential contributors that a challenger has lost viability." Our analysis, relying on Senate data rather than House data, helps validate and complement Krasno et al.'s conclusions. Like Krasno et al., we find that spending in earlier periods affects spending later in the campaign. However, in addition, we find that polling results influence changes in challenger spending. Polls, probably more so than FEC reports, serve as a visible cue to potential contributors regarding the viability of the candidates.

To conclude, candidate spending during Senate campaigns is far from static, and changes in spending from early October to early November are principally related to the competitiveness of the race. Although this is true for all candidates, it is especially important for challengers. Incumbents, with one eye on the spending of the challengers and one eye toward the polls, change their spending accordingly. Challengers have less control of their destinies. Their ability to alter their spending is dependent on their prior spending levels and on polls indicating they have a chance to win.

Identifying the forces that alter candidate spending during the campaign provides a general look at the tactics of the candidates. An inquiry into the types of messages candidates buy with their campaign funds provides a more specific and detailed examination of candidate strategies. After all, these messages are how voters come to know the candidates. Candidates' propaganda, blitzing across the airwaves and delivered in speeches, are the basis upon which voters often form evaluations of the competing candidates. An interesting and largely unexplored question is: How does the nature of the campaign alter the messages candidates produce for voters? Also, does the content of media attention devoted to the campaign and the closeness of the race lead candidates to emphasize different types of campaign themes? As outlined in chapter 1, we certainly think so. It is time now to examine these questions systematically.

Understanding the Content of Candidates' Campaign Messages

Some messages produced by candidates focus strictly on a candidate's personal traits, such as Nancy Kassebaum's message in Kansas in 1990 concerning her integrity and experience. Other messages are exclusively about issues, such as Neil Rolde's call in Maine in 1990 to establish a national health care system. Between these two extremes, messages often consist of a mixed discussion of the candidate's traits and policy positions. Page (1978) suggests that candidates develop issue priorities around topics where widespread consensus exists among voters (e.g., clear air and water, an educated society, a growing economy), while stressing the candidates' positive personal characteristics. Page (1978: 178) explains, "A candidate who takes a specific policy stand is bound to alienate those who disagree; but a candidate who promises peace, progress, and prosperity, and projects an image of warmth and honesty, is likely to please almost everyone."

The probability of a candidate producing Page's ideal message is related directly to the dynamics of the campaign. As discussed in chapter 1, candidates in competitive races with aggressive opponents and an interested and vigilant press produce messages that focus more on issues, even at the expense of traits. The pressures of competition, engaged reporters, and skilled opponents force the candidates to address the issues of the day. Comparatively, candidates in races where one candidate has a secure lead and the media are busy reporting about other campaigns are likely to stay away from issues altogether.

Beyond the fact that we expect more issue discussion in highly intense campaigns compared to low-key campaigns, there may exist some subtle differences in how incumbents, challengers, and candidates seeking open seats react to the dynamics of the campaign environment. For example, incumbents may always stress fewer issues in order to direct constituent attention toward their areas of expertise (Fenno, 1978, 1996; Mayhew, 1974). Challengers and candidates in open seats, in contrast, have an incentive to discuss a number of society's ills as examples of the failure of current policy.

Discussions with the campaign managers reveal that candidates are very much interested in presenting information to voters about both issues and personal traits. According to the campaign managers, issues are indeed a central component of most campaigns. Seventy-three percent of the managers mentioned an issue as a main theme of their campaign.[16] Furthermore, almost half (46 percent) of the managers mentioned an issue first, suggesting the importance of issues to these campaigns.

In addition to asking managers about the campaigns' main themes, we also asked them to identify the specific policy positions their candidates stressed in the campaigns. Six responses were recorded.[17] Responses ranged from zero to six, with a mean of 2.57 and a standard deviation of 1.46. These data provide us with a direct look at the actual types of issues candidates emphasize in their electoral bids. We have grouped these issues into nine categories and presented the data in figure 3.1.

Overall, candidates talk about the economy more than any other issue, reflecting their belief in the centrality of economic issues in Senate elections (Hibbing and Alford, 1982; Stein, 1990). In addition, like presidential and House candidates, Democrats and Republicans present different topics in their campaigns for the U.S. Senate (Goldenberg and Traugott, 1984; Westlye, 1991; Geer, 1992; West, 1993; Herrnson, 1995). The differences are noticeable in two substantive areas: economic issues and social programs, reflecting differences in the established constituencies of the two parties (Baumer and Gold, 1995; Page, 1978; Axelrod, 1972, 1982).

Republicans are almost twice as likely to focus on economic issues compared to Democrats (34 percent compared to 19 percent). For example, U.S. House representative Lynn Martin (R) of Illinois tried to emphasize her fiscal conservatism during her campaign against Senator Paul Simon in 1990. Martin took a "no new taxes" pledge and publicly opposed the 1990 budget compromise package offered by President George Bush and House and Senate leaders because the package included a tax increase. Republican Alan Keyes (R) of Maryland also made the economy the centerpiece of his campaign against two-term senator Paul S. Sarbanes in 1988. Throughout

---

[16] The exact wording of the question was, "What were the main themes that you tried to stress in [candidate's name]'s campaign for the Senate." We coded up to six responses for each candidate.

[17] The exact wording of the question was, "What policy positions did your campaign try to emphasize?" We should note that even though we inquired about the candidates' "policy positions," most managers simply enumerated the issues they emphasized during the campaign, with only a handful articulating the candidates' actual positions.

the campaign, Keyes touted his economic program of free markets and private-sector job creation.

Democrats, in contrast, prefer to focus on social programs such as health care, education, and the environment. They are twice as likely as Republicans to talk about these issues in their campaigns (28 percent compared to 14 percent). Senator Frank Lautenberg (D) of New Jersey highlighted his efforts to combat pollution and protect the environment when running for reelection in 1988. Lautenberg reminded New Jersey voters of his work as chairman of the Superfund, Recycling, and Solid Waste Management Subcommittee. He ran advertisements heralding his leadership on legislation aimed at combating ocean pollution. Senator John D. Rockefeller (D) of West Virginia, in his first reelection bid in 1990, chose to emphasize health care issues. Rockefeller showcased his work as chairman of the Finance Subcommittee on Medicare and Long-Term Care and as chairman of the Pepper Commission, a bipartisan group of health care policymakers. Rockefeller explained the importance of developing a national health care policy since an estimated 350,000 residents of West Virginia had no health care coverage.

An examination of the issues emphasized by incumbents, challengers, and open-race candidates reveals a somewhat different story. First, these three types of candidates do not differ in their emphasis on economic issues and social programs. However, challengers, for obvious reasons, are more likely than incumbents to call for changes in government such as term limits and campaign finance reform (10 percent compared to 1 percent). For example, Lieutenant Governor Mike DeWine of Ohio ran as an "outsider" in his 1992 campaign against Senator John Glenn, repeatedly calling for congressional term limits. Incumbents, in contrast, are more likely than other candidates to mention personal traits when queried about their policy positions. These responses indicate that some incumbents equate personal characteristics with issues (12 percent for incumbents compared to 1 percent for challengers and 4 percent for candidates in open races).

While candidates devote a considerable amount of time to articulating their policy priorities during their campaigns, candidates also try to cultivate favorable personal images. These impressions are important because citizens often consider the candidates' personalities when casting their votes (e.g., Kinder, 1986; Markus, 1982; Miller, 1990; Rapoport et al., 1989). In particular, research aimed at explaining individuals' vote choices demonstrates that evaluations of the candidates' traits significantly affect voting decisions in presidential and subpresidential elections (e.g., Goldenberg et al., 1988; Markus, 1982; Kinder, 1986).

Kinder (1986), exploring the structure of citizens' trait assessments, identified four distinct trait dimensions: competence, leadership, integrity, and empathy. Kinder defines competence as traits dealing with managerial and

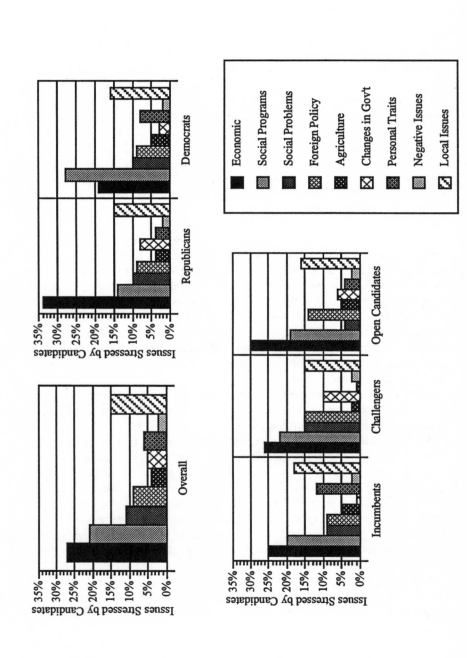

Figure 3.1. Campaign manager data: policies stressed by candidates in Senate campaigns. The *economic* category includes discussion of general economic issues, inflation, jobs, unemployment, taxes, budget, and interest rates. The *social program* category includes discussion of health, elderly, education, environment, and welfare. The *social problems* include drugs, AIDS, day care, abortion, civil rights, prayer in school, death penalty, crime, family values, and gun control. *Foreign policy* includes issues dealing with defense, foreign aid, Central America, apartheid, Gulf War, Panama, Israel, Yugoslavia, imports and exports. *Agriculture* focuses on farm policy. *Changes in government* include campaign finance, term limits, and "time for a change." The items that constitute *personal traits* fall into three areas: integrity, leadership, experience. *Negative issues* include any issue that was presented in a negative way, regardless of the category. *Local issues* were specific enough that they did not fall into one of the other issue categories.

technical skills (e.g., hard-working, intelligent, knowledgeable, experienced), while leadership involves more "mythical and heroic" traits (e.g., inspiring, strong, independent). The integrity dimension is associated with traits such as honesty, trustworthiness, and morality, while empathy is reflected by the candidates' compassion and understanding (e.g., sensitive, kind, really cares, in touch). Additional research by Kinder and others suggests that the dimension of empathy is less central to voters' impressions of candidates than competence, leadership, and integrity (Kinder, 1986; Kinder and Abelson, 1981; Kinder and Sears, 1985; Markus, 1982; Miller et al., 1986).

Studies of House members and U.S. senators suggest that politicians understand that positive personal images will increase their chances of victory (Fenno, 1978, 1996). In fact, Fenno (1978) found that House members try to develop a "presentation of self" that includes, above all, trust. House members tend to emphasize "qualification, identification, and empathy" as central building blocks of constituents' trust. Members of Congress and U.S. senators demonstrate their qualifications by talking about their experience, their accomplishments in Congress, their honesty, and their "good character" (Fenno, 1978, 1996: 325). They try to convey a sense of identification by stressing commonalities between constituents and themselves (e.g., "I was born in this county and graduated from the local high school"). They stress empathy by expressing sympathy for the problems facing their constituents.

To examine the role that personal traits play in Senate campaigns, we once again look to the interviews with the campaign managers. When we asked managers to identify the main themes emphasized in their messages, they mentioned fewer traits than issues. On average, they mentioned one trait compared to approximately two issues. However, incumbents were far more likely than nonincumbents to mention traits as a major theme. As an illustration, when we look at the managers' first responses to the main-themes question, incumbent managers mentioned a personal trait over half of the time (52 percent). In contrast, managers for candidates in open races presented a trait as a first response only 15 percent of the time, and managers for challengers offered a personal trait first only 7 percent of the time.[18]

We can also investigate the types of personal characteristics emphasized by the candidates since we asked campaign managers to identify the personal traits they discussed during their campaigns.[19] In figure 3.2 we display the managers' responses. We organize the responses according to Kinder's (1986) four trait dimensions (i.e., competence, leadership, integrity, and empathy). In addition, we include a category for references to specific elected experience (e.g., discussion of constituency service, highlighting of particu-

---

[18] Democrats and Republicans are equally likely to mention traits in their campaigns.

[19] The exact wording of the question for the traits was, "What personal characteristics did you emphasize in your campaign?"

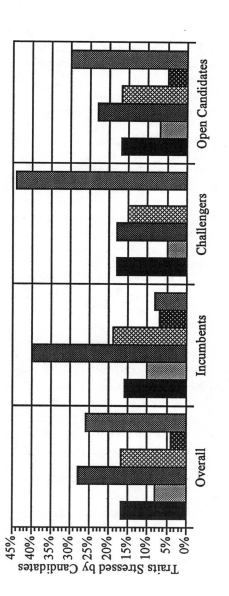

Figure 3.2. Campaign manager data: trait characteristics stressed by candidates in Senate campaigns. The *competence* category includes the following traits: knowledgeable, intelligent, effective, competent, independent, hardworking. The *leadership* category includes the following traits: inspiring and strong leader. The *empathy* category includes the following traits: compassion, sensitivity, nice person, ties with state, and average person. The *integrity* category includes references to the candidate's honesty and trustworthiness. The *specific elected experience* category includes references to candidate's seniority, committee assignments, and voting positions. The *background* category includes discussion of candidate's career: occupations outside of the U.S. Senate, war record, and special life experience.

lar committee assignments), and a category for general background (e.g., war record, special life experience, career outside of Senate) (Fenno, 1996). Responses falling into these last two categories are used by candidates to document and illustrate their competence and leadership abilities. Incumbents can rely on specific elected experiences to emphasize these traits. Nonincumbents, on the other hand, are relegated to discussing their backgrounds as a way of validating their experiences and leadership skills.

The data in figure 3.2 demonstrate that candidates highlight a variety of different personal traits. Overall, 17 percent of the candidates focus on their competence, while 7 percent emphasize their leadership abilities when running for the U.S. Senate. Senator George Mitchell, for example, ran for reelection in 1988 with the slogan, "Leadership that Works for Maine and the Nation." Candidates also make reference to these traits indirectly by talking about specific experience as U.S. senators (e.g., "My experience on the Foreign Relations Committee provides me with valuable insights") or by indicating that their background is relevant for service in the Senate (e.g., "As a successful entrepreneur, I know how to create jobs and vitalize the economy"). If we combine the general discussion of competence and leadership with the concrete examples drawn from elective and nonelective experience (i.e., competence, leadership, specific elected experience, and background), we account for more than half of the trait mentions by the managers.

Messages also focus on candidates' empathy by showing them as caring, as in touch with the constituents, and as nice people. For example, one manager for a senator reported that the campaign relied extensively on television ads to emphasize the senator as "a good and decent guy."[20] Another campaign sought to present the senator as a "good ol' boy," while a third senator emphasized his closeness with his constituents by using the campaign slogan, "One of us representing us."

Finally, according to their managers, candidates often highlight their integrity during their campaigns. When Senator John Chafee of Rhode Island ran for reelection in 1988, he often compared himself to an experienced and reliable doctor whose judgment you can trust (*Congressional Quarterly*, 1988). Another campaign manager emphasized his candidate's honesty by explaining that the senator "always seeks the truth and lets the chips fall where they may." Many other managers simply named integrity as one of several traits used to describe their candidates. For example, one campaign manager characterized a former House member in his bid for a Senate seat as "honest, trustworthy, public servant, and a family man."

The data in figure 3.2 also reveal that the status of the candidates influences the traits the candidates choose to emphasize. Nonincumbents neces-

---

[20] We withhold the name of the candidates when presenting information from the campaign manager interviews since these interviews were confidential.

sarily focus more extensively on their backgrounds as a way of demonstrating their competence and leadership qualities.[21] Incumbents, in contrast, talk about their empathy frequently, stressing their sensitivity more than any other trait. Sitting senators need not emphasize their experiences since their leadership qualities are likely to be superior to those of their opponents. Instead, their positions of power may lead citizens to view them as out of touch and part of the "Washington establishment." To combat this potential problem, senators spend a considerable amount of time demonstrating that they empathize with their constituents.

The responses from the campaign managers illuminate the general messages candidates thought would convince voters to support their candidacies. To analyze more closely the substance of the candidates' messages, we turn to candidates' commercials. Data from commercials provide us with the exact content of candidates' messages delivered during campaigns rather than a general summary of the messages supplied by the managers. The messages embedded in the ads are what the voters see and use when assessing candidates.

With the political advertising data, we examine whether the closeness of the race and the campaign coverage affect the content of commercials aired by candidates. Are candidates more likely to discuss issues and present their positions on issues when races are heated and the media are paying close attention? Do candidates alter which issues they talk about depending on how close the race appears? Does the context of a campaign force candidates to discuss issues at the expense of traits? We attempt to answer these questions in the following pages.

The Likelihood of Issue Discussion

To examine how competition and media coverage influence the amount of issue discussion in candidates' ads, we first examined the content of each ad to determine if it contained any mention of an issue. Each ad was coded so that the "major" and "minor" messages of the ad were identified. If the ad focused only on the economy, for example, then the economy was coded as the major message. If, however, the ad stressed the strong leadership qualities of a candidate and explained that the candidate took leadership positions on a variety of issues, including the economy and health care, then leadership was coded as the major emphasis and the economy and health care were considered minor emphases. Of the 594 ads that were analyzed, 80 percent stressed issues in some way, and 36 percent of the ads made an issue the major focus of the ad.

---

[21] There is no significant difference in the types of traits emphasized by Democrats and Republicans.

In this first analysis, we are interested in identifying the forces that moti-vated candidates to mention issues in their ads, either in a minor or major way. That is, under what conditions do candidates feel compelled at least to mention issues in their ads? To answer this question, we coded each ad a "1" if it included any discussion of issues and "0" if no issues were mentioned.[22]

To measure competition, we used polls taken between September 16 and September 30.[23] Polls in September precede the airing of most of the candi-dates' commercials, since candidates air the bulk of their commercials in the last month of their campaigns. FEC reports reveal that the vast majority of candidate spending comes between October 1 and Election Day.[24]

To determine if media discussion about issues during the early days of the campaign influenced the likelihood that candidates would pursue issues in their ads, we measured the amount of issue discussion in the newspapers for the month of September. These measurements precede the airing of most advertisements. Candidates may be more likely to discuss issues if they are involved in races where the press is discussing policy generally, or if the press has identified particular issue concerns in the state.[25]

To detect if a candidate's status is related to the likelihood of discussing issues, we simply include binary variables to represent incumbents, chal-lengers, and candidates in open seats. Given the tabular analysis presented earlier, we expect incumbents to be less likely to discuss issues compared to nonincumbents.

Finally, we know that in House and Senate races candidates often monitor the strategies of their rivals during campaigns in order to adopt an effective counterstrategy (Fenno, 1978, 1996).[26] We found a similar pattern for Senate

---

[22] In the analyses in this chapter and the following chapter, the advertisement—and not the candidate—is the unit of analysis. The candidate is not the unit of analysis because the number of advertisements for each candidate is not identical. As discussed in chapter 2, we stratified our sample of advertisements by candidate, selecting four ads per candidate, if available. For some candidates, especially underfunded nonincumbents, four ads were not available. In the present analysis, if we examine the amount of issue and trait discussion by candidate, some candidates would receive less issue or trait discussion simply because they have fewer advertisements in the sample. To avoid these problems, we have chosen to rely on the advertisement as the unit of analysis.

[23] Competition ranges from 0 (0 points separating the opponents in the polls) to 72 (72 points separating the opponents in the polls).

[24] In fact, 60 percent of all campaign spending occurred after October 1 for the Senate races contested between 1988 and 1992.

[25] The amount of issue coverage for the candidate was operationalized by dividing the amount of issue coverage by the total number of paragraphs printed about the race.

[26] It may be the case that perceptions of an opponent's campaign will be more influential when the race is close. Although we tested for this multiplicative relationship between competi-tion and beliefs about the opponent's strategy in this chapter, we found no evidence for such a conditional relationship.

TABLE 3.3

Logit Analysis of Political Advertising Data: Explaining Whether an Issue Is Mentioned in an Ad

	Unstandardized Logit Coefficient	Standard Error	Beta	Level of Significance
Competition	− .009	.003	− .34	p < .01
Media coverage	.002	.002	.11	n.s.
Incumbent	.17	.14	.21	n.s.
Challenger	.06	.14	.07	n.s.
Opponent's campaign	.06	.13	.07	n.s.
Constant	.67	.16		p < .01
N = 594				
% of cases correctly predicted = 80				

Notes: Issue Mention is a binary variable where 1 = an issue was mentioned in the ad, 0 = no issue was mentioned. *Competition* is measured from poll results taken September 16 to October 1. Competition ranges from 0 (0 points separating candidates in preelection polls) to 72 (72 points separating candidates). *Media coverage* is the proportion of paragraphs about issues during the month of September. *Incumbent* and *Challenger* is a binary variable where 1 = incumbent, 0 = otherwise. *Opponent's campaign* is a binary variable where 1 = candidate mentioned an issue first when asked the main themes of the opponent's campaign, 0 = otherwise. The estimate for open-race candidates is also the intercept for the equation (see Knoke and Burke, 1980). The p-values are based on one-sided tests because each hypothesis is directional.

campaigns in our study. We asked managers to articulate the main themes presented by their opponents. Ninety-nine percent of managers readily mentioned at least one theme, and 75 percent mentioned two. These interviews clearly suggest that managers were well aware of their competitors' strategies. We hypothesize that candidates who view their opponents as running issue-oriented campaigns may spend more time dealing with issues in their own campaigns. If a manager mentioned an issue first when evaluating the opponent's campaign, we considered the manager to view the opponent as running an issue-oriented campaign.[27]

In summary, we expect that competition, media coverage, perceptions of the opponent's strategy, and the status of the candidate will explain whether candidates focus on issues in their commercials. Based on our sample of 594 ads, we conducted a logistic regression analysis.[28] The results are presented in table 3.3.

[27] The first mentions, because they represent "top-of-the-head" responses, are likely to describe the managers' perceptions of their opponents' major campaign emphasis (Taylor and Fiske, 1978; Zaller and Feldman, 1992). Thirty-one percent of candidates mentioned an issue first when asked to list the main themes of their opponents' campaigns.

[28] A logit analysis was necessary because the dependent variable was dichotomous.

An examination of the findings suggests that polls measuring the level of competition in the race influence whether candidates decided to discuss issues in their ads. Candidates are more likely to broach the topic of issues if the race is close and to stay away from issue discussion when the polls predict a safe lead for one candidate, if all other things are equal. The measure tapping competition has the strongest beta coefficient in the model and is the only variable that is statistically significant.

To ease the interpretation of the Maximum Likelihood Estimate MLE coefficient for competition, we recalculated the coefficient in terms of probabilities. We calculated an average change in probabilities across differing levels of competition for all candidates because the results indicated that the likelihood of discussing issues does not vary according to the status of the candidate.[29] According to the logit analysis, a candidate has a .71 chance of discussing an issue in an ad when the race is too close to call (i.e., competition = 0), on average, compared to a .59 probability when one candidate leads by 60 percentage points in the polls.

In contrast, media coverage that focuses on issues during September does not pressure candidates to discuss issues in their ads. For example, if editors and reporters identify specific issues in September as representing key issues in the upcoming campaign and devote a high proportion of coverage to them, candidates do not necessarily feel obliged to address them.[30] Likewise, the opponents' strategies do not appear to affect candidates' decisions about whether to discuss issues in their ads. Candidates react to the polls, not to the tactics of their opponents.

In sum, our findings suggest that competition affects the likelihood of policy discussion in campaigns. In particular, candidates running in hard-fought campaigns are more likely to focus on policy matters than candidates

[29] Both of the variables measuring the status of the candidates are far from statistically significant.

[30] We also included in the model a variable that measured campaign managers' perceptions that the media was covering issues. This variable is potentially valuable because we know that perceptions, rather than reality, often shape behavior. The coefficient measuring managers' perceptions failed to reach statistical significance.

In addition, we looked at whether candidates who were ideologically extreme were more likely to mention issues in their ads. To measure a candidate's ideological extremism, we relied on the campaign manager's description of the candidate. However, the ideology of the candidate was not related to the candidate's likelihood of mentioning an issue in an ad ($p < .10$). We also looked at whether Democrats and Republicans differed in their propensity to mention issues. Again, we found no differences ($p < .10$). We also looked at whether the heterogeneity of the state and the number of moderates in the state were related to the candidate's likelihood of mentioning issues in the ads. Both of these measures were based on the state survey data presented in Wright et al. (1985). We found that neither variable was related to the candidate's discussion of issues in the ads ($p < .10$). Finally, we examined whether a candidate's level of spending affected the candidate's likelihood of mentioning an issue in an ad. We found no relationship between spending levels and propensity for issue discussion in the ads ($p < .10$).

running in lopsided contests. These findings indicate that the scope of information available to voters depends on the closeness of the campaign. This
difference in the issue dialogue may affect the way citizens think about policy when making decisions about candidates. Although we find that competition alters the likelihood of issue discussion, does it change the probability
that candidates will actually articulate positions on the issues they discuss?
We turn to addressing this question in the next analysis.

The Likelihood of Taking Positions on Issues

Candidates' general discussions of issues may reveal their policy priorities,
but such rhetoric does not necessarily identify candidates' actual positions
on issues. Candidates can provide significantly more information to voters
by specifying their actual stands on issues. For example, Bruce Herschensohn of California spent a great deal of time articulating his stands on a
number of issues during his campaign against Representative Barbara Boxer
in 1992. Using political advertisements as well as campaign speeches,
Herschensohn told voters he opposed any cuts in the defense budget, favored
a flat income tax, supported offshore oil drilling, and opposed massive federal disaster relief. Such a litany of position taking goes well beyond identifying policy priorities and offers citizens important cues about the candidate's likely behavior if elected to the U.S. Senate.

To investigate the forces that encourage candidates to take positions on
issues, we again relied on the political advertising data. If an issue was
mentioned in an ad, either as the major or minor message, coders recorded
whether the candidate took a position on the topic. Candidates took positions
in 53 prercent of the ads in which an issue was the major message. When an
issue was the minor emphasis, candidates took a position 36 percent of the
time.

To measure the clarity of position taking, we coded each advertisement to
determine whether the candidate took a clear position in the ad.[31] A commercial received a score of 1 if at least one clear position was mentioned in the
ad. Ads that included no discussion of the candidate's issue positions received a score of 0.[32] To explain position taking, we examined polls in Sep-

---

[31] We restrict our analysis to ads where the major emphases were on issues. This decision
yields 216 ads for analysis.

[32] We initially developed a scale with three values: candidates received a "0" if they talked
about an issue without taking a position (e.g., talked about the environment but failed to indicate whether they favored or opposed increased regulation); candidates received a "1" if they
offered a mixed position on an issue (e.g., decreased spending for Head Start programs, increased spending for science programs in secondary schools); candidates received a "2" if they
staked out a clear position on an issue by either advocating the maintenance of current policy, or

TABLE 3.4

Logit Analysis of Political Advertising Data: Explaining Whether Candidates Take Issue Positions

	Unstandardized Logit Coefficient	Standard Error	Beta	Level of Significance
Competition	−.008	.004	−.24	p < .05
Media coverage	.003	.002	.15	p < .10
Incumbent	−.29	.21	−.29	p < .10
Challenger	−.32	.23	−.29	p < .10
Opponent's campaign	−.02	.17	.02	n.s.
Constant	.35	.24		n.s.
N = 216				
% of cases correctly predicted = 58				

Notes: Issue clarity is a binary variable where 1 = candidate stated at least one issue position clearly, 0 = candidate was never clear on issue position. *Competition* is measured from poll results taken September 16 to October 1. Competition ranges from 0 (0 points separating candidates in preelection polls) to 72 (72 points separating candidates). *Media coverage* is the proportion of paragraphs about issues during the month of September. *Incumbent* and *Challenger* are binary variables; for example, 1 = incumbent, 0 = otherwise. *Opponent's campaign* is a binary variable where 1 = candidate mentioned an issue first when asked the main themes of the opponent's campaign, 0 = otherwise. The estimate for open-race candidates is also the intercept for the equation (see Knoke and Burke, 1980). The p-values are based on one-sided tests because each hypothesis is directional.

tember, media coverage in September, status of the candidates, and perceptions of the opponent's strategy. As before, we believe that competitive races with an active press will increase the probability that candidates will take clear positions on the issues in their advertisements.

The findings from the analysis are presented in table 3.4. Similar to our earlier results, the closeness of a race encourages candidates to take clear stands on issues. The negative and statistically significant coefficient for competition demonstrates that as races become more competitive (i.e., fewer points separate the opponents in preelection polls), senatorial candidates, on average, are more likely to offer clear stands on issues.

To clarify the interpretation of the logit coefficient for competition, we

discussing the need for significant change (e.g., increased spending for Head Start and increased spending for science programs in secondary schools). Preliminary analysis revealed that no candidate offered mixed positions on issues in their ads. Thus, the scale was reduced to two values (i.e., no issue position = 0, clear issue position = 1). Each issue position was coded separately, then summed to create a cumulative issue scale. The frequency distribution for this scale indicated that once candidates decided to articulate an issue position, they focused on more than one issue, usually two. Therefore, the distribution on the scale was not linear. Given this distribution, we decided to recode the scale into two categories where 0 = no issue positions were stated in the ad, 1 = at least one clear issue position was mentioned in the ad.

once again estimate the average likelihood of a candidate's taking a clear position on an issue when the race is a dead heat compared to when one candidate leads by a safe margin. The probability of a candidate's taking a clear position when competition is at its peak is .56 (i.e., competition = 0), compared to .44 (i.e., competition = 60) when the race is nearly uncontested.

In addition to competition, media coverage and the status of the candidate also influence candidates' likelihood of taking positions on issues. The positive coefficient for media coverage suggests that when press coverage of issues increases, candidates are more likely to take positions on issues. In contrast, the two negative coefficients for the incumbent and challenger variables indicate that these candidates are less likely than candidates in open races to declare positions on matters of public policy.[33]

In summary, we have provided evidence that competition not only influences the amount of issue discussion in candidates' ads but also alters whether candidates take clear stands on the issues they are discussing. As the competitiveness of the race intensifies, candidates respond by talking more about issues and offering clearer choices to voters by staking out specific stands on policy matters. In less competitive campaigns, candidates seem content to talk about issues without indicating their actual positions. If the pressures related to competition motivate candidates to take positions on issues, then it seems reasonable that the closeness of the race may also motivate candidates to address controversial issues. In the next section, we look at whether the dynamics of a campaign affect the issue agenda of candidates.

The Likelihood of Discussing Certain Issues

Some issues in American politics are characterized by dramatically divergent viewpoints; examples include abortion, school prayer, gun control, the death penalty (Miller and Shanks, 1996). Individuals' positions on these issues tend to be unbending; hence, finding common ground is difficult, and locating compromise is unlikely. Discussions focusing on these topics quickly turn into emotionally charged debates, with exchanges becoming heated and often bitter. These types of issues have caused divisions within the electorate for as long as reliable polling data have been available (Page and Shapiro, 1992).

[33] Remember that the constant is the estimate for candidates in open races. The incumbent and challenger coefficients are interpreted as the differences between these candidates, respectively, and the constant. In addition, similar to earlier analysis, we look at whether (1) managers' perceptions of media coverage about issues, (2) the ideology of the candidate, (3) the party of the candidate, (4) the heterogeneity of the state, (5) the number of moderates in the state, and (6) the level of candidate spending influence the likelihood of taking a clear position. Each of these variables fails to reach statistical significance ($p < .10$).

Such divisive issues are often referred to as "positional" issues. It is difficult for candidates to discuss these issues without revealing a relatively clear position. The topics do not lend themselves to ambiguity. Candidates taking positions on these issues are likely to assuage a minority of voters yet alienate, or even anger, a majority of voters. When candidates take positions on these issues, it is often because they are intentionally appealing to an ideological or single-issue minority of voters, or they are forced to take a stand by a close race, or they are challenged by a strong opponent, or they are harassed by a diligent press.

Candidates left to their own devices would much rather discuss "valence" issues, where a vast majority of voters agree broadly on goals, without much concern for specifics. These issues are tailor-made for campaigns. They allow candidates to produce commercials that are clear on ends, but ambiguous on means. For example, the complexities of jobs, health care, education, the environment, and crime can be discussed in terms of full employment, comprehensive and quality health care, an educated society, clean air and water, and secure neighborhoods.

We were interested in whether the dynamics of the campaign cajole candidates into leaving the safety of the valence issues for the controversy of positional issues. We categorized all of the major issues discussed in the candidates' ads as either valence or positional issues.[34] Candidates discussed a positional issue in 32 percent of the ads, while 77 percent of these ads discussed a valence issue.[35] On average, candidates discussed nearly two valence issues per ad, with no mention of a positional issue.

We gave each advertisement a score based on the number of valence and positional issues discussed in the ad. Each positional issue mentioned was given a score of -1; and each valence issue mentioned was given a score of $+1$. Therefore, if a candidate ran an ad where abortion (-1) and school prayer (-1) were mentioned, then the ad received a score of -2. If a second candidate produced a commercial highlighting the candidate's views on education $(+1)$ and health care $(+1)$, then the ad received a score of $+2$. Finally, if a third candidate developed an ad discussing abortion (-1) and education $(+1)$, then the ad received a score of 0.[36]

To explain the types of issues candidates present to voters, we once again

---

[34] The valance issues were identified as the economy, inflation, employment, jobs, health care, care of the elderly, education, day care, the environment, drugs, crime, and campaign finance reform. The positional issues were identified as taxes, term limits, pay raises for members of Congress, abortion, civil rights, school prayer, death penalty, gun control, foreign aid, apartheid, support for the Gulf War, and aid to Israel.

[35] Thirty-two percent plus 77 percent sum to greater than 100 percent because some candidates discuss more than one issue in an ad.

[36] The scale ranged from -2 (two or more positional issues were discussed) to 3 (three or more valence issues were discussed) and had the following distribution: $-2 = 1$ percent; $-1 = 13$ percent; $0 = 16$ percent; $1 = 45$ percent; $3 = 7$ percent.

TABLE 3.5

OLS Regression Analysis of Political Advertising Data: Explaining Relative Emphasis on Positional or Valence Issues

	Unstandardized Regression Coefficient	Standard Error	Beta	Level of Significance
Competition	.01	.003	.10	p < .05
Media coverage	.002	.002	.04	n.s
Incumbent	.25	.12	.12	p < .05
Challenger	.02	.12	.01	n.s.
Opponent's campaign	.01	.11	.01	n.s
Party	.30	.08	.14	p < .01
Constant	3.08	.14		p < .01
N = 594				
R^2 = .05				

Notes: Positional-valence scale is an interval measure ranging from -2 to 3. *Competition* is measured from poll results taken September 16 to October 1. Competition ranges from (0 points separating candidates in preelection polls) to 72 (72 points separating candidates). *Media coverage* is the proportion of coverage in September that is related to issues. *Incumbent* and *Challenger* are binary variables; for example, 1 = incumbent, 0 = otherwise. *Opponent's campaign* is a binary variable where 1 = candidate mentioned an issue first when asked the main themes of the opponent's campaign, 0 = otherwise. *Party* is a binary variable where 1 = Democrat, and 0 = Republican. The estimate for open-race candidates is also the intercept for the equation (see Lewis-Beck, 1980). The p-values are based on one-sided tests because each hypothesis is directional.

examine the impact of polls, media coverage, candidate status, and perceptions of the opponent's strategy. In addition, we include a measure of the candidate's party. In recent years, Republican candidates have concentrated much of their efforts on some highly visible positional issues (e.g., abortion, tax reform). Therefore, partisan differences in the discussion of positional issues is likely.

The data are analyzed with OLS regression and the findings are presented in table 3.5. Consistent with all prior analyses in this chapter, competition alters the strategies of candidates. The positive coefficient indicates that as the race becomes less competitive, candidates are more likely to discuss valence issues in their ads. The gut-wrenching positional issues that so often divide voters into bitter and competing camps are discussed more frequently in the closest of campaigns.

Two additional forces influence candidates' choice of strategies. First, the party of the candidate influences whether a candidate is more likely to discuss positional issues than valence issues. The sign of the coefficient suggests that, as expected, Republicans are more likely to discuss positional issues than Democrats. Second, we find incumbents are more likely than other candidates to steer clear of positional issues and to emphasize valence issues in their campaigns. Nonincumbents, in contrast, may feel a greater need to discuss positional issues as a way of drawing attention to their candidacies.[37]

At this point in our analysis there is evidence that competition significantly influences the amount of issue discussion by candidates, which issues are presented to voters, and how clearly candidates discuss public policy. Candidates monitor the polls as early as September and devise and adjust their campaign strategies accordingly. The ads that blitz the airwaves in October are very much a product of the level of competition in September. Competition appears to be the primary force on the campaign trail shaping campaign strategies of candidates. However, is competition powerful enough to push aside candidates' discussion of their personal traits in favor of issue discussion?

Allocating Scarce Resources: Traits versus Issues

The interviews with the campaign managers illustrate that candidates, especially incumbents, believe personal traits are an important element of a successful campaign strategy. However, the desire to promote positive traits creates a dilemma for candidates. By focusing on their own personal characteristics, candidates limit the amount of time they can spend discussing other topics such as policy priorities or criticisms of their opponents. Since resources are limited, time is scarce, and voter attention is fickle (Page, 1978), candidates must weigh the relative merits of illustrating their positive personal traits against discussing other types of messages. Commercials, typically thirty seconds in length, force candidates to decide which topics are most important to their campaigns.

Candidates prefer to discuss personal traits because these messages lead voters to develop positive images. However, as we have demonstrated, competitive elections force candidates to focus more extensively on the issues. Therefore, candidates in close races have less opportunity to emphasize their traits during their campaigns. Candidates running in noncompetitive contests, in contrast, feel less constrained by the factors inherent in tight races and have more freedom to illustrate their personal strengths in their commercials.

In this analysis we examine whether the dynamics of the race are related to the balance of trait and issue discussion in candidates' advertisements. For

---

[37] Again, we look at whether (1) managers' perceptions of media coverage about issues, (2) the ideology of the candidate, (3) the heterogeneity of the state, (4) the number of moderates in the state, and (5) the level of candidate spending influence the type of issues that candidates discuss in their ads. None of these variables reaches statistical significance ($p < .10$).

TABLE 3.6

OLS Regression Analysis of Political Advertising Data: Explaining Relative
Emphasis on Candidate's Traits or Issues

	Unstandardized Regression Coefficient	Standard Error	Beta	Level of Significance
Competition	−.01	.005	−.13	p < .05
Media coverage	.004	.003	.07	p < .10
Incumbent	−.08	.23	−.03	n.s.
Challenger	−.21	.25	−.07	n.s.
Opponent's campaign	.29	.21	.11	p < .10
Constant	.36	.26		p < .10
N = 311				
R^2 = .03				

Notes: Issue-trait scale is a interval measure ranging from −2 to 2. *Competition* is measured
from poll results taken September 16 to October 1. Competition ranges from 0 (0 points separating candidates in preelection polls) to 72 (72 points separating candidates). *Media coverage* is
the proportion of coverage in September that is related to issues. *Incumbent* and *Challenger* are
binary variables. *Opponent's campaign* is a binary variable where 1 = candidate mentioned an
issue first when asked the main themes of the opponent's campaign, 0 = otherwise. The estimate for open-race candidates is also the intercept for the equation (see Lewis-Beck, 1980). The
p-values are based on one-sided tests because each hypothesis is directional.

each advertisement, we determined whether traits or issues were a major or
minor emphasis of the commercial. Based on this coding scheme, we developed a 5-point scale ranging from 2 (the major emphasis of the advertisement is an issue, with no mention of traits) to −2 (the major emphasis of
the advertisement is traits, with no mention of issues).[38]

To explain how candidates allocate commercial time between issue and
trait discussion, we once again expect that competition, media coverage, status of the candidates, and perceptions of the opponents' strategies will shape
candidates' decisions. The results presented in table 3.6 indicate that competition motivates candidates to focus more exclusively on issues, while the
lack of competition allows candidates to concentrate more on traits. The
significant and negative regression coefficient for competition indicates that
as a race becomes more lopsided, candidates focus more exclusively on traits
than on issues. The standardized coefficient for competition (−.13) is the

---

[38] The five points on the scale are the following: 2 = major issue and no trait; 1 = major
issue and minor trait or minor issue and no traits; 0 = major issue and major trait or minor
issue and minor trait; −1 = major trait and minor issue or minor trait and no issues; −2 =
major trait and no issues. The scale had the following distribution: 2 = 26 percent; 1 = 26
percent, 0 = 17 percent, −1 = 16 percent, −2 = 15 percent. Ads which did not mention the
candidate's own traits or issues (i.e., ads focusing on the candidate's opponent) were not included in the analysis.

largest in the model, indicating that competition has the greatest impact on the balance between issue and trait discussion in the candidates' ads.

Two additional variables influence candidates' relative emphases on traits or issues: media coverage and perceptions of what the opponents are talking about.[39] The coefficient representing media coverage indicates that as the reporters and editors increase their discussion of issues, candidates respond by shifting their focus away from traits and toward issues. We have shown in this chapter, for the first time, that perceptions about the opponents' campaigns shape candidates' strategies. That is, if candidates perceive their opponents as running issue-oriented campaigns, then they are likely to adjust their strategies accordingly.[40]

Summary

An examination of the candidates' political advertisements reveals that candidates present different campaign messages depending on the competitiveness of the contest. As races become more competitive, the dialogue of the campaign changes markedly from a description of the candidates' personalities to a debate about issues. In particular, in closely contested races, candidates talk more about issues, venture into controversial issue arenas, and declare clearer positions on issues.

In contrast, when one candidate has a commanding lead in the polls, candidates are more reluctant to debate public policy and are more likely to talk about benign topics such as their own personal characteristics. In these races, candidates do not spend much time discussing their policy priorities; they rarely present ads focusing on controversial issues, and they usually shy away from presenting clear positions on issues. Instead, these candidates prefer to focus on their personal strengths and to extol their experience, empathy, and integrity.

The status of the candidate has a marginal effect on the content of cam-

---

[39] None of the rival factors examined in this chapter (managers' perceptions of media coverage, the ideology of the candidate, the party of the candidate, the heterogeneity of the state, the number of moderates in the state, and the level of candidate spending) are significantly related to a candidate's preference for issues versus traits ($p < .10$).

[40] We examined whether incumbents and nonincumbents differed in their responsiveness to the closeness of the race. To test this hypothesis, we examined the conditional relationship between status (incumbent versus nonincumbent) and poll standings in explaining the four dependent variables examined in the advertising analysis (i.e., whether an issue is mentioned in an ad, the clarity of issue positions, the willingness to focus on positional versus valence issues, and the relative emphasis on issues versus traits). The conditional relationship was significant ($p < .10$) in only one case. In deciding between positional and valence issues, incumbents are more likely than nonincumbents to respond to the closeness of the race. The unstandardized coefficient for poll*status is .01 with a standard error of .006.

paign messages. Compared to challengers, incumbents are somewhat more likely to discuss traits, shy away from taking positions on issues, and avoid discussing controversial topics.

Surprisingly, the news media have only a modest influence on the messages of candidates. We hypothesized that when the news media focused on issues, candidates would respond by producing ads to reflect this discussion. After all, the news media may be representing the interests of constituents in the state. While campaign managers certainly read local papers in September, media discussion of policy had only a weak impact on whether candidates took positions on issues and whether they shifted some of their resources from discussing traits to talking about issues.

Finally, we have found that candidates rarely react to their opponents' strategies when developing their own campaign themes, even though the campaign managers we interviewed were quick to identify the main messages of their opponents' campaigns. Candidates devise their own strategies to match their strengths and then make adjustments according to the level of competition in the race.

Examining the substantive topics on which candidates focus is only one element of a comprehensive campaign strategy. An equally important decision is whether candidates decide to criticize their opponents. In the next chapter we move from a discussion of campaign content to an exploration of the tone of the campaign. We look at how the dynamics of campaigns push candidates to run more negative commercials. The crucial question is: What forces move candidates to criticize their opponents' views on issues as well as their opponents' personal characteristics?

Four

Attack Politics

UNDERSTANDING THE DETERMINANTS

OF NEGATIVE CAMPAIGNING

DURING electoral campaigns, negative advertising can be both beneficial and nefarious. On the one hand, critical commentary and debates about current and proposed public policies can be informative. Similarly, open and frank dialogue about the personality characteristics of potential leaders is often enlightening. On the other hand, critical discussions sometimes lead to inaccurate assertions, unsubstantiated allegations, and defamation of the candidates' reputations and character.

To be sure, negative campaigning is not a new phenomenon. In the 1828 presidential election between Andrew Jackson and John Quincy Adams, handbills were circulated during the campaign that charged Jackson with "ordering . . . executions, massacring Indians, stabbing Samuel Jackson in the back, murdering one soldier who disobeyed his commands, and hanging three Indians" (Jamieson, 1984: 7). Among recent elections, many political pundits viewed George Bush's relentless attack of Michael S. Dukakis during the 1988 presidential campaign as one of the most infamous examples of negative campaigning (West, 1993). Sabato (1989) called the 1988 election "a dreary, highly negative, and trivial general election campaign."

Today, candidates for virtually every level of office rely on negative advertising to some extent (Johnson-Cartee and Copeland, 1991). A brief perusal of the *Congressional Quarterly Weekly Reports* illustrates the pervasiveness of negative campaigning in recent Senate campaigns. When describing the 1992 open race in Colorado, *CQ* (1992: 3346) reports, "The well-financed Considine has been blanketing the state since September with a barrage of sometimes caustic, sometimes witty attacks. Some say it is the longest, nastiest political assault waged in modern-day state history."

Negative campaigning, a common tactic in open races (Herrnson, 1995), is also embraced by both challengers and incumbents. Three-term senator John Glenn in his 1992 reelection bid "made a tactical decision to engage DeWine early, criticizing him for overdrafting checks and accusing him of having an undistinguished congressional record" (*CQ*, 1992: 3351). Challenger DeWine, not to be outdone, asked the question throughout the campaign, "What on earth has John Glenn done?" A majority of voters apparently decided Glenn had done enough; he captured 51 percent of the vote.

In developing critical messages, candidates attack their opponents' stands on issues as well as criticize their opponents' character. For example, House representative Connie Mack of Florida ran an aggressive ideological campaign against House representative Buddy MacKay, defining the 1988 campaign as a choice between a conservative and a liberal. Mack's ads, with the tag line "Hey, Buddy, you're liberal," criticized a number of MacKay's stands, including his opposition to a balanced budget amendment and his refusal to support military aid to the Contras (*CQ*, 1988).

Challenger Joseph Lieberman chose to attack Senator Lowell Weicker's maverick persona in his successful bid for Connecticut's U.S. Senate seat. Playing off Weicker's longtime slogan, "Nobody's Man but Yours," Lieberman's television ads asked, "Nobody's Man but Whose?" Throughout the campaign, Lieberman criticized Weicker by suggesting that Weicker was hiding behind the "maverick" label to keep from being held accountable for his actions (*CQ*, 1988).

Negative campaigning is pursued for the simple reason that candidates and campaign consultants view it as effective (Kern, 1989). These beliefs are not unfounded. Political scientists, psychologists, and communication scholars have often demonstrated that negative information is more influential than positive information (e.g., Hamilton and Zanna, 1974; Johnson-Cartee and Copeland, 1991; Lau, 1985). But why?

There are at least two general explanations for the effectiveness of negative campaigning, both originating from work in social psychology. First, because the preponderance of information that people receive in their daily lives is positive (e.g., at work, school, home, and among friends and family), negative information is more unique and consequently more salient (Campbell et al., 1976; Lau, 1985). Although this phenomenon is well documented by social psychologists studying normal social life, the critical question is whether it applies to political information. Do voters remember negative information about candidates more readily than positive information? Studies of political advertisements suggest that the answer is yes (Jamieson, 1992; Kern, 1989). Researchers employing experimental designs demonstrate that negative ads are more memorable than positive ads (Basil et al., 1991; Lang, 1991; Newhagen and Reeves, 1991).

A second explanation for the effectiveness of negative campaigning rests on the assumption that most people, most of the time, are risk averse. To limit their risk, people acquire and retain information about the costs of particular outcomes (Lau, 1985). In a political campaign, information about costs (i.e., negative information) is especially welcome if it leads voters to avoid undesirable outcomes (e.g., increased taxes if a particular candidate is elected). Lau (1985), examining the 1968, 1972, and 1980 presidential campaigns, provided evidence for the importance of negative information. In particular, Lau showed that voters who cared about the outcome of the election weighed negative information more heavily than positive information when developing affective evaluations of the candidates.

Given this line of research, there are clear incentives for candidates to "go negative." At the very least, it appears that voters are more likely to recall negative than positive information. Additionally, if the negative information is linked with political outcomes with which voters are uncomfortable, they may use the negative information when forming their impressions of the candidates.

While negative campaigning has advantages, such a strategy is not without problems and is hardly a panacea for candidates. To see the potential costs of negative campaigning, we turn to the Ohio senatorial campaign in 1988. Senator Howard Metzenbaum was seeking his third term. Many political observers believed Metzenbaum was vulnerable. First, he was born in 1917, and some in Ohio thought that, at age seventy-one, his age was a liability. Second, he was one of the most liberal senators in the U.S. senate, unquestionably "out of step with a majority of Ohioans." Third, Metzenbaum's return of the $250,000 he received when connecting two citizens in a business deal smacked of impropriety. And, finally, Michael Dukakis was unlikely to provide any coattails for Metzenbaum.

As anticipated, a quality challenger emerged. George Voinovich had been elected three times as mayor of Cleveland and had served as lieutenant governor in the late 1970s. Voinovich raised a significant sum of money and established a sizable campaign organization. During the campaign, he attacked Metzenbaum early and often. He criticized him in speeches, in commercials, and in fliers. The range of his assault covered issues, ideology, and personality. Although Voinovich trailed in the polls, the race was close until Voinovich claimed that Metzenbaum was "soft" on child pornography. This assertion generated immediate criticisms by the media and other political elites (e.g., Senator John Glenn) who charged that Voinovich's attack was untrue and grossly unfair. Metzenbaum's pollster, who detected an immediate surge in support for Metzenbaum, observed, "the kiddie porn charges were simply unbelievable. You can't go out and beat someone over the head caveman style" (Pfau and Kenski, 1990: 54). Officials within Voinovich's campaign organization cited this episode as a key reason for Voinovich's loss. This example demonstrates that negative campaigning can most certainly backfire. In fact, the backlash may be far worse than any maximum benefit resulting from a negative message.

There is systematic evidence that the case of Ohio is not an anomaly. Experiments consistently demonstrate that viewers develop negative impressions of the candidate airing the "attack" ad, even if the candidate does not appear in the advertisement (Basil et al., 1991; Garramone, 1984; Kahn and

Geer, 1994).[1] More generally, people simply dislike negative advertisements more than positive ones. They often find a steady stream of negative information offensive (Johnson-Cartee and Copeland, 1991). Indeed, Ansolabehere et al. (1994) show that negative advertisements may actually demobilize the electorate and create more cynical citizens. Thus, candidates airing "attack" commercials may hinder their chances of victory by inadvertently depressing turnout among potential supporters.[2]

In summary, there are potential benefits and costs of negative campaigning. Candidates must be prudent when developing a negative strategy. They must decide whether to pursue a negative strategy at all, and if so, they need to decide carefully the content of the attack. In the following pages we will examine several common strategies used by candidates to convince voters that their opponents are not worthy of being U.S. senators. In addition, we will determine whether the use of these strategies varies with the competitiveness of the race, the media coverage of the campaign, and the characteristics of the candidates. For example, are certain types of campaigns characterized simply by more "mudslinging" by candidates? Or, are citizens given valuable information about the senatorial contestants in such contests? To answer such questions, we will examine the candidates' political advertisements.[3]

Examining the Determinants of Negative Campaigning

Candidates' decisions about engaging in negative campaigning are far from random; they are carefully scripted by the candidates and their advisers. Candidates' decisions regarding the production of negative advertisements are affected by at least three sets of factors: the candidates' standings in the polls, the media coverage of the campaign, and the characteristics of the candidates.

The Importance of Competition

We contend that the level of competition in a race encourages all candidates to become more negative. However, the underlying rationale for presenting a negative message varies with the status of the candidate. Incumbents en-

---

[1] However, the backlash is less pronounced when the attacking candidate is not shown in the commercial (Johnson-Cartee and Copeland, 1991).

[2] More recently, Finkel and Geer (1997), analyzing ads from presidential campaigns, find that negativity is unrelated to turnout.

[3] We did not use the campaign manager data because managers rarely identified a negative theme as one of the main themes in their campaign. In fact, only 10 percent of the managers volunteered any type of negative theme. However, managers were more likely to view their opponent's campaign as negative; more than one-third of the managers said their opponent emphasized at least one negative theme in their campaign.

gaged in close races will be more likely than safe incumbents to adopt negative campaign strategies. In competitive contests, senators need to increase support while eroding the coalition that exists for the challenger. Such a strategy requires that incumbents present the electorate with a favorable picture of their candidacy, while simultaneously painting an unattractive portrait of the challenger.

Incumbents who enjoy a substantial lead in the polls, on the other hand, do not need to include negative themes when designing their campaign strategy. These senators simply need to maintain support among their constituents. They can restrict the focus of their message to highlight their own personal attributes (e.g., leadership), what they have accomplished for the state (e.g., pork), and their favorite policy priorities (e.g., Kennedy and health insurance; Nunn and defense; Moynihan and welfare). There is no reason for a safe incumbent to mention the name of the opponent, since the opponent's level of support is significantly weaker than the incumbent's.

Ironically, the strategies of challengers who are way behind in the polls are similar to those of incumbents who are way ahead. That is to say, both sets of candidates have reasons to avoid producing negative ads. Challengers running in lopsided races need to spend time introducing themselves to voters and explaining why they are viable alternatives to the more popular incumbents. Until challengers have at least established some recognition of their candidacies, they cannot afford to focus primarily on the negative qualities of the sitting senators.

In addition, challengers sometimes enter races against entrenched incumbents knowing they cannot win. These challengers may view their campaigns as ways to increase their chances for victory in future electoral bids, or they may want the visibility of a candidacy for nonpolitical reasons. It makes little sense, then, to waste energy attacking an unbeatable incumbent. These candidates need to build name recognition, develop favorable impressions among voters, and perhaps locate sources of future funding. Finally, challengers sometimes enter elections to increase public awareness for a particular issue. For example, state representative Neil Rolde, in his uphill battle against heavily favored GOP incumbent William S. Cohen, toured Maine to drum up interest for a national health care system. Criticizing Cohen would not have advanced Rolde's cause.

Long-shot challengers, then, have clear incentives to avoid exclusively negative campaigns. While we do not expect their campaigns to be purely positive, since they must convince voters to reject the incumbents, we do believe these challengers will rely on negative themes less often than their more competitive counterparts. Challengers running in close contests, on the other hand, are able to spend more time attacking their opponents. These candidates are more widely known and liked by the electorate. Compared to their noncompetitive colleagues, they already have established a favorable image with many voters, and they do not need to spend as much time convincing voters of their attractiveness as potential senators. Instead, they can allocate significantly more time and resources to explaining why citizens need to replace the sitting senators.[4]

The Role of the News Media

While the competitiveness of the race leads candidates to rely more heavily on negative campaigning, the news media's treatment of the race may also influence the candidates' choices of strategies. If the media's early coverage of the campaign contains criticisms of the candidates, then candidates may feel more at ease attacking their opponents in their commercials. Since the news media have already published attacks of the candidates, a candidate who begins to air critical commercials may not be viewed as the first to "go negative." In addition, candidates may believe that their attack advertisements will receive coverage in the press if the media show a willingness to publicize negative information about the race. Finally, if the news media are attacking candidates early in the campaign on matters of public policy, candidates may defend their positions while attacking their opponents' positions later in the campaign.

Characteristics of the Candidates

In general, we expect incumbents to be less negative than challengers and candidates in open races. Incumbents are more likely to avoid talking about their opponents. Challengers, in contrast, always need to convince voters why the sitting senators should be replaced. Therefore, challengers, regardless of the closeness of the race, need to document the liabilities of the incumbents.[5] We also believe that candidates in open races will engage in negative campaigning more often than races involving incumbents. Candidates in open races may view their polling numbers as volatile; thus, they may believe their support is "soft." The candidates' insecurities regarding their support among potential supporters may lead them, in open races, to rely more heavily on negative campaigning.

Finally, as we discussed in chapter 3, candidates often monitor the cam-

[4] We expect that the strategies of candidates in open races will also be contingent on the closeness of the race. That is, open-race candidates in competitive races will tend to go negative, while open-race candidates who either have large leads or are trailing badly in the polls will be more likely to refrain from negative advertising.

[5] Kaid and Davidson (1986), in their study of fifty-five commercials for three U.S. Senate races in 1982, find challengers are significantly more likely to air negative advertisements, compared to incumbents.

paigns of their rivals in order to maximize the effectiveness of their own strategies. Therefore, candidates who view their opponents as running negative campaigns may be more likely to rely on negative themes in their own campaigns. Candidates who view their opponents as attacking their candidacies may feel compelled to respond by producing and airing their own negative advertising.

In summary, we expect poll standings, media coverage, the status of the candidates, and perceptions of the opponents' strategies to explain the candidates' willingness to attack their opponents in their advertising. When candidates decide to attack their opponents, they can rely on a multitude of strategies. For example, candidates can raise questions directly or indirectly about their opponents' integrity, political expertise, strength of character, or leadership qualities when attacking the opponents' personal attributes.

Candidates may decide to avoid personal attacks and criticize their opponents on policy matters. If candidates choose such a strategy, they have several options at their disposal. They can point out problems with the opponents' policy agendas. They can criticize their rivals for specific policy positions. Candidates also like to blame their opponents for unpopular policy outcomes produced by their opponents' positions on issues. For instance, a candidate may explain that welfare programs endorsed by the opponent, such as AFDC, have created a permanent cycle of poverty in this country that reaches across generations. Or, a candidate may charge that the opponent's support of welfare programs has contributed to the growing national debt. We explore the likelihood of candidates using these strategies in the following pages.

Criticizing the Opponent on the Issues

When examining the relationship between candidates' strategies, competition, and media coverage, we must be cognizant of the possible reciprocal relationships among these three components. For example, although we theorize that the closeness of the race affects the likelihood that a candidate will run a negative commercial, it is altogether possible that the airing of a negative commercial may make the race closer. Voters may learn something negative about the candidate who is ahead in the race and transfer support to the trailing candidate. Likewise, because the media often react to candidate behavior, it is quite likely that negative commercials could produce more negative coverage by the press.

To minimize our worry that candidates' decisions to "go negative" may be driving both competition and media coverage, we once again use polling data and media coverage from September. This lessens our concern because candidates' first waves of ads, those appearing in September or even early

October, tend to simply introduce the candidates to voters and "trace compact narrative histories of the candidate's life" (Diamond and Bates, 1984: 307). It is unlikely that candidates would blitz the airwaves with negative ads until they have introduced the positive aspects of their candidacies (Alger, 1996; Just et al., 1996). Thus, the chance that negative ads would air in advance of polls and media coverage published in September is minimal.

Criticizing the Opponent's General Policy Agenda

We turn first to an examination of a typical negative strategy used by candidates. Candidates often develop messages pointing out problems with their opponents' policy agendas. This strategy is not used specifically to criticize an opponent's actual issue position, but rather to attack the opponent's policy priorities. For example, S. B. Woo, in his 1988 challenge of Senator William Roth of Delaware, criticized Roth for being negligent on child welfare issues, including public education. Similarly, Robert McMillan used the tag line "Where was Pat" to illustrate Senator Patrick Moynihan's negligence regarding the problem of ocean pollution.

To determine if candidates employ this strategy, we coded each ad in our sample for whether a candidate criticized the opponent's policy priorities. Those ads where candidates criticized their opponents' policy agendas were coded "1," and those ads not containing criticisms of general policy priorities were coded "0." In the campaigns in our study, candidates pointed out problems with their opponents' policy priorities in 18 percent of their advertisements.

We employed logistic regression to determine whether competition and media coverage in September, as well as the characteristics of the candidates, are related to the likelihood of candidates employing this strategy. The results are presented in table 4.1. The findings show that candidates contesting close races are much more likely than their noncompetitive counterparts to point out problems with their opponents' issue agendas. The beta coefficient for poll standings is by far the largest in the model, at least double the size of all the remaining coefficients.

By calculating specific probabilities based on the unstandardized coefficients, we can more clearly illustrate the impact of competition on a candidate's willingness to critique the opponent's policy priorities. For instance, in lopsided races (competition = 60), candidates have only a .21 probability of pointing out deficiencies in the opponents' agendas. However, candidates running in the most competitive contests (competition = 0) have a .39 probability of attacking their rivals' issue priorities.

While candidates clearly consider their poll standings when they decide to

TABLE 4.1

Logit Analysis of Political Advertising Data: The Likelihood of Criticizing an Opponent's Policy Agenda

	Unstandardized Logit Coefficient	Standard Error	Beta	Level of Significance
Competition	−0.01	.004	−.60	p < .01
Media coverage	0.008	.008	.14	n.s.
Challenger	0.24	.12	.30	p < .05
Open	−0.07	.16	−.08	n.s.
Opponent's campaign	−0.006	.13	−.01	n.s.
Constant	−0.59	.17		p < .01
N = 594				
% of cases correctly predicted = 82				

Notes: Discussion of opponent's policy agenda is a binary variable where 1 = candidate's political advertisement criticized the opponent's policy agenda, 0 = candidate's political advertisement contains no criticisms. *Competition* is measured by poll results published September 16 to October 1. Competition ranges from 0 (0 points separating candidates in preelection polls) to 72 (72 points separating candidates). *Media coverage* was operationalized as the proportion of coverage containing criticisms during the month of September. *Challenger* and *Open* are binary variables; for example, 1 = challenger, 0 = otherwise. *Opponent's campaign,* based on information from the campaign manager data, is a binary variable where 1 = the candidate mentioned that the opponent was pursuing a negative theme before mentioning other themes, 0 = the candidate did not mention a negative theme first. The estimate for incumbent is also the constant for the equation (see Knoke and Burke, 1980). The p-values are based on one-sided tests because the hypotheses are directional.

attack their opponents' policy concerns, they are less affected by the news media's coverage of the race or by their perceptions of their opponents' strategies.[6] In the model presented in table 4.1, neither of these factors had a significant impact on a candidate's likelihood of presenting negative messages.

Finally, controlling for the closeness of the race, challengers are significantly more likely than incumbents to point out problems with their opponents' agendas.[7] As discussed earlier, challengers may be more likely to

---

[6] The variable measuring negative coverage in the media was based on the number of criticisms published in the largest circulating newspaper during the month of September. More specifically, the variable was operationalized as the number of paragraphs containing criticisms about the candidates/total number of paragraphs about the candidates. The coverage of criticisms include criticisms articulated by the candidates, campaign officials, public figures, potential voters, and reporters. To measure perceptions of the opponent's strategy, we rely on the campaign manager survey where managers were asked to indicate the main themes of their opponent. If a manager mentioned a negative theme first, we considered the manager to view the opponent as running a negative campaign.

[7] To examine the impact of status on the likelihood of pursuing a negative campaign, we

attack their opponents because they need to offer potential supporters reasons for rejecting the sitting senators. Incumbents, in contrast, can often campaign without ever discussing the challengers' policy agendas. While we find challengers to be more negative than incumbents, candidates contesting open races are not more likely than incumbents to criticize their opponents' policy priorities.[8]

Criticizing an Opponent's Position on an Issue

Candidates often want to go beyond a discussion of opponents' policy agendas and criticize specific issue positions. In our sample of political commercials, candidates criticize their opponents' positions on issues in 17 percent of their advertisements. They identify the rivals' positions by reading legislative votes, examining statements in speeches and commercials, and following responses to reporters' questions. For example, Republican Pete Dawkins of New Jersey aired political advertisements showing Frank Lautenberg as voting for tax increases on seventeen different occasions while serving in the U.S. Senate. These positions, portrayed as hard facts, illustrate the opponent's issue positions and indicate the direction public policy may take if the opponent wins.

Each ad was coded a "1" if a candidate criticized a specific policy position of the rival candidate on one or more issues, and "0" if no such criticism was mentioned. To determine under what conditions candidates are likely to employ this strategy, we again turn to explanations based on the candidates' poll standings, the media coverage of the race, and the characteristics of the candidates.

In addition, we look at whether candidates of different parties vary in their propensity to criticize their opponents' policy views. According to national polling data, more Americans viewed themselves as conservative rather than

---

include two binary variables (challenger = 1, else = 0; candidate in open race = 1, else = 0) in the logit model. With these two variables, we can see whether challengers and open-race candidates are significantly more (or less) likely to attack their opponent's agenda, compared to the baseline group of incumbents (see Lewis-Beck, 1980). In this analysis, we use incumbents as the baseline group because of our expectations that they would be the least likely to go negative.

[8] In examining the candidate's likelihood of attacking the opponent's agenda, we also looked at the impact of several additional variables. First, relying on the campaign manager data, we examined whether candidates who viewed the news media's characterization of the campaign as negative were more likely to attack their opponents' agenda. We also examined whether ideologically extreme candidates, based on ratings offered by the candidate's manager, were more likely to criticize their opponents' priorities. In addition, we looked at whether the candidates' party affected their likelihood of pursuing this type of negative message. Finally, we looked at whether campaign spending influenced criticisms of an opponent's agenda. The results of the logit analysis showed that none of these variables were statistically significant (p < .10).

TABLE 4.2
Logit Analysis of Political Advertising Data: The Likelihood of Criticizing the
Opponent's Issue Positions

	Unstandardized Logit Coefficient	Standard Error	Beta	Level of Significance
Competition	−0.01	.004	−.49	p < .01
Media coverage	−0.007	.009	−.14	n.s.
Challenger	0.32	.13	.41	p < .01
Open	0.29	.16	.31	p < .05
Opponent's campaign	−0.07	.14	−.08	n.s.
Party	−0.34	.13	−.45	p < .01
Constant	0.52	.18		p < .01
N = 594				
% of cases correctly predicted = 83				

Notes: The dependent variable is a binary variable where 1 = candidate's political advertisement contains at least one criticism of the opponent's issue position, 0 = candidate's political advertisement contains no criticisms. *Competition* is measured by poll results published September 16 to October 1. Competition ranges from 0 (0 points separating candidates in preelection polls) to 72 (72 points separating candidates). *Media coverage* was operationalized as the proportion of coverage containing criticisms during the month of September. *Challenger* and *Open* are binary variables; for example, 1 = challenger, 0 = otherwise. *Opponent's campaign*, based on information from the campaign manager data, is a binary variable where 1 = the candidate mentioned that the opponent was pursuing a negative theme before mentioning other themes, 0 = the candidate did not mention a negative theme first. The estimate for incumbent is also the constant for the equation (see Knoke and Burke, 1980). Party is a binary variable where 1 = Democrat, 0 = Republican. The p-values are based on one-sided tests because the hypotheses are directional.

liberal during the 1988–1992 period. In fact, according to a 1990 CBS/New York Times Poll, 34 percent of respondents classified themselves as conservative, compared to 23 percent who viewed themselves as liberal.[9] Given that the public was more conservative than liberal, Republican candidates, compared to Democrats, had more of an incentive to criticize their opponents' positions on issues. It is interesting to note that only 2 percent of the ads ever mentioned the words liberal or conservative, either in a positive or a negative way. The goal of candidates is to link the opponents to certain issue positions, clearly hoping to paint the opponents as too liberal without actually relying on the word "liberal."

We estimated a logistic regression analysis specifying the circumstances and characteristics of candidates that explain when one candidate will attack another's issue positions. The results are presented in table 4.2. Three factors

[9] These numbers were stable for the 1988–1992 period (Erikson and Tedin, 1995). The exact wording of the ideological question was, "How would you describe your views on most political matters? Generally, do you think of yourself as liberal, moderate, or conservative?"

are important for understanding why candidates discuss their opponents' policy stands. First, and most important, is the closeness of the contest, as indicated by the statistical significance of the unstandardized coefficient and the large standardized coefficient for competition. In addition, and as expected, Republican candidates criticize their opponents' policy positions more often than Democrats. Finally, when compared to incumbents, challengers and candidates contesting open races are more likely to focus on their rivals' issue positions in their political communications.

To illustrate the significance of competition, party, and status, we graphically represent the probabilities derived from table 4.2 in figure 4.1. The graphs indicate that the closeness of the election pushes each type of candidate to focus more attention on the opponents' issue positions. For example, Republican challengers have only a .27 probability of detailing their opponents' stands on issues in noncompetitive contests. However, in cases where these challengers are running even with incumbents, they have a .43 probability of talking about their rivals' position on policy matters.

While challengers spend the most time talking about their opponents' views on policy, figure 4.1 shows that incumbents are least likely to mention these types of themes in their campaigns. Republican incumbents in lopsided contests have a .21 probability of identifying the policy positions of their opponents. In hard-fought contests, Republican incumbents have a .35 probability of criticizing their opponents' stands on issues.

Finally, figure 4.1 also shows that Republicans tend to criticize their opponents' stands on issues more frequently than Democrats. Given that a plurality of voters consider themselves conservative, Republican candidates, more than their Democratic counterparts, tried to characterize the ideological position of their rivals by attacking their opponents' issue positions.

While candidates' poll standings, party, and status influence the candidate's likelihood of drawing attention to their rivals' stands on issues, negative coverage in the news media and perceptions of the opponents' strategies once again fail to influence the candidates' reliance on negative campaigning.[10]

Although identifying rivals' positions on issues is a popular strategy used by candidates, it is not always appropriate. Candidates, especially incumbents, may find it difficult to criticize their opponents' issue stands because opponents may lack a public record detailing their views. Second, in some cases, opponents' positions on the salient issues of the day may be more popular than the candidates' positions. Third, candidates may unintentionally encourage some people to vote for their opponents by publicizing the oppo-

---

[10] Perceptions of media coverage, the ideological extremism of the candidate, and level of campaign spending each fail to influence the candidate's likelihood of criticizing the opponent's issue positions ($p < .10$).

A. Republicans

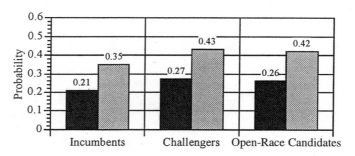

B. Democrats

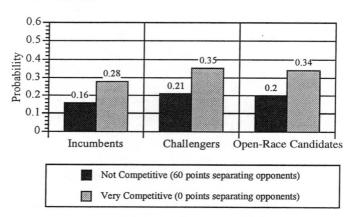

Figure 4.1. How competition affects the probability of discussing the opponent's position on issues. These probabilities are based on the unstandardized estimates presented in table 4.2. We calculate the probabilities by varying the party of the candidates and the level of competition in the race while holding all remaining variables at their means (see King, 1989: 105).

nents' position on an issue, even if the issue tends to be unpopular. For example, even though more people are pro-choice than pro-life on the abortion issue (Erikson and Tedin, 1995), a pro-choice candidate may convince some voters (i.e., voters holding a pro-life position) to endorse the opponent by publicizing the opponent's pro-life stance. When it is difficult or politically risky to attack the opponents' positions on the issues, candidates may adopt more generic policy critiques. Specifically, candidates can blame their opponents for unpopular policy outcomes. In the next section, we examine the circumstances leading candidates to employ such strategies.

Blaming Opponents for Policy Outcomes

To be sure, blaming the opponent for unfortunate policy consequences is a popular strategy; 20 percent of all the advertisements in our sample contain criticisms of the opponent for failed policy. For example, in the 1990 campaign between U.S. House representative Robert Smith and former U.S. senator John Durkin, Smith tried to blame Durkin for the spending excesses of the federal government. Smith criticized Durkin for supporting massive spending programs, such as the federal bailout of New York City, and explained that such support contributed to the ballooning federal budget.

We coded each ad a "1" if it contained some criticism of the opponent for an unfavorable policy outcome, and "0" if no links were made between the opponent and an unfavorable outcome. Once again, we explain candidates' decisions to employ this strategy by looking at competition, media coverage, candidate status, and perceptions of the opponents' behavior. As before, the data were subjected to logistic regression analysis. The findings are presented in table 4.3.

Consistent with our previous findings, candidates become increasingly more likely to blame their opponents for adverse policy outcomes as their races become more competitive. The unstandardized coefficient for competition easily defeats the null hypothesis. In addition, challengers and candidates contesting open races are much more likely than incumbents to criticize their opponents for unfavorable policy outcomes. Incumbents are the least likely to employ this strategy because their challengers often lack government experience, making it difficult to attack them for negative policy outcomes.[11]

To highlight the importance of status and competition, we calculate some illustrative probabilities based on the data in table 4.3. First, incumbents in lopsided races (competition = 60) have only a .18 probability of blaming their opponents for unfortunate policy outcomes, while incumbents in the most competitive races (competition = 0) have a .29 probability of using such a strategy. Challengers, in contrast, are always more likely than incumbents to blame their opponents for negative policy outcomes. In noncompetitive races, challengers have a .30 probability of relying on this strategy. In the closest races, challengers employ this tactic much more often. They have a .44 probability of pursuing this type of negative message in highly competitive races.

To summarize, we find that competition does indeed have a powerful and consistent impact on how candidates campaign for the U.S. Senate. As races become more hard-fought, candidates react by increasing their policy attacks

[11] Once again, perceptions of media coverage, ideological extremism of candidate, party of candidate, and campaign spending are insignificant (p < .10).

TABLE 4.3

Logit Analysis of Political Advertising Data: The Likelihood of Blaming the Opponent for Unfavorable Policy Outcomes

	Unstandardized Logit Coefficient	Standard Error	Beta	Level of Significance
Competition	-0.008	.004	$-.30$	$p < .05$
Media coverage	-0.002	.008	$-.03$	n.s.
Challenger	0.65	.12	.79	$p < .01$
Open	0.48	.15	.48	$p < .01$
Opponent's campaign	0.13	.12	.14	n.s.
Constant	-0.91	.18		$p < .01$
$N = 594$				
% of cases correctly predicted = 80				

Notes: The dependent variable is a binary variable where 1 = candidate's political advertisement blames opponent for unfavorable policy, 0 = candidate's political advertisement does not hold opponent responsible for policy. *Competition* is measured by poll results published September 16 to October 1. Competition ranges from 0 (0 points separating candidates in preelection polls) to 72 (72 points separating candidates). *Media coverage* was operationalized as the proportion of coverage containing criticisms during the month of September. *Challenger* and *Open* are binary variables; for example, 1 = challenger, 0 = otherwise. *Opponent's campaign*, based on information from the campaign manager data, is a binary variable where 1 = the candidate mentioned that the opponent was pursuing a negative theme before mentioning other themes, 0 = the candidate did not mention a negative theme first. The estimate for incumbent is also the constant for the equation (see Knoke and Burke, 1980). The p-values are based on one-sided tests because the hypotheses are directional.

on their opponents. Specifically, they question opponents' policy priorities, they criticize opponents' positions on issues, and they blame opponents for unfortunate policy outcomes.

In addition, senators are significantly less likely than nonincumbents to rely on policy attacks. Compared to challengers and candidates in open races, incumbents spend less time criticizing their opponents' positions on issues and blaming their opponents for unfortunate policy outcomes. They cannot use these tactics as readily because their challengers often lack political records to criticize.

Finally, candidates do not consider media coverage of the race or perceptions of their opponents' strategies when developing negative advertisements about policy. Candidates are not more likely to rely on negative policy attacks when coverage of the race is more negative. Similarly, candidates who view their opponents as running negative campaigns are not more likely to attack their rivals on issue grounds, compared to candidates who do not view their opponents as critical.

While debates about the direction of public policy are crucial for shaping the quality of life in a democracy, issues are not always the central focus of a candidate's campaign. The personal traits of the candidates sometimes dominate races for the U.S. Senate. To be sure, such traits are especially conducive to negative attacks. The candidates' personal problems (e.g., financial improprieties, drinking problems) or lack of leadership (e.g., missed votes on the floor of the U.S. Senate) are sometimes so tempting that candidates cannot resist leveling personal attacks, even at the expense of discussing the issues of the day.

Negative Information about Personal Traits

Examples of personal attacks are plentiful in the senatorial elections contested between 1988 and 1992. For example, Democrat Tony Smith, when challenging Senator Frank H. Murkowski of Alaska in 1992, criticized the senator for accepting honoraria, for taking more than a dozen junkets, and for being named "the greediest senator" by the *Washington Times* for his enthusiastic support of Senate pay raises. Smith's attacks were aimed at presenting Murkowski as a self-serving incumbent who was more interested in making money than in helping his constituents back home. In our sample of commercials, we found that candidates criticize their opponents on personal grounds 14 percent of the time.

When developing negative messages about the opponents' personal traits, campaigns need to protect the sponsoring candidates from potential backlash. Since citizens often develop negative impressions of candidates who flagrantly attack their rivals' personal traits (Basil et al., 1991; Garramone, 1984; Kahn and Geer, 1994), campaigns shield their candidates by creating advertisements where surrogates or announcers deliver critical messages about the opponents' personal failings. For example, in our sample of advertisements for the 1988–1992 Senate candidates, only 15 percent of negative advertisements contain negative personal messages delivered by the candidates, while 75 percent of the negative ads rely on announcers or surrogates to detail personal attacks.

In figure 4.2 we present the types of personal attacks used by candidates in their commercials. The first four categories ("incompetent," "lacks leadership," "insensitivity," "lacks integrity") correspond to Kinder's (1986) four trait dimensions (i.e., competence, leadership, integrity, and empathy). The next two categories tap criticisms of the opponents' records and behavior in the U.S. Senate or other political office ("negative Washington ties," "negative voting record"). The "lacks background" category contains comments questioning the opponents' qualifications for the U.S. Senate, and "negative campaigning" includes criticisms of the opponents for running negative campaigns. Finally, we have included an "other category" for negative personal themes not encompassed in the eight previous categories.

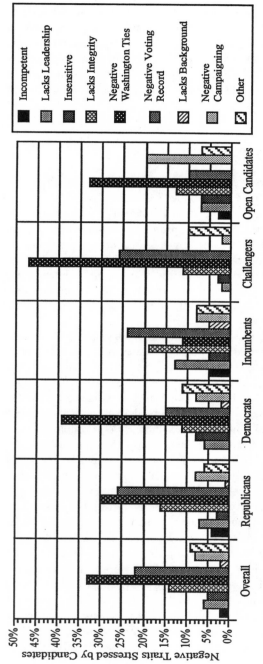

Figure 4.2. Political advertising data: negative traits stressed in Senate campaigns. The *incompetent* category includes negative references to the following traits: knowledgeable, intelligent, effective, competent, independent, hardworking. The *lacks leadership* category includes negative references to the following traits: inspiring, strong leader. The *insensitive* category includes negative references to the following traits: compassionate, sensitive, nice person, ties with state, and average person. The *lacks integrity* category includes negative references to the candidate's honesty and trustworthiness. The *negative Washington ties* category includes negative comments about the candidate's behavior in Washington (i.e., House bank overdrafts, frequent use of honoraria, ties to Washington interest groups, abuses of office privileges). *Negative voting record* includes criticisms of candidate's record in elective office (i.e., absenteeism, votes hurting the state's interests, flipflops in voting). *Lacks background* category includes negative references to candidate's political experience. *Negative campaigning* includes criticisms of candidate for running a negative campaign.

The data reveal that when Senate candidates decide to attack the personal traits of their rivals, they spend a lot of time criticizing their opponents' behavior in office, with complaints about connections in Washington generating the most discussion. For example, in 1988, Democrat William Gray of Vermont aired an advertisement criticizing U.S. House representative James M. Jeffords for his behavior in Washington. The television advertisement portrayed Jeffords (whose fund-raising total of nearly $1 million doubled that of Gray) as playing the "Washington Game," in which he receives campaign contributions, votes a certain way, then receives more money.

Similarly, in Indiana in 1990, state representative Baron Hill (D) attacked his opponent, Senator Daniel R. Coats (R), for his negative ties to Washington. Unlike Gray, Hill used humor to remind voters that Coats mailed more than 13.1 million pieces of mail to Indiana residents, all at taxpayers' expense. Hill's advertisement showed letters spewing forth from a mailbox, forcing several women to open umbrellas to protect themselves from the downpour.

While negative references to Washington were the most common type of personal attack, candidates frequently criticized their opponents' voting records. In the 1988 Mississippi race, U.S. House representative Wayne Dowdy (R) attacked U.S. House representative Trent Lott's (D) voting record *and* ties to Washington when he aired an ad claiming that Lott cast votes hurting Mississippi while the government provided him with a $50,000 per year "chauffeur." The advertisement showed a dark-glassed limousine driving through the countryside while an announcer accused Lott of viewing life through a "tinted window."

Although not as common as criticisms about opponents' lives in political office, 14 percent of the negative personal messages raise questions about opponents' integrity. In 1990, for example, state senator Bill Cabannis questioned Alabama senator Howell Heflin's integrity and voting record when he ran commercials painting Heflin as a two-faced "pol" who drawls soothing rhetoric when back home but frequently votes with Democratic liberals in Washington. In New Hampshire during the 1992 election, Democrat Jon Rauh raised doubts about Governor Judd Gregg's integrity when he focused on the governor's failure to serve his country during the Vietnam War. Rauh, a retired corporate executive who served in the army, criticized Gregg for eluding the Vietnam draft on a medical exemption for acne, bad knees, and sleep walking.

The data from the advertisements also suggest that the status of the candidate plays a more consequential role than his party in explaining the substance of the personal attacks.[12] Nonincumbents spend a great deal of time

[12] The only statistically significant difference between Democratic and Republican candidates was in the category of "negative voting record." Twenty-six percent of ads produced by GOP

trying to use their opponents' Washington experiences as liabilities. Nearly 50 percent of ads produced by challengers attacked the incumbents' "Washington ties." Harry Lonsdale, in his uphill challenge of Oregon senator Mark Hatfield in 1990, sought to undermine Hatfield's integrity by voicing concern over the incumbent's ready acceptance of political action committee (PAC) money and honoraria. In the 1992 California race between U.S. House representative Barbara Boxer and Bruce Herschensohn, Herschensohn tried to exploit Boxer's personal record in Washington by airing advertisements explaining that Boxer had written 143 overdrafts at the House bank and had abused other House perquisites.

To isolate the forces that encourage candidates to criticize personal traits, we estimated a logit equation examining the candidates' probability of attacking their opponents on personal grounds. The dependent variable was coded "1" if the advertisement contains some personal criticism of the opponent, and "0" if the ad contains no negative information about the opponent's personality. The results are presented in table 4.4. Consistent with our previous findings, we found that the likelihood of launching a personal attack increases dramatically with the competitiveness of the contest. The findings show that challengers and candidates in open races are more likely than incumbents to air negative-trait commercials in their reelection bids.[13]

To demonstrate how candidates' standings in the polls and their status influence campaign strategies, we graphed some illustrative probabilities derived from the findings in table 4.4. As figure 4.3 demonstrates, competition strongly enhances candidates' preferences for negative trait advertisements. In noncompetitive races, Senators seeking reelection have only a .19 probability of airing personal attacks. In contrast, Senators who find themselves in dead heats have a much greater likelihood (probability of .37) of attacking their opponents on personal grounds.

Challengers and open-race candidates are more likely than senators to utilize negative personal themes in their electoral contests. In addition, these candidates rely more heavily on attacks in close contests. For example, in noncompetitive races, challengers have a .27 probability of utilizing negative personal attacks. However, in the most competitive contests, challengers have almost a 50-50 probability (i.e., .47) of attacking the incumbents on personal grounds.

When deciding to attack rivals on personal traits, candidates are influenced by their poll standings and by their status. However, consistent with our earlier findings, the news media's coverage and the candidates' percep-

---

candidates criticized their opponents' voting records, while only 15 percent of Democratic ads focused on their rivals' voting records.

[13] A candidate's likelihood of attacking the opponent on personal grounds is not affected by perceptions of media coverage, ideological extremism of the candidate, party of the candidate, and campaign spending (p < .10).

TABLE 4.4
Logit Analysis of Political Advertising Data: The Likelihood of Relying on
Negative Personal Appeals

	Unstandardized Logit Coefficient	Standard Error	Beta	Level of Significance
Competition	−0.01	.004	−.55	p < .01
Media coverage	−0.007	.008	−.11	n.s.
Challenger	0.44	.12	.51	p < .01
Open	0.23	.14	.22	p < .05
Opponent's campaign	−0.09	.12	−.09	n.s.
Constant	0.44	.16		p < .01

N = 594
% of cases correctly predicted = 78

Notes: The dependent variable is a binary variable where 1 = candidate's political advertisement contains a criticism about the opponent's traits, 0 = candidate's political advertisement does not contain a criticism about the opponent's traits. *Competition* is measured by poll results published between September 16 and October 1. Competition ranges from 0 (0 points separating candidates in preelection polls) to 72 (72 points separating candidates). *Media coverage* was operationalized as the proportion of coverage containing criticisms during the month of September. *Challenger* and *Open* are binary variables; for example, 1 = challenger, 0 = otherwise. *Opponent's campaign*, based on information from the campaign manager data, is a binary variable where 1 = the candidate mentioned that the opponent was pursuing a negative theme before mentioning other themes, 0 = the candidate did not mention a negative theme first to describe the main themes of the opponent. The estimate for incumbent is also the constant for the equation (see Knoke and Burke, 1980). The p-values are based on one-sided tests because the hypotheses are directional.

tions of their opponents' campaigns fail to influence the candidates' willingness to criticize their opponents.

The Conditional Relationship between Competition and Status

One of the main conclusions of this chapter is that the closeness of the race encourages candidates to rely more heavily on negative appeals. However, certain candidates may be more responsive to the competitiveness of the contest. In particular, we expect sitting senators to be most sensitive to the closeness of the race when choosing between a positive and negative campaign strategy.

Incumbents exhibit greater variance in the tone of their campaign strategies because, unlike challengers and open race candidates, they largely refrain from waging attacks in lopsided races. For instance, in races where one candidate has at least a 40-point lead in preelection polls, incumbents attack their rivals in only 6 percent of their ads. In contrast, challengers and open-

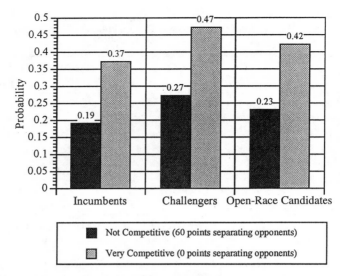

Figure 4.3. How competition affects the probability of using negative personal appeals. These probabilities are based on the unstandardized estimates presented in table 4.4. We calculate the probabilities by varying the status of the candidates and the level of competition in the race, while holding all remaining variables at their means (see King, 1989: 105).

race candidates running in these noncompetitive races attack their opponents almost 50 percent of the time.[14]

Since incumbents start out by campaigning positively in lopsided races, they have a greater opportunity to move in a negative direction as the race becomes more hotly contested. Therefore, we expect competition to play a more powerful role for these candidates. Challengers and open-race candidates, in contrast, use attacks even in perceived "blowouts," especially compared to incumbents.

In addition, incumbents are likely to have the resources necessary to alter their campaign strategies if their lead appears to be dwindling. More specifically, incumbents can afford to air positive appeals when they have a comfortable lead in the polls; if their lead is threatened, incumbents often have the campaign funds available to create and air negative advertisements. Nonincumbents are less likely than sitting senators to have the money needed to alter their strategies dramatically during the course of the campaign.

To explore the conditional relationship between status and competition, we reestimate the regression equations presented earlier (i.e., Tables 4.1–4.4)

[14] This difference between incumbents and nonincumbents is statistically significant at $p <$ .01.

TABLE 4.5

An Examination of the Conditional Impact of Status and Competition on Negativity (Unstandardized Logit Coefficients with Standard Errors)

	Criticize Agenda	Criticize Position	Blame Policy	Criticize Trait
Competition*Incumbent	−.013 (.008)[b]	−.02 (.01)[a]	−.02 (.01)[a]	−.03 (.009)[a]
Competition	−.008 (.005)[b]	−.003 (.005)	−.002 (.005)	−.005 (.005)
Incumbent	.13 (.21)	.18 (.23)	−.23 (.22)	.16 (.21)
Media coverage	.007 (.008)	−.01 (.01)	−.003 (.008)	−.008 (.008)
Opponent's campaign	.02 (.13)	−.08 (.13)	.15 (.12)	−.05 (.12)
Constant	−.60 (.21)[a]	−.50 (.16)[a]	−.44 (.15)[a]	−.30 (.15)[b]
N = 594				
% of cases correctly predicted	82%	83%	80%	78%

Notes: Criticize Agenda is a binary variable where 1 = candidate's political advertisement criticized the opponent's policy agenda, 0 = candidate's political advertisement contains no criticisms. *Criticize Position* is a binary variable where 1 = candidate's political advertisement contains at least one criticism of the opponent's issue position, 0 = candidate's political advertisement contains no criticisms. *Blame Policy* is a binary variable where 1 = candidate's political advertisement blames opponent for policy, 0 = candidate's political advertisement does not hold opponent responsible for policy. *Criticize Trait* is a binary variable where 1 = candidate's political advertisement contains a criticism about the opponent's traits, 0 = candidate's political advertisement does not contain a criticism. *Competition* is measured by poll results published September 16 to October 1. Competition ranges from 0 (0 points separating candidates in pre-election polls) to 72 (72 points separating candidates). *Incumbent* is a binary variable where 1 = incumbent, 0 = otherwise. *Media coverage* was operationalized as the proportion of coverage containing criticisms during the month of September. *Opponent's campaign*, based on information from the campaign manager data, is a binary variable where 1 = the candidate mentioned that the opponent was pursuing a negative theme before mentioning other themes, 0 = the candidate did not mention a negative theme first. The p-values are based on one-sided tests because the hypotheses are directional.
[a]p < .05
[b]p < .10

by adding the requisite interaction terms.[15] With the inclusion of the interaction term, we can assess whether the impact of competition on the propensity for negative advertising varies for incumbents and nonincumbents.[16] The results of the conditional analysis are presented in table 4.5. In figure 4.4, we use the data in table 4.5 to illustrate the conditional relationship between status and competition.

[15] For example, in replicating the analysis in table 4.1, we include five independent variables: (1) competition, (2) incumbent (1 = incumbent, 0 = nonincumbent), (3) opponent's campaign, (4) media coverage, (5) competition*incumbent. If competition*incumbent is positive and statistically significant, then incumbents are more likely than nonincumbents to air more negative issue appeals as the race tightens.

[16] With the additive analyses presented in Tables 4.1–4.4, it is impossible to assess whether the importance of competition varies with the status of the candidate.

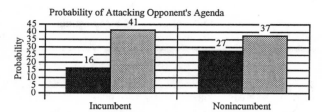

Probability of Attacking Opponent's Agenda

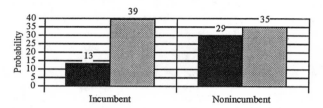

Probability of Discussing Opponent's Issue Positions

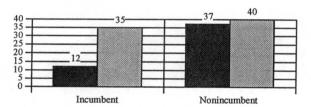

Probability of Blaming Opponent for Unfavorable Outcome

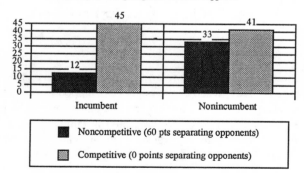

Probability of Using Negative Personal Appeals

Figure 4.4. Competition and the probability of "going negative" among incumbents and nonincumbents. These probabilities are based on the results of the multiplicative analysis (see table 4.5). We calculate the probabilities by varying the status of the candidates and the level of competition in the race while holding all remaining variables at their means for each of the four regression equations (see King, 1989: 105).

According to the findings, competition is consistently more important for incumbents than nonincumbents. Compared to challengers and candidates in open races, incumbents respond much more dramatically to their standings in the polls. In close races, incumbents are compelled to attack their opponents' policy agendas, to link their opponents with unpopular positions on issues, to blame their opponents for unfavorable policy consequences, and to describe their opponents with unfavorable personal traits. For example, safe incumbents (competition = 60) have only a 12 percent probability of attacking their opponents in personal terms, while vulnerable incumbents (competition = 0) are likely to use such a strategy about half the time (45 percent probability). In comparison, nonincumbents running in lopsided races have a 33 percent probability of relying on personal attacks, while their competitive counterparts have a 41 percent probability of using such a strategy.

Overall, the impact of competition on negativity is conditioned by the status of the candidates. In particular, incumbents respond most strongly to the closeness of the race when deciding whether to run a negative campaign. Differences in the competitiveness of the race have a profound effect on the incumbents' likelihood of relying on "attack" advertising.

Summary

Candidates alter their campaign strategies depending on the closeness of the contests. As races become more competitive, candidates change the substance and tone of their campaign messages. In chapter 3, we showed that as campaigns become more hard-fought, candidates prefer to emphasize policy matters instead of focusing on their personal strengths. In the present chapter, we demonstrate that the competitiveness of the contests also enhances the negativity of the campaigns, especially among incumbents. As preelection polls tighten, candidates respond by attacking their opponents on a variety of dimensions. They escalate their policy attacks by discussing their rivals' policy agendas, by revealing their opponents' unpopular positions on issues, and by blaming their competitors for unfavorable policy outcomes. Candidates also increase their personal attacks in competitive races, questioning opponents' integrity, voting records, and ties to the "Washington establishment."

While the closeness of the campaign clearly influences how candidates choose to campaign, characteristics of the candidates are also related to the negativity of campaign messages. We show that incumbents, on average, engage in negative campaigning less frequently than challengers and candidates in open races. For example, incumbents are less likely than challengers to criticize their opponents' agendas, to attack their opponents' positions on issues, and to blame their rivals for unfortunate policy outcomes, all other things being equal. Senators also rely less frequently on personal attacks than nonincumbents. However, incumbents are most sensitive to the closeness of the race, escalating their attacks when they find themselves in competitive contests.

Finally, the findings in this chapter, coupled with the findings from chapter 3, show that candidates do not react to their opponents' strategies or to media coverage when developing positive or negative appeals. For example, candidates who perceive their opponents as running negative campaigns do not consistently respond by criticizing their opponents. Similarly, candidates who view their rivals as running issue-oriented campaigns do not subsequently emphasize issues in their own campaigns. Furthermore, coverage in the press is not related to the substance or tone of the candidates' campaign messages. The tone of news coverage and the amount of policy discussion in the news do not affect the content or negativity of the candidates' commercials.

Since competition consistently and powerfully influences how candidates campaign, citizens witnessing a hard-fought contest are given considerably more information than citizens residing in a state featuring a lopsided contest. As races become more competitive, candidates respond by offering more details about their own policy preferences; this information can help citizens make intelligent choices on election day. Even negative information, prevalent in close races, can provide people with helpful details about the candidates. For example, when Wisconsin senator Bob Kasten framed his 1992 general election contest in traditional ideological terms by portraying his opponent, state senator Russ Feingold, as a "tax and spend" liberal, Kasten was giving voters useful cues about the candidates. The issue and ideological discussion during the campaign, while probably exaggerated, may have informed voters about authentic policy differences between the candidates.

There are always questions about the accuracy of the information presented in negative ads. One way to address this is to turn to the now popular "ad watches" conducted by newspapers. In these articles reporters and editors attempt to "set the record straight" for the voters. An examination of ad watches between 1988–1992 suggests that the public is presented with accurate information in approximately 51 percent of candidates' commercials. However, validating the information disseminated by candidates is not the only role the media play during campaigns. The news media are crucial sources of campaign information for voters on a range of campaign-related topics (e.g., candidates' issue positions, candidates' records, candidates' backgrounds). In the next chapter, we look at how the news media cover senatorial campaigns and whether the coverage depends on the competitiveness of the race and the behavior of the candidates.

Part Three

THE NEWS MEDIA'S COVERAGE
OF CAMPAIGNS

Five

Deciding What Is News

THE MEDIA'S COVERAGE OF SENATE CAMPAIGNS

THE NEWS MEDIA play a central role in today's political campaigns. Citizens receive more electoral information from the news media than directly from the candidates (Graber, 1989). In addition, people view the information they receive from the media as more credible than information disseminated by candidates via campaign speeches and political commercials (Joslyn, 1984). Without question, the media are a potent force for generating, maintaining, and improving discussion during modern campaigns.

In chapter 1, we argued that news organizations consider both the closeness of the race and the behavior of the candidates when allocating coverage during a campaign. These factors have a pervasive influence on the type and quality of coverage devoted to any campaign. In this chapter, we begin by describing news coverage of the 1988 and 1990 Senate races in Wyoming as a way of illustrating how press patterns vary depending on the activities of the candidates and the competitiveness of the race. The Wyoming examples show how the amount, tone, style, and general professionalism of coverage are altered by the dynamics of the campaign.

In 1988 two-term U.S. senator Malcolm Wallop (R) nearly lost his reelection bid to state senator John P. Vinich (D). Polls in September indicated Wallop led by only 10 points, and in the final days of the campaign the race was too close to call. During the campaign, Wallop tried to stress his seniority and experience while Vinich repeatedly criticized Wallop for spending too much time attending to the national conservative agenda and ignoring the needs of Wyoming voters. During the campaign, Wallop spent over $1.3 million, while Vinich spent about $500,000. Wallop won reelection by a narrow margin; he secured approximately 1,400 more votes than Vinich.

Two years later, Senator Alan Simpson, Wallop's junior colleague, did not face a fierce challenge in his reelection bid. Simpson led his opponent, Kathy Helling, by 40 points in September, with the lead remaining unchanged during the course of the campaign. Simpson ran a low-key campaign devoid of serious policy discussion. Helling tried to emphasize abortion and social security, but her meager war chest of $6,000 limited greatly the reach of her message. In the end, Simpson easily defeated Helling, capturing almost 65 percent of the vote.

The *Casper Star-Tribune*, the largest circulating newspaper in Wyoming, covered these races quite differently. Over one hundred articles were published about the Wallop-Vinich race, while only forty-five articles were devoted to Simpson-Helling. Furthermore, in the race between Simpson and Helling, the *Tribune* devoted the bulk of its coverage to Simpson. Over five hundred paragraphs focused on Simpson, including discussion of his voting record, his position on impending legislation in the U.S. Senate, and his activities at home. In contrast, Kathy Helling, a graduate student of social work, received only one hundred paragraphs of coverage during the entire campaign.

An article published in the Casper paper in October 1990 epitomizes the coverage of the race: "Schoolchildren and tourists who come to Washington expecting to find the Senate a showcase of oratory in the tradition of Daniel Webster or Henry Clay typically find reality a disappointing bore. Unless, that is, they encounter Alan K. Simpson of Wyoming" (Lewis, 1990: B1). Later in the article, the author explains that Simpson does not have any strong opposition in his reelection campaign. After amassing a war chest of nearly $1 million early in the process, "no Democrat of much stature would take him on. Simpson [faces] an abortion opponent, Kathy Helling, who emerged from a field of contenders that included a patient in a mental hospital and a convicted felon" (Lewis, 1990: B1). This article clearly paints Simpson as a national figure, while Helling is portrayed as the best of a group of misfits.

The coverage allocated to the Wallop-Vinich contest was much more extensive and not as one-sided.[1] During the campaign season, about one thousand paragraphs in the Casper paper focused on Wallop's campaign and his actions as a U.S. senator. Vinich, while receiving less news attention than Wallop, accumulated more than eight hundred paragraphs of coverage in the *Tribune*. Unlike Helling, Vinich's coverage in the paper allowed him to articulate a number of criticisms of Wallop as well as discuss his own policy priorities and positions.

An article published on October 2, 1988, characterizes the tone and content of coverage of the 1988 race. This article, appearing on the front page of the paper, featured the headline, "Vinich Charges Wallop Lies about His Record, Running for 3rd Senate Term." The article begins, "U.S. Sen. Malcolm Wallop 'lied to the people 12 years ago . . . and he's lying to the people again 12 years later,' Democratic U.S. Senate candidate John Vinich said at a Tuesday news conference" (Winters, 1988). During the course of the article, Vinich also criticizes Wallop's record on various issues, "suggesting that when 'commodity programs are being cut for hungry kids in Green

---

[1] We should note that differences in coverage patterns in the 1988 and 1990 campaigns are not due to differences in endorsement decisions. The *Casper Star-Tribune* did not endorse Wallop in his 1988 campaign nor Simpson in his 1990 campaign.

River, Wyoming . . . Malcolm's philosophy is telling them to tighten their belts'" (Winters, 1988). Finally, the article devotes several paragraphs to Vinich's own position on various issues, including the environment, energy, and the line-item veto.

Differences in the coverage of these two races may have affected how citizens viewed the political rivals. The sheer amount of coverage devoted to these two campaigns is related to voters' level of knowledge about the candidates.[2] Kathy Helling, who was virtually ignored by the *Casper Star-Tribune*, never became widely known among potential voters. The NES/SES surveys showed that only 36 percent of the Wyoming respondents recognized Helling's name after the election, while nearly all of the respondents (96 percent) recognized Vinich's.[3]

In addition to influencing people's awareness of the candidates, the news media can also affect the type of information acquired by potential voters. For example, studies of presidential campaigns show that when the news media focus on the horse race (i.e., who is ahead and who is behind in the polls), people think about campaign issues rather than policy issues (Brady and Johnston, 1987; Joslyn, 1984; Patterson, 1980). Furthermore, Bartels (1988) demonstrates that the news media's emphasis on the horse race affects people's assessments of the candidates' viability, which may be related to their eventual vote choices.

In the 1988 Wyoming race, readers were given a great deal of information about the competitive nature of the contest. The news about the horse race may have led people to view Vinich as a viable challenger, encouraging citizens to develop more favorable views of Vinich's candidacy. Kathy Helling was routinely described as a underfunded "long-shot" candidate. Needless to say, this type of media characterization did not encourage positive evaluations of her candidacy.[4]

Beyond influencing candidates' name recognition and viability, press coverage can also influence people's issue priorities. Studies of national and local news sources indicate that the press can influence the agendas of citizens (e.g., Erbring et al., 1980; Iyengar and Kinder, 1987; Iyengar et al., 1982; MacKuen, 1981; Weaver et al., 1981). More specifically, news organizations, by giving a great deal of attention to certain issues (e.g., crime), while ignoring other issues (e.g., the environment), can affect which issues citizens view as important.

---

[2] Patterson (1980) and Aldrich (1980) both document an impressive relationship between the amount of news coverage a candidate receives and voters' recognition of the candidate during presidential nomination campaigns.

[3] Of course, Vinich was probably better known than Helling at the start of the campaign.

[4] While eighty-eight paragraphs discussed the horse race during the Wallop-Vinich campaign in the *Casper Star-Tribune*, only eleven paragraphs focused on this topic during the Simpson-Helling contest.

Furthermore, by focusing on certain issues and avoiding others, the news media can prime voters to think about specific topics when evaluating candidates (Hetherington, 1996; Iyengar et al., 1982; Iyengar and Kinder, 1987). In the 1988 race in Wyoming, Vinich stressed the importance of the economy in his campaign. He harangued Senator Wallop for ignoring the economic plight of Wyoming residents and tried to highlight how he would revive the state's sluggish economy.

Vinich, by focusing on the economy in his political speeches and commercials, hoped to encourage the news media to follow his message, thereby leading citizens to view the economy as an important issue. Vinich appeared to be successful. The economy received a great deal of press attention during the campaign, with almost ninety paragraphs focusing on the economy in the *Casper Star-Tribune*. When NES/SES respondents from Wyoming were asked to identify the main issues of the 1988 campaign, respondents mentioned the economy more than any other issue.[5] Since citizens viewed the economy as an important campaign issue, they may have compared Wallop's and Vinich's ability to deal with the economy when developing overall impressions of the two candidates. In the end, the priming of the economy by Vinich and the *Tribune* may have created more negative assessments of Senator Wallop.

Finally, the news media can alter people's preferences by showering certain candidates with praise while criticizing others. Both experimental and quasi-experimental studies (e.g., Paletz and Vinegar, 1977; Robinson, 1976; Steeper, 1978), as well as aggregate time-series analyses (MacKuen, 1983; Page and Shapiro, 1987), suggest that the news media can produce significant changes in public opinion.

In the races for Wyoming's two Senate seats, Senator Wallop received much more critical coverage than Senator Simpson. In fact, almost four times as many criticisms were published about Wallop during his reelection than about Simpson two years later (i.e., 130 criticisms vs. 33 criticisms, respectively). The critical nature of Wallop's coverage may have contributed to people's more negative evaluations of his candidacy. During the NES/SES postelection survey, Wallop was given an average score of 52 degrees on the standard feeling thermometer, while Simpson's score was significantly higher, averaging 64 degrees.[6]

The Wyoming examples illustrate the complex interplay among candidate strategies, news coverage, and voter awareness. Editors and reporters, by responding to the closeness of the race and the behavior of the candidates, shape the information voters read and hear about the candidates. Since people rely on press accounts to gain information and perspective on electoral

---

[5] It is possible, of course, that voters viewed the economy as a crucial issue long before the onset of the campaign.

[6] The feeling thermometer is used to assess how warm or cold respondents' feelings are toward the candidate, on a scale ranging from 0 to 100, 0 representing cold and 100 measuring warm.

campaigns, it is vitally important to explore how the media decide to cover a particular contest. What are the forces that influence the decisions of editors and reporters when they craft stories about the campaign and candidates?

Factors Affecting News Coverage of Political Campaigns

To understand how media elites make decisions regarding the treatment of campaigns, it is necessary to recognize the organizational, professional, and political pressures faced by news executives and news reporters.[7] These pressures lead news personnel to consider the following factors when covering political campaigns: (1) the competitiveness of the race, (2) the behavior and experience of the candidates, (3) the characteristics of the newspaper, and (4) the presence of competing news events.

Competitiveness of Campaigns

As discussed in chapter 1, the economic incentive operating in newsrooms, as well as journalistic norms regarding the "newsworthiness" of a story, lead newspapers to devote more resources to the coverage of competitive races. The outcomes of close contests are uncertain, making these races more interesting to readers. Editors respond by allocating more resources and reporters to the coverage of competitive campaigns.

In addition, the standard criteria of newsworthiness lead reporters and editors to focus on competitive elections, since these campaigns are likely to contain more drama and conflict than low-key campaigns. Indeed, Westlye (1991), in his four case studies of Senate elections, provides evidence that the amount of news coverage was significantly higher in the two races that were competitive than in the two noncompetitive ones.

The tone of coverage may also change with the competitiveness of the campaign, with close races generating more critical coverage. As we have seen in chapter 4, the candidates' likelihood of pursuing a negative campaign increases with the competitiveness of the race. Because news professionals value conflict when reporting the news (Cook, 1996), stories about competitive campaigns are likely to represent the negative tone of the candidates' messages.

The Behavior of the Candidates

Organizational incentives and professional norms also lead news personnel to consider the actions of the candidates when deciding how to cover a

---

[7] As discussed in chapter 2, we concentrate on campaign coverage in newspapers.

campaign. Reporters and editors tend to react to campaign activity when preparing stories about the candidates. These activities, often referred to as "media events," include press releases by the candidates, press conferences, interviews with reporters, campaign rallies, and campaign stops with small gatherings of potential voters, such as luncheons and business meetings. All of these events are designed to capture the media's attention and, ideally, to create "news."

Candidates' abilities to "make news" are linked directly to money (Cook, 1989). Resources are needed to contact news organizations, to pay for transportation around the state, to hire advance people to organize events and rallies, and to produce pamphlets, advertisements, and position papers that reporters can utilize when researching stories. Fenno (1996) observed the interplay between money and its ability to generate media coverage when he traveled with candidates running for the U.S. Senate. He found that candidates with money were able to obtain media attention; without it, they struggled to have their statements and events recognized by the press.

Nevertheless, Fenno (1996: 93) recommends that the "interaction [of] money and media" be examined more thoroughly. On the campaign trail, he found it difficult to sort out the exact nature of the relationship between money and media coverage. He witnessed numerous situations where it appeared that a lack of money was related to an absence of press coverage (Fenno, 1996: 87–93). However, it was also possible that the lack of media attention was related to a noncompetitive race, or an uninteresting campaign message, or competing news events. A review of the literature on senatorial and congressional campaigns provides little guidance regarding the complex relationship between candidate spending and media coverage. In this chapter we investigate the connection between money and media attention, while holding constant many of the rival forces that may also be related to media coverage.

Besides the link between coverage and spending, newspapers may devote more coverage to incumbents compared to challengers, irrespective of spending levels. Traditional standards of reporting require authoritative figures as sources. The local media depend heavily on sitting senators for news about Washington (Bennett, 1996; Cook, 1989; Gans, 1980; Hallin, 1986; Hess, 1996; Trish, 1997), thus producing more coverage of incumbents relative to challengers. Incumbents may receive more favorable coverage than their challengers because local reporters are reluctant to offend the senators by critically covering their campaigns and thereby risk losing important sources.

The seniority of sitting senators and the political experience of nonincumbents may also affect press coverage. For example, senators with more seniority may receive more press coverage since these individuals are more likely to hold important committee assignments and prominent leadership positions. Similarly, nonincumbents who have held prior political office may have more experience dealing with the press. Consequently, these candidates may be more successful in achieving coverage of their candidacies, compared to their less experienced counterparts.

Characteristics of the Newspaper

The political bias of a particular newspaper can also determine how candidates are treated in the press. While a number of researchers have argued that reporting by the news media reflects a political bias, the exact nature of the news media's slant has been difficult to document (Davis, 1996). Some researchers (e.g., Lichter et al., 1986) cite the liberal leaning of many reporters and editors as evidence for a liberal bias in the news media.[8] However, other scholars argue that the news-gathering process is shaped by the news corporations' capitalist orientation, creating news content that reflects the organizations' conservative bias (Bagdikian, 1990; Chomsky and Herman, 1989; Parenti, 1993). While scholars have articulated reasons why the news media may be liberal or conservative, empirical evidence validating either claim has been lacking (Davis, 1996).

Page (1996), examining news media coverage of three discrete events, demonstrates that the partisan loyalties and policy preferences of newspaper owners (both liberal and conservative leanings) are reflected in the newspapers' editorials. Furthermore, Page demonstrates that these political preferences sometimes spill over into news stories. Page argues that the editorials of the newspapers and the slant of the news stories correspond because owners hire, encourage, and promote employees who hold similar views. Editors and reporters with alternative views, in contrast, tend either to adapt or depart.

Given Page's findings from these three case studies, it is reasonable to hypothesize that candidates receiving a newspaper's editorial endorsement will enjoy more favorable coverage during the campaign, compared to candidates who fail to secure the newspaper's endorsement. For example, articles written about the endorsed candidate may be more positive in tone and rely more heavily on complimentary adjectives.

In addition to a systematic bias in coverage, the sheer size of a newspaper may affect the amount of news attention given to a Senate campaign. Newspapers range dramatically in the number of column inches devoted to news (as opposed to advertising). In our study, the newspaper with the smallest news hole was the *New York Daily News* with 735 column inches, while the largest

[8] Weaver and Wilhoit (1986) examine a more representative sample of journalists than Lichter et al., (1986) and find journalists to be more centrist than liberal in their ideology.

newspaper was the *Boston Globe* with 6,183 column inches. Newspapers with more room for news may devote more coverage to Senate campaigns.[9]

Competing News Events

News personnel are likely to consider the presence of competing news stories when deciding how to cover a Senate campaign. In particular, when allocating resources during the campaign season, editors consider the presence of other important elections, like presidential and gubernatorial campaigns (Kahn, 1991). The presence of such newsworthy events may influence the number of reporters assigned to the Senate campaign as well as the amount of space available for stories about the Senate contestants.

We also look at whether the size of the population in a state affects coverage patterns. We reason that editors making decisions about which stories to print will have a wider selection of newsworthy stories in states with millions of people than in states with only a few hundred thousand.[10] Therefore, in large states, fewer stories may be printed about the Senate campaign, since a variety of alternative stories will be competing for news space.

In the following section, we examine how the closeness of the campaign, the candidates' spending, the characteristics of the newspaper, and competing news events influence press treatment of U.S. Senate campaigns. We look at three types of coverage patterns: (1) quantity and placement of campaign stories, (2) the substance of campaign coverage, and (3) the tone of campaign stories.

The Amount and Prominence of Coverage

We begin by looking at the number of paragraphs published about the candidates as well as the prominence of campaign coverage. The amount and prominence of coverage can directly influence citizens' awareness of the candidates. For instance, in low-key races where the underdog is greatly underfunded and news attention is quite limited, candidates will have a difficult time increasing voter recognition of their candidacies. As races become

[9] The mean news hole for our sample is 3,881 column inches with a standard deviation of 1,138 column inches.

[10] By including the population of the state in the analysis, we are also providing a necessary control for spending differences that are purely a function of the size of the state. We could simply divide spending by population, but we would lose the control for competing news stories. By including population in our analysis, we control for any forces that may covary with the size of the state (i.e., spending, rival stories).

more competitive, newspapers will carry more stories about the campaigns and will display these stories more prominently in the newspaper. Citizens reading these newspapers are likely to become more familiar with these candidates, if not directly through the substance of the articles, then incidentally from repeated exposure to the candidates' names.

In general, news coverage of Senate elections varies a great deal. Campaigns receive, on average, 812 paragraphs during the course of a campaign. Incumbents' names appear, on average, in 55 percent of the paragraphs, while 42 percent of the paragraphs mention the challengers, and the remaining 3 percent do not mention either candidate by name. Nonetheless, not all races receive equivalent attention in the news. In our study, the 1988 race in New York between Daniel Patrick Moynihan and Robert McMillan received the least amount of coverage; only 67 paragraphs were published about the race during the entire campaign. In contrast, the 1990 contest in North Carolina between Jesse Helms and Harvey Gantt received the most coverage, with 3,070 paragraphs published in the *Raleigh News and Observer.*

To understand how candidates' standings in the polls and their level of campaign activity influence newspaper coverage, we developed OLS equations to explain the number of paragraphs published about the race as well as the number devoted to each of the two contestants. We examined news coverage between October 1 and Election Day. We restricted our analysis to this period in order to ensure that poll standings and candidate spending occur before newspaper coverage. It is necessary to use measures of spending and poll standings that occur before campaign coverage, given the potential reciprocal relationships among coverage, money, and poll standings.[11]

The analysis presented in table 5.1 shows that the level of competition clearly influences the amount of press attention given to the race in general. For example, a one-point change in poll standings is associated with a change of 15 paragraphs in coverage, on average. This translates into a whopping 908-paragraph difference in the number of paragraphs published in a "toss-up" race (i.e., zero points separating candidates in the polls), compared to a race where one candidate leads by 60 points, holding all other things equal.

Competition also affects the amount of press attention given to incumbents and challengers (see table 5.1B). The coefficients representing competition in these equations have a similar effect on the amount of coverage devoted to incumbents and challengers. That is, a one-point increase in the closeness of the race is associated with the publication of seven more para-

---

[11] In the case of poll standings, we look at polls published between September 16 and September 30. With regard to candidate spending, we look at expenditures between late August and late September.

TABLE 5.1
OLS Regression Analysis Explaining the Amount of Campaign Coverage

A. Amount of Coverage Devoted to Senate Campaign

	Unstandardized Coefficient (standard error)		Beta
Competition	−15.13	(2.21)[a]	−.56
Incumbent spending	42.76	(18.09)[b]	.20
Challenger spending	23.35	(19.82)	.10
Gubernatorial campaign	−362.52	(83.44)[a]	−.39
Presidential campaign	−247.26	(85.64)[a]	−.25
Size of newspaper	0.02	(0.04)	.06
Population of state	−42.34	(93.84)	−.04
Constant	982.41	(551.83)	

$R^2 = .48$
N = 96

B. Amount of Coverage Devoted to Each Senate Candidate

	Incumbent/Open Winner			Challenger/Open Loser		
	Unstandardized Coefficient (standard error)		Beta	Unstandardized Coefficient (standard error)		Beta
Competition	−7.44	(1.17)[a]	−.52	−7.32	(1.03)[a]	−.56
Incumbent spending	31.50	(10.89)[a]	.25	27.15	(9.60)[a]	.23
Challenger spending	8.38	(10.86)	.06	8.30	(9.57)	.07
Gubernatorial campaign	−203.63	(44.80)[a]	−.42	−161.14	(39.49)[a]	−.36
Presidential campaign	−151.51	(46.17)[a]	−.29	−83.09	(4.07)[a]	.17
Size of newspaper	0.009	(0.02)	.04	0.01	(0.02)	.08
Population of state	−44.55	(50.43)	−.09	−9.93	(44.45)	−.02
Constant	639.05	(296.10)[a]		356.13	(261.01)	
R^2	.48			.50		
N	96			96		

Notes: The dependent variable is the number of paragraphs about the race or candidate. *Competition* ranges from 0 (0 points separating candidates in preelection polls) to 72 (72 points separating candidates). The following variables are logged to base 10: *incumbent spending, challenger spending, population of state. Gubernatorial Campaign* is a binary variable where 1 = concurrent gubernatorial campaign, 0 = otherwise. *Presidential campaign* is a binary variable where 1 = presidential year, 0 = otherwise. *Size of newspaper* is the number of column inches devoted to news. All p-values are two-tailed except in the following cases where our expectations are clearly directional: competition, gubernatorial campaign, presidential campaign, size of newspaper.
[a] p < .05
[b] p < .10

graphs, on average, for incumbents and challengers.[12] The impact of competition can be seen more clearly if we compare coverage patterns in dead heats (competition = 0), with coverage in races where one candidate has a large and probably insurmountable lead (competition = 60). The results of the regression equation show that incumbents or challengers involved in extremely close races receive about 420 more paragraphs of coverage, on average, than their colleagues running in the most lopsided contests, holding everything else constant.

As hypothesized, poll standings are not the only factor that editors consider when deciding how much attention to give to the candidates' campaigns. News organizations also appear to respond to the activities of incumbents. The statistically significant coefficient for incumbent spending suggests that their campaign activities influence the amount of news attention given to the race and to the candidates. Incumbents are able to generate more coverage of their candidacies when they spend more money during their campaigns (see table 5.1B). However, the substantive findings are rather meager compared to competition. That is, the unstandardized coefficient for incumbent spending indicates that a *ten-fold* increase in spending by incumbents is associated with a 31-paragraph increase in incumbent coverage, on average, holding everything else constant.[13] In dramatic contrast, only a 4-point change in the level of competition would produce the same amount of change in coverage for incumbents ($-7.44*4 = 29$ paragraphs).

Interestingly, the findings suggest that incumbents also affect the number of paragraphs written about their opponents. To be sure, spending by incumbents is not intended to encourage greater coverage of their opponents. Campaign activity by incumbents, driven by their spending, is most likely generating coverage of the challengers for one of two reasons, or both. First, journalists respond to campaign events orchestrated by incumbents' spending (e.g., press conferences, rallies). However, in the name of fair play, reporters are likely to report something about the challengers. In this case, the challenger receives "spillover" coverage generated by incumbent spending.

[12] We examine two categories of candidates: (1) incumbents and open winners, and (2) challengers and open losers. In the remainder of the chapter we will refer to the incumbent/open winner category as the incumbent category, and the challenger/loser category as the challenger category. In each analysis in this chapter, we initially included an open-race variable to see whether coverage patterns differed for candidates running in open races compared to candidates running in incumbent races. However, the variable tapping open races never reached statistical significance and was dropped from the analysis.

[13] The tenfold interpretation is necessary because we logged spending to base 10. For both challenger and incumbent spending, outliers are created because of heavy spending in some small states (e.g., Wyoming, Maine, Vermont, Idaho), even controlling for the size of the state. This is typical in Senate elections, and logging is the solution used by previous scholars (e.g., Abramowitz, 1988; Green and Krasno, 1990). This allows us to keep all of the cases for analysis instead of discarding the outliers (Tufte, 1975).

Second, we know that incumbents are using some of their money to draw attention to their opponents' weaknesses. That is, money is used to produce negative ads or negative press releases, and these messages receive attention in the press. Later in this chapter, we will examine the specific impact of incumbent spending in more detail when we look at the relationship between spending and the tone of media coverage.

Campaign spending by challengers, in contrast, does not encourage more coverage of their candidacies or those of their opponents.[14] This insignificant relationship is potentially disastrous for challengers who need news coverage to draw attention and support to their candidacies. When interviewed, the campaign managers of challengers often referred to this problem by complaining about the lack of media attention devoted to their campaigns. They felt that irrespective of what they tried to accomplish, the media often ignored their efforts. Fenno (1996) heard similar complaints from candidates and campaign workers while on the campaign trail.

Finally, the size of the state and the size of the newspaper do not appear to affect the amount of coverage devoted to a campaign.[15] However, newspapers are quite sensitive to the amount of space available for a senatorial campaign when confronted with competing high-profile campaigns. In particular, a concurrent gubernatorial or presidential campaign drastically influences the amount of coverage devoted to each of the senatorial candidates. Senators seeking reelection during a presidential year receive, on average, 151 fewer paragraphs of coverage than their colleagues running during the off-year. Similarly, Senate challengers vying with gubernatorial candidates for coverage receive, on average, 161 fewer paragraphs than challengers who do not compete with gubernatorial candidates for the media spotlight.

Even though all candidates hope for large *amounts* of positive coverage, they also yearn to have news about the campaign displayed prominently by the press so that it is easily seen by potential voters. In particular, articles that appear on the front page are more likely to grab the attention of readers, while articles buried in the back section of the paper may be noticed only by the most observant reader. Similarly, discussion of the candidates' campaigns may be portrayed prominently by appearing in the headline rather

[14] In addition to campaign spending, other characteristics of the candidates also fail to influence coverage patterns ($p < .10$). In particular, the prior political experience of nonincumbents, the seniority of the incumbent, the gender of the candidate and whether the candidate was involved in a scandal do not influence overall coverage of the race or coverage of individual candidates. In addition, these characteristics fail to influence the various coverage patterns examined in the remainder of this chapter (with one exception, the variable measuring the quality of the challenger in table 5.6). Finally, coverage of candidates in open races does not differ significantly from coverage of candidates in incumbent races in the present analysis and throughout the chapter ($p < .10$).

[15] The unstandardized coefficients for news hole and population are statistically insignificant in each of the three regression equations.

then relegated to the last few paragraphs of a long article. Candidates who receive more prominent news coverage may have an easier time increasing voter recognition and interest in their campaigns.

The results in table 5.2 indicate that competition influences powerfully the placement of news about the candidates. Furthermore, incumbent spending, and not challenger spending, continues to affect coverage patterns. Finally, Senate candidates receive more prominent coverage when they are not competing with a presidential or gubernatorial campaign for coverage.

In general, competition has the most dramatic impact on the prominence of coverage, compared to the remaining factors in the model. For example, when opponents are running even in the polls, nine more stories, on average, appear on the front page, compared to races where one candidate enjoys a 60-point lead.[16] Figure 5.1A portrays graphically the differences in front page coverage across levels of competition. These differences are substantial, since campaigns receive, on average, only about ten front-page stories during the course of a campaign.

When we look at the number of times incumbents and challengers are mentioned in the headline of an article, we find a similar pattern. The findings in table 5.1B reveal that as races become more hard-fought, incumbents and challengers have an easier time obtaining prominent coverage. Irrespective of status, every 10-point increase in the competitiveness of the race is associated with between three and four additional headline mentions for the candidates. Figure 5.1B demonstrates that incumbents who are running even with their challengers in preelection polls receive twenty-one more headline mentions, compared with their counterparts who are running 60 points ahead of their opponents. Similarly, challengers who are running even with their rivals receive twenty-three more headline mentions than challengers in lop-sided contests (i.e., competition = 60).

Incumbent spending, although statistically significant in explaining the likelihood of front-page articles and the likelihood of headline mentions, has far less influence than competition. For example, a tenfold increase in incumbent spending yields, on average, less than one additional headline about incumbents (i.e., 0.83) and approximately one additional headline for challengers (i.e., 1.02), all other things being equal. Challenger spending is statistically unrelated to the prominence of coverage.

In summary, these results show that newspapers clearly consider the nature of the campaign when deciding where to place stories, how prominently to feature the candidates, and how much coverage to devote to them. Competitive campaigns simply receive a greater amount of coverage and more

[16] This number is gleaned from the findings in table 5.2A. The unstandardized coefficient for competition (i.e., −.15) was used to calculate estimates of front-page stories across differing levels of competition, holding all remaining variables at their means. The same procedure was used to provide estimates from table 5.2B.

TABLE 5.2
OLS Regression Analysis Explaining the Prominence of Campaign Coverage

A. Number of Front-Page Stories Devoted to Senate Campaign

	Unstandardized Coefficient (standard error)		Beta
Competition	−0.15	(.04)[a]	−.37
Incumbent spending	0.70	(.36)[c]	.19
Challenger spending	−0.02	(.36)	−.04
Gubernatorial campaign	−3.69	(1.49)[a]	−.26
Presidential campaign	−5.52	(1.53)[a]	−.37
Size of newspaper	0.0001	(.0007)	.02
Population of state	−2.74	(1.68)	−.19
Constant	27.56	(9.84)[b]	
R^2 = .28			
N = 96			

B. Number of Headline Mentions Devoted to Each Senate Candidate

	Incumbent/Open Winner			Challenger/Open Loser		
	Unstandardized Coefficient (standard error)		Beta	Unstandardized Coefficient (standard error)		Beta
Competition	−0.35	(0.05)[a]	−.55	−0.38	(0.04)[a]	−.63
Incumbent spending	0.83	(.49)[c]	.15	1.02	(0.42)[b]	.19
Challenger spending	0.68	(.49)	.12	0.44	(.42)	.08
Gubernatorial campaign	−8.03	(2.02)[a]	−.37	−6.58	(1.75)[a]	−.32
Presidential campaign	−6.92	(2.08)[a]	−.30	−5.74	(1.80)[a]	−.26
Size of newspaper	0.0003	(0.0009)	.03	0.005	(0.0008)	.06
Population of state	−1.98	(2.28)	−.09	−1.86	(1.97)	−.09
Constant	32.66	(13.37)[b]		28.24	(11.56)[c]	
R^2	.45			.54		
N	96			96		

Notes: The dependent variable is the number of paragraphs about the race or candidate. *Competition* ranges from 0 (0 points separating candidates in preelection polls) to 72 (72 points separating candidates). The following variables are logged to base 10: *incumbent spending, challenger spending, population of state. Gubernatorial campaign* is a binary variable where 1 = concurrent gubernatorial campaign, 0 = otherwise. *Presidential campaign* is a binary variable where 1 = presidential year, 0 = otherwise. *Size of newspaper* is the number of column inches devoted to news. All p-values are two-tailed except in the following cases where our expectations are clearly directional: competition, gubernatorial campaign, presidential campaign, size of newspaper.
[a] p < .01
[b] p < .05
[c] p < .10

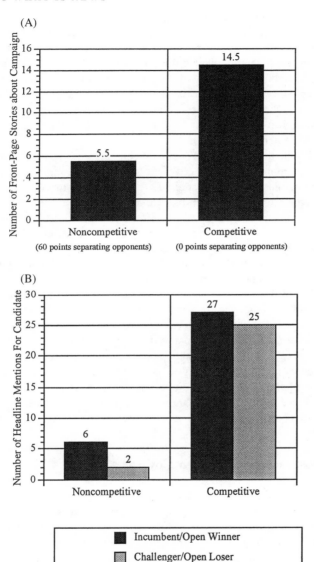

Figure 5.1. (A) The relationship between front-page coverage and competition. (B) The relationship between headline mentions and competition. The point estimates are based on the unstandardized regression coefficients presented in table 5.2. We calculate the point estimates by varying the level of competition in the race while holding all remaining variables at their means (Lewis-Beck, 1980).

prominent coverage than lackluster ones. Citizens observing intense campaigns have an opportunity to learn more about the candidates. Furthermore, an abundance of news stories may actually increase voter interest in the contest. In contrast, people residing in states where a safe incumbent is coasting to another victory will receive little news about the race in the newspaper. Since it will be far more difficult for these citizens to learn about the senator's challenger, these individuals may remain uninterested in the campaign and may even decline to vote in the November election (Caldeira et al., 1985; Filer et al., 1993).

In addition, incumbents are able to generate marginally more coverage and slightly more prominent coverage of their campaigns and their opponents' campaigns with their spending. Challengers, in contrast, cannot increase media attention by spending more money during their electoral bids. This disadvantage, not previously documented by researchers, represents one more obstacle challengers face in their uphill battle for election.

Finally, campaigns contested concurrently with Senate campaigns profoundly affect coverage of the Senate contestants. Candidates who compete with presidential and gubernatorial campaigns struggle to receive news attention during the electoral season. Less news is published about these candidates, and the attention they receive is less likely to appear on the front page or in the headlines. The tendency for news coverage of Senate candidates to decrease when gubernatorial or presidential campaigns are being contested may be most problematic for underdogs. These candidates need to acquire news attention in order to generate name recognition and to raise needed campaign funds. In addition, free media attention is important for many of these poorly funded candidates in order to increase public support for their campaigns.

The Substance of Campaign Coverage

Explaining the absolute amount of media coverage about the candidates is only part of the story concerning press coverage. The substance of the news coverage is as important as the sheer quantity of press attention. What is being said about the candidates, in addition to how many times, is ultimately what influences voters' attitudes and preferences. People rely on the information in the news to identify the party affiliation of the candidates, the candidates' positions on important policy matters, and their personal characteristics. A wealth of research findings links these characteristics directly to voters' decisions about which candidate to support (Converse and Markus, 1979; Markus, 1982; Page and Jones, 1979; Rahn et al., 1990). In addition, voters sometimes consider their assessments of the candidates' viability when choosing between candidates (Bartels, 1988; Brady and Johnston,

1987). When newspapers provide a plethora of policy, trait, and horse-race information during an election, citizens have an easier time making informed judgments about the candidates.

Newspapers vary a great deal in their efforts to familiarize people about the issues. On average, about 154 paragraphs about issues are published during a Senate campaign, with incumbents averaging 190 paragraphs, open candidates about 175, and challengers about 109. However, these averages conceal a great deal of variation. For example, in the lopsided 1990 race between Senator Alan Simpson and Kathy Helling of Wyoming, only 62 paragraphs discussed Helling's policy priorities. In contrast, two years earlier, the same newspaper in the same state devoted 332 paragraphs to state senator John Vinich's views about issues during his competitive challenge of Senator Malcolm Wallop.

The personal characteristics of candidates receive strikingly less attention than issues, averaging about 54 paragraphs during the course of the campaign. However, trait information is more pervasive for incumbents who emphasize their experience and leadership during the campaign.[17] Incumbents receive, on average, 72 trait paragraphs, while only about 32 paragraphs focus on a challenger's personality, and 65 paragraphs, on average, discuss the personal characteristics of the candidates contesting open seats.

In Wyoming's low-key campaign in 1990, only 23 paragraphs were published about the personal characteristics of Senator Simpson and a meager 3 paragraphs discussed Helling's personal traits. In contrast, two years earlier in Wyoming, the *Casper Star-Tribune* spent significantly more time describing Senator Wallop and Vinich in terms of personal traits: 96 paragraphs focused on Wallop's traits and 37 on Vinich's.

In addition to presenting information about issues and traits, newspapers spend some time describing the viability of the candidates. This "horse-race" information often focuses on the candidates' standings in the most recent polls. Newspapers also describe the strength of the dueling campaign organizations as well as the candidates' ability to secure resources, such as endorsements by important political figures (e.g., the president, the state's governor) and important groups in the state (e.g., endorsement by the state's teachers' union).

The discussion of the horse race in the newspapers is not as prevalent as trait or issue information. In fact, issue coverage is about three times more common than details about the horse race. Only about 40 paragraphs are published about the candidates' viability, on average, with incumbents, challengers, and open-race candidates receiving approximately the same amount of attention. However, in some races the press is preoccupied with the horse

---

[17] In chapter 6, we will explicitly examine the correspondence between the candidate's campaign message and the message disseminated by the press.

race. As an example, in the 1990 Wyoming race, only about 10 paragraphs mentioned the challenger's viability, while six times as many paragraphs described Vinich's viability in 1988.

In the following section, we examine newspaper coverage of issues, traits, and the horse race. We hypothesize that coverage is affected by the closeness of the race, the behavior of the candidates, competing news events, and the characteristics of the newspapers. We expect the amount of substantive coverage to change with the competitiveness of a campaign and the actions of the candidates. Finally, the presence of competing news events will influence coverage.

Issue Coverage in Senate Campaigns

As we saw in chapter 3, information about issues is sometimes available directly from candidates. However, people will have a far easier time making policy distinctions if their state newspapers spend time covering the issues during the campaign. In table 5.3 we examine the amount of coverage dedicated to the issues. The results suggest that citizens witnessing closely contested campaigns are presented with substantially more news about issues than citizens watching less competitive races.[18] The unstandardized coefficient for competition suggests that every 1-point change in poll standings will produce, on average, a 3-paragraph change (3.13 for incumbents, 3.05 for challengers) in issue coverage.[19] Thus, a 10-point swing in the polls yields, on average, about a 30-paragraph difference in issue coverage. An examination of the beta coefficients indicates that competition, compared to the other forces in the model, has the most powerful influence on the amount of issue coverage devoted to the candidates. The similarity of the unstandardized coefficients for competition in the incumbent and challenger models indicates that the competitiveness of the race equally influences all candidates, irrespective of status.

Spending by the incumbent marginally influences coverage patterns. Sitting senators who spend more money during their reelection campaign can increase the amount of news attention given to issues. Once again, incumbents can generate more media attention for their own campaigns and their opponents' campaigns. For example, every tenfold increase in spending by

[18] The dependent variable is the number of paragraphs mentioning issues.

[19] When we examine the proportion of coverage devoted to issues in each campaign (i.e., number of paragraphs about issues/total number of paragraphs about the campaign), we find the same pattern. That is, the statistically and substantively important variables in the models remain the same. Competition strongly influences the proportion of news devoted to issues. The unstandardized coefficient for competition is significant at the $p < .001$ level for incumbents and challengers.

TABLE 5.3

OLS Regression Analysis Explaining the Amount of Issue Coverage

A. Amount of Issue Coverage Devoted to Incumbent/Open Winner

	Unstandardized Coefficient (standard error)		Beta
Competition	-3.13	$(.51)^a$	$-.52$
Incumbent spending	9.97	$(4.77)^b$	$.19$
Challenger spending	-6.09	(4.76)	$-.11$
Gubernatorial campaign	-74.09	$(19.63)^a$	$-.36$
Presidential campaign	-72.15	$(20.23)^a$	$-.33$
Size of newspaper	0.01	(0.01)	$.08$
Population of state	-17.87	(22.09)	$-.08$
Constant	300.15	$(129.74)^b$	
$R^2 = .41$			
$N = 96$			

B. Amount of Issue Coverage Devoted to Challenger/Open Loser

	Unstandardized Coefficient (standard error)		Beta
Competition	-3.05	$(.42)^a$	$-.60$
Incumbent spending	7.83	$(3.89)^b$	$.17$
Challenger spending	-5.94	(3.87)	$-.13$
Gubernatorial campaign	-46.40	$(15.99)^a$	$-.27$
Presidential campaign	-27.10	$(16.48)^c$	$-.15$
Size of newspaper	0.01	(0.01)	$.09$
Population of state	-4.37	(18.00)	$-.02$
Constant	179.20	$(105.68)^c$	
$R^2 = .45$			
$N = 96$			

Notes: The dependent variable is the number of paragraphs about issues for the candidate. *Competition* ranges from 0 (0 points separating candidates in preelection polls) to 72 (72 points separating candidates). The following variables are logged to base 10: *incumbent spending, challenger spending, population of state*. *Gubernatorial campaign* is a binary variable where 1 = concurrent gubernatorial campaign, 0 = otherwise. *Presidential campaign* is a binary variable where 1 = presidential year, 0 = otherwise. *Size of newspaper* is the number of column inches devoted to news. All p-values are two-tailed except in the following cases where our expectations are clearly directional: competition, gubernatorial campaign, presidential campaign, size of newspaper.

[a]p < .01
[b]p < .05
[c]p < .10

incumbents is associated with about 8 more paragraphs being published about the issue priorities of the challenger (7.83 to be exact). Spending by challengers, in contrast, does not influence the newspaper's coverage of issues.

Concurrent gubernatorial and presidential campaigns also affect the amount of news available about the senatorial candidates. For example, when Senate candidates are competing with gubernatorial candidates for news attention, they receive much less coverage of their issue priorities. Incumbents who are running for reelection at the same time as gubernatorial candidates receive, on average, 74 fewer paragraphs than their colleagues who do not face such a crowded electoral field. Challengers are also affected by concurrent guber-natorial campaigns, receiving about 46 fewer paragraphs of issue coverage when they compete with gubernatorial candidates for news space. A similar pattern is seen for presidential campaigns.

When journalists cover campaigns, they not only discuss the candidates' policy priorities, but they can also present more detailed information about the candidates' positions on specific policy matters. In our study, an average of 32 paragraphs is devoted to the incumbents' positions on issues during the campaign, 20 paragraphs focus on the challengers' stands, and 40 paragraphs on those of open-race candidates. However, as races become more hard-fought, the press is more willing to present detailed information about the candidates' standings on policy matters.[20] In addition, news attention to the candidates' issue positions also increases when the Senate candidates are not competing with presidential and gubernatorial candidates for news space. Finally, the spending activity of incumbents produces more news coverage of their own policy stands, but it does not affect the amount of press atten-tion devoted to their opponents' issue positions.

Figure 5.2 illustrates the dramatic relationship between the closeness of the contest and the amount of news coverage devoted to discussion of the

---

[20] In OLS regression equations predicting the number of paragraphs devoted to the issue posi-tions of incumbents and challengers, competition is consistently the most influential variable. In the equation predicting the number of paragraphs devoted to the incumbents' issue positions, the unstandardized coefficient for competition is $-.59$ with a standard error of .13 (beta $= -.42$). The following variables are also statistically significant at the $p < .10$ level: concurrent gubernatorial race (the unstandardized coefficient is -14.01 with a standard error of 4.89, beta $= -.29$), presidential year (the unstandardized coefficient is -20.25 with a standard error of 5.04, beta $= -.40$), and incumbent spending (the unstandardized coefficient is 1.90 with a standard error of 1.19, beta $= .15$).The R^2 for the model is .33. In an OLS regression predicting the number of paragraphs devoted to the challengers' issue positions, the unstandardized coeffi-cient for competition is $-.69$ with a standard error of .11 (beta $= -.55$). The following variables are also statistically significant at the $p < .10$ level: concurrent gubernatorial race (the unstandardized coefficient is -5.19 with a standard error of 4.20, beta $= -.11$) and presiden-tial year (the unstandardized coefficient is -7.48 with a standard error of 4.33, beta $= -.17$). The R^2 for the model is .37.

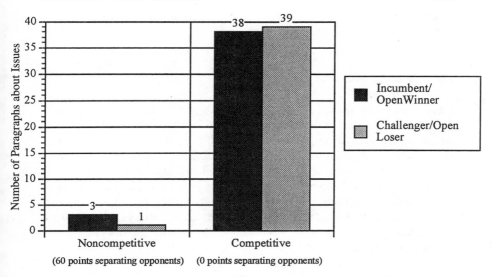

Figure 5.2. The relationship between competition and coverage of issue positions. The point estimates are based on the OLS regression analysis discussed in note 20. We calculate the point estimates by varying the level of competition in the race while holding all remaining variables at their means (Lewis-Beck, 1980).

candidates' issue stands. About 38 paragraphs discuss the incumbents' issue positions in the most competitive races, while only about 3 paragraphs discuss the stands of incumbents in the most lopsided races. We find a similar pattern for challengers. As figure 5.2 illustrates, challengers running in the most competitive contests receive, on average, 39 paragraphs devoted to their issue positions, while challengers receive a single paragraph discussing their stands on issues when they are contesting the most lopsided races. In general, every 10-point increase in the closeness of the race is associated with about 6 more paragraphs being published, on average, about the candidates' policy positions.

These results persuasively document the importance of competition for understanding how newspapers cover issues during campaigns. Journalists spend substantially more time focusing on the issue priorities and issue positions of competitive candidates for the U.S. Senate. In less intense races, the press largely ignores policy concerns. These dramatic differences affect whether citizens are introduced to the issues of the campaign. Since journalists cover issues a great deal in competitive contests, the news media can alter people's issue priorities in these campaigns by focusing intensely on certain policy areas. In more lopsided races, campaign coverage is not plentiful enough to alter the public's agenda. In the end, the press may change voters' preferences about policy or increase people's ability to draw issue distinctions among the candidates.

Trait Coverage in Senate Campaigns

Candidates understand that citizens are more likely to vote for candidates they like, admire, and trust. As we discussed in chapter 3, candidates often adopt slogans and develop commercials to highlight their positive personal characteristics. In contrast, when covering campaigns, the news media are not very interested in describing the candidates' personal characteristics. Earlier in the chapter, we demonstrated that journalists prefer to focus on issues rather than traits. On average, issues receive about three times as much coverage as traits. However, newspapers do not always ignore traits in their coverage of campaigns. In our sample, the focus on traits ranged from no emphasis at all for Bill Grant in his 1992 challenge of Bob Graham in Florida, to 299 trait mentions for Robert Kerrey in the 1988 Karnes-Kerrey race in Nebraska.

The model in table 5.4 demonstrates that newspapers are likely to spend more time covering the traits of the candidates when the outcome of the campaign is uncertain. For incumbents and challengers alike, every one-point change in poll standings is associated with a one-paragraph change in trait coverage. As campaigns change from one-sided affairs (e.g., competition = 60) to hotly contested (e.g., competition = 0), candidates can expect that sixty additional paragraphs will be devoted to their personal characteristics.

Activities of the candidates, captured by spending, have a smaller impact on the amount of personal trait coverage in the press than coverage of issues. Spending by incumbents fails to influence trait coverage. However, for the first time in these analyses, the level of challenger spending does have a minor impact on news coverage. Specifically, challengers who spend more money can increase the amount of press attention given to the incumbents' traits. The unstandardized coefficient for challenger spending (i.e., 4.83) means that every tenfold increase in spending is associated with about five additional paragraphs written about the incumbents' personalities. Of course, if the challenger's money is well spent, the substance of this additional trait coverage will be negative. We address the tone of trait coverage later in this chapter.

Finally, the presence of competing news events continues to influence the quantity of press coverage. Candidates competing for space with other prominent campaigns receive substantially less coverage of their personal traits. Overall, the closeness of the race, the behavior of the challenger, and the presence of other campaigns can determine how much personal information

TABLE 5.4
OLS Regression Analysis Explaining the Amount of Trait Coverage

A. Amount of Trait Coverage Devoted to Incumbent/Open Winner

	Unstandardized Coefficient (standard error)		Beta
Competition	-1.03	$(.27)^a$	$-.37$
Incumbent spending	2.27	(2.50)	.09
Challenger spending	4.83	$(2.50)^c$	.19
Gubernatorial campaign	-28.11	$(10.30)^a$	$-.30$
Presidential campaign	-19.79	$(10.61)^b$	$-.19$
Size of newspaper	-0.0008	(0.005)	$-.02$
Population of state	-10.50	(11.59)	$-.11$
Constant	121.49	$(68.07)^c$	
$R^2 = .26$			
$N = 96$			

B. Amount of Trait Coverage Devoted to Challenger/Open Loser

	Unstandardized Coefficient (standard error)		Beta
Competition	-1.00	$(.18)^a$	$-.51$
Incumbent spending	1.61	(1.71)	.09
Challenger spending	0.41	(1.70)	.02
Gubernatorial campaign	-10.61	$(7.02)^c$	$-.16$
Presidential campaign	-9.76	$(7.24)^c$	$-.14$
Size of newspaper	0.001	(0.003)	.05
Population of state	-2.92	(7.91)	$-.04$
Constant	61.54	(46.43)	
$R^2 = .30$			
$N = 96$			

Notes: The dependent variable is the number of paragraphs about traits for the candidate. *Competition* ranges from 0 (0 points separating candidates in preelection polls) to 72 (72 points separating candidates). The following variables are logged to base 10: *incumbent spending, challenger spending, population of state. Gubernatorial campaign* is a binary variable where 1 = concurrent gubernatorial campaign, 0 = otherwise. *Presidential campaign* is a binary variable where 1 = presidential year, 0 = otherwise. *Size of newspaper* is the number of column inches devoted to news. All p-values are two-tailed except in the following cases where our expectations are clearly directional: competition, gubernatorial campaign, presidential campaign, size of newspaper.
[a] $p < .01$
[b] $p < .05$
[c] $p < .10$

about the candidates is printed in the state newspaper. In an off-year campaign, when the candidates are even in the polls, when the challenger is spending a great deal of money, and when no gubernatorial campaign is being contested, incumbents can expect to receive about 147 paragraphs, on average, devoted to their personal characteristics. In stark contrast, during a presidential year with a concurrent gubernatorial race, incumbents enjoying a 60-point lead can expect to see only nine paragraphs, on average, that discuss their personalities. These variations suggest that the likelihood voters will evaluate candidates' traits when casting their ballots depends to some degree on the amount and focus of media coverage.

Horse-Race Coverage

Scholars studying presidential campaign coverage consistently document the dominance of the horse race over more substantive coverage such as policy and trait discussions. Patterson (1980), in his landmark study of coverage of the 1976 presidential campaign, found that over 50 percent of all the news on the election was about who was winning or losing, and about strategy and logistics. Only about 30 percent of the election news involved the substance of the election, such as issues and candidates' personal qualities. More recent studies, examining the 1980, 1984, 1988, and 1992 presidential elections, continue to document the same pattern. Whether researchers study television or newspapers, primaries or general election campaigns, coverage of presidential elections is dominated by the horse race (e.g., Buchanan, 1991; Just et al., 1996; Kerbel, 1995; Lichter et al., 1988; Patterson, 1993; Robinson and Sheehan, 1983).

In Senate races, coverage of the horse race is much less prevalent (Kahn, 1991). This lack of coverage is due potentially to the fact that public opinion polls of statewide races are less common than surveys of presidential contests. The data in figure 5.3 dramatize the scarcity of horse-race coverage and the emphasis on policy. Furthermore, the proportion of space devoted to the horse race does not increase as races become more competitive.

Newspapers clearly devote more space to issues, traits, and the horse race as races become more competitive. However, editors do not change the proportion of space devoted to these three topics. Regardless of the closeness of the campaign, issues dominate and horse-race concerns are least important, trailing coverage of traits. When races become closer, editors expand the space for campaign news, spending more time focusing on both substantive news and campaign news. Unlike presidential campaigns, where horse-race information appears to "squeeze out" more substantive coverage, editors and reporters covering Senate campaigns reserve a certain amount of space for policy and trait discussions, regardless of the closeness of the race.

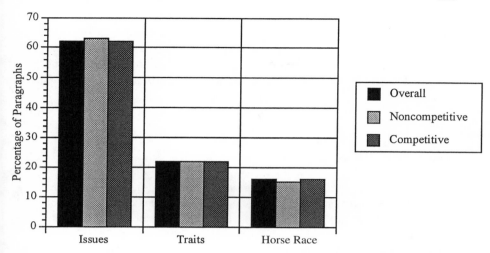

Figure 5.3. Percentage of campaign coverage devoted to issues, traits, and horse race. *Issue coverage* mentions the candidates' issue positions or issue priorities, *trait coverage* discusses the candidates' personal characteristics, and *horse-race coverage* focuses on campaign news such as the candidates' standings in the polls, strategy, and hoopla. *Noncompetitive races* are races where 60 points separate the candidates in early polls. *Competitive races* are races where candidates are tied in early polls. Overall, ninety-six races are examined, with 47,900 paragraphs devoted to either issues, traits, or horse race.

In summary, poll standings influence all types of news content. Issue coverage is most responsive to changes in the candidates' levels of support. The size of the unstandardized coefficient for competition is much larger for issues (−3.13 for incumbents, −3.05 for challenger) than for traits (−1.03 for incumbents, −1.00 for challengers), or compared to horse-race coverage (−.64 for incumbents, −.74 for challengers).[21] While every 10-point change in the closeness of the election produces about a 30-paragraph change in issue coverage, the same 10-point change produces a 10-paragraph change in trait coverage and about a 7-paragraph change in horse-race coverage.

In addition, news organizations also pay attention to the behavior of the

[21] These numbers are gleaned from comparing the effects of polls across tables 5.3, 5.4, and a similar analysis of horse-race coverage. In the model predicting the number of horse-race paragraphs devoted to the incumbent, the following variables were statistically significant at $p <$ .10: competition (the unstandardized coefficient is −.64 with a standard error of .20) and presence of gubernatorial race (the unstandardized coefficient is −16.5 with a standard error of 7.7). The R^2 for the model is .25. In the model predicting horse-race paragraphs devoted to the challenger, the following variables were statistically significant at $p <$ .10: competition (the unstandardized coefficient is −.74 with a standard error of .19), presence of gubernatorial race (the unstandardized coefficient is −15.3 with a standard error of 7.4), and presidential year (the unstandardized coefficient is −13.3 with a standard error of 7.6). The R^2 for the model is .30.

candidates, especially incumbents. In general, incumbents who spend more money can escalate the amount of news attention given to their own candidacies and to their opponents' campaigns. Furthermore, newspapers are very sensitive to space constraints; editors consistently allocate less coverage to Senate races contested in the same year as gubernatorial and presidential elections.

The Tone of Coverage

When covering campaigns, journalists view their role as informing citizens about the competing candidates and their alternative agendas for governance (Clarke and Evans, 1983; Cook, 1996). However, when the press gives more favorable coverage to certain candidates, news personnel may be able to persuade citizens to alter their opinions about the political contestants. Even if journalists are simply reporting the facts (e.g., one candidate has a three-to-one funding advantage over the opponent), the reporting may reflect positively on one candidate and negatively on the other. Similarly, when reporters print criticisms of one candidate leveled by the opponent's campaign, these negative comments may lead citizens to form negative impressions of the criticized candidate. While these criticisms may form the basis of a legitimate news story (i.e., stated in an interesting way in a press conference or political advertisement), they nevertheless may sway voters' preferences.

We were curious whether the closeness of the race and the activities of candidates influence the tone of campaign coverage, all other things being equal. The competitiveness of the campaign may lead to more critical coverage of the candidates, since candidates step up their attacks on one another as races become closer (see chapter 4). Campaign coverage of competitive races may simply mirror the critical tone of the candidates' messages. News organizations enjoy reporting attacks by candidates because they believe such coverage delivers large audiences (Bennett, 1996). Second, candidates who campaign more vigorously, as reflected by their campaign spending, may generate more positive coverage of their own campaigns and more critical coverage of their opponents.

In addition, a newspaper's endorsement decision may affect the tone of coverage given to the candidates. Candidates who are successful in securing the newspaper's endorsement may be described more favorably in the news, while more critical comments may be published about candidates who fail to receive the newspaper's endorsement.

In general, incumbents have an easier time garnering favorable press. In our study, 23 percent of the articles written about incumbents are positive, 15 percent of the articles published about challengers are favorable in tone, and the remainder are considered neutral.[22] This advantage is not surprising since many Senators have established good relationships with local reporters, and reporters are wary about damaging such relationships by covering the Senators in an unfavorable light (Cook, 1989; Fenno, 1996). In open races, 20 percent of the articles written about the winners are positive in tone, while the losers are covered more negatively. Only 11 percent of the articles devoted to open losers are positive.[23]

However, incumbents do not always bask in a positive media spotlight. When we look at the number of criticisms printed in a newspaper during a campaign season, we find incumbents are criticized an average of fifty-four times, with criticisms ranging from only one aimed at Senator Jim Sasser in his 1988 reelection campaign to 299 criticisms of Senator Jesse Helms during his race against Harvey Gantt in 1990.

To examine the tone of news coverage, we looked at the number of criticisms published in the local newspapers. The findings displayed in table 5.5 reveal that candidates are much more likely to be criticized in the newspapers when they are engaged in hard-fought campaigns.

Once again, competition is by far the most important factor in the incumbent and challenger models. For incumbents and challengers, there is about a one-to-one correspondence between changes in poll standings and changes in candidate criticisms. For example, every 10-point increase in the closeness of the campaign is associated with ten additional criticisms published in the newspaper. Such a relationship suggests that the news media may be following the lead of the candidates by reporting more negative comments about the contestants in the most competitive races.

The presence of a gubernatorial campaign also influences the number of criticisms published about the candidates. According to the unstandardized coefficients in the models, incumbents who are not competing with gubernatorial candidates for coverage can expect to be criticized about twenty-one times more than incumbents who are running campaigns during gubernatorial races. Challengers also receive fewer critical comments in the news when they are running at the same time as gubernatorial candidates. However, the relationship is less powerful for challengers who can expect ten fewer criticisms, on average, when their campaigns correspond with gubernatorial elections.

The level of spending by incumbents and challengers does not affect the number of criticisms reported in the press. That is, candidates who spend more extravagantly on political commercials, on targeting potential suppor-

---

[22] This difference, while not overly dramatic, is statistically significant at p < .01. The p-value is based on the difference-in-proportions test.

[23] This difference between open winners and open losers is statistically significant at p < .01. Again, the p-value is based on the difference-in-proportions test.

TABLE 5.5

OLS Regression Analysis Explaining Number of Criticisms Published in Newspaper

A. Number of Criticisms about Incumbent/Open Winner

	Unstandardized Coefficient (standard error)		Beta
Competition	−0.95	(.17)[a]	−.45
Incumbent spending	1.95	(1.59)	.10
Challenger spending	1.98	(1.57)	.10
Gubernatorial campaign	−21.02	(6.55)[a]	−.29
Presidential campaign	−8.24	(6.96)	−.11
Endorsement	−13.22	(3.90)[a]	−.29
Size of newspaper	0.002	(0.003)	.07
Population of state	0.23	(7.47)	.003
Constant	51.17	(43.88)	
R^2 = .48			
N = 96			

B. Number of Criticisms about Challenger/Open Loser

	Unstandardized Coefficient (standard error)		Beta
Competition	−0.79	(.13)[a]	−.53
Incumbent spending	0.98	(1.20)	.07
Challenger spending	−0.33	(1.18)	−.02
Gubernatorial campaign	−10.16	(4.92)[b]	−.20
Presidential campaign	−3.48	(5.23)	−.06
Endorsement	−2.88	(2.93)	−.09
Size of newspaper	0.002	(0.002)	.10
Population of state	3.09	(5.61)	.06
Constant	20.67	(32.96)	
R^2 = .41			
N = 96			

Notes: The dependent variable is the number of criticisms published about the candidate. *Competition* ranges from 0 (0 points separating candidates in preelection polls) to 72 (72 points separating candidates). The following variables are logged to base 10: *incumbent spending, challenger spending, population of state. Gubernatorial campaign* is a binary variable where 1 = concurrent gubernatorial campaign, 0 = otherwise. *Presidential campaign* is a binary variable where 1 = presidential year, 0 = otherwise. *Endorsement* is an ordinal variable where 1 = incumbent/winner endorsed, 0 = no endorsement, −1 = challenger/loser endorsed. *Size of newspaper* is the number of column inches devoted to news. All p-values are two-tailed except in the following cases where our expectations are clearly directional: competition, gubernatorial campaign, presidential campaign, size of newspaper, endorsement.

[a] $p < .01$
[b] $p < .05$

ters with direct mail, and on making numerous speeches across the state are not guaranteed more critical coverage than their opponents.

Finally, the endorsement decisions of newspapers significantly influence the tone of campaign coverage given to incumbents.[24] Newspapers that endorse incumbents print twenty-six fewer criticisms, on average, than newspapers that endorse the Senators' challengers (i.e., a two-point movement on the endorsement scale). However, the newspaper's endorsement decision does not affect the number of criticisms published about challengers.[25]

To examine the "endorsement effect" for incumbents in more detail, we look exclusively at criticisms initiated by reporters.[26] When reporting criticisms of the incumbents, journalists often rely on the challengers or other officials (e.g., politicians in the state, campaign officials) as sources. However, on occasion, journalists level criticisms against candidates without indicating sources. The likelihood of journalists making unattributed criticisms is strongly associated with the newspaper's endorsement decision. In fact, in a model predicting the number of criticisms initiated by journalists, we find the paper's endorsement decision to be the most important factor.[27]

To further explore the amount of critical coverage given to the candidates, we employ a second measure of tone. More specifically, we look at the number of negative adjectives published about each candidate. When reporters cover campaigns, they often use unflattering terms (e.g., inexperienced, erratic, uninformed) when describing candidates. The use of negative adjectives averaged fourteen per race for incumbents, eight per race for challengers, and eighteen per race for candidates contesting open seats. As an illustration, fifty-nine negative adjectives were published about Senator

[24] The endorsement variable is coded 1 if the incumbent/open winner is endorsed; 0 if neither candidate is endorsed; −1 if the challenger/open loser is endorsed.

[25] In addition to examining the amount of critical coverage in the press, we also examined the proportion of critical coverage devoted to each candidate. When we change our dependent variable (i.e., critical coverage of candidate/total coverage of candidate), we find the same pattern of findings. In the OLS model predicting the proportion of critical coverage devoted to the incumbent, the competitiveness of the race and the newspaper's endorsement decision continue to statistically affect coverage patterns ($p < .06$). Similarly, in the OLS model examining the proportion of critical coverage devoted to the challenger, competition influences coverage patterns ($p < .02$).

[26] We also examined the proportion of coverage devoted to the candidates' negative traits (e.g., negative trait coverage about incumbent/total coverage of incumbent) . We find that competition strongly affects the proportion of critical trait coverage devoted to the incumbent ($p < .01$), while endorsement decisions ($p < .09$) and the quality of the challenger ($p < .02$) affect the proportion of critical trait coverage devoted to the challenger.

[27] The significant variables ($p < .10$) in the OLS model predicting unattributed criticisms of the incumbent are: endorsement decision (unstandardized coefficient is −1.35 with standard error of .36, beta = .35), competition (unstandardized coefficient is −.05 with standard error of .02, beta = .27), and the presence of governor's race (unstandardized coefficient is −1.86 with standard error of .62, beta = .32). The R^2 for the model is .36.

TABLE 5.6
OLS Regression Analysis Explaining Negative Trait Coverage

A. Number of Negative Traits about Incumbent/Open Winner

	Unstandardized Coefficient (standard error)		Beta
Competition	−0.43	(.10)[a]	−.42
Incumbent spending	0.99	(.90)	.11
Challenger spending	1.65	(.89)[c]	.18
Gubernatorial campaign	−6.96	(3.68)[b]	−.20
Presidential campaign	−1.06	(3.91)	−.03
Endorsement	−3.48	(2.20)[c]	−.15
Size of newspaper	.0006	(.002)	.03
Population of state	−1.63	(4.20)	−.04
Constant	31.48	(24.68)	
$R^2 = .31$			
$N = 96$			

B. Number of Negative Traits about Challenger/Open Loser

	Unstandardized Coefficient (standard error)		Beta
Competition	−39	(.09)[a]	−.51
Incumbent spending	0.31	(.71)	.04
Challenger spending	0.67	(.69)	.10
Gubernatorial campaign	−2.02	(2.89)	−.08
Presidential campaign	−2.96	(3.05)	−.11
Endorsement	2.64	(1.71)[c]	.16
Size of newspaper	0.001	(0.001)	.13
Population of state	.91	(3.25)	.03
Challenger quality	−1.04	(.51)[b]	−.23
Constant	7.29	(19.22)	
$R^2 = .28$			
$N = 96$			

Notes: The dependent variable is the number of negative traits published about the candidate. Competition ranges from 0 (0 points separating candidates in preelection polls) to 72 (72 points separating candidates). The following variables are logged to base 10: *incumbent spending, challenger spending, population of state. Gubernatorial campaign* is a binary variable where 1 = concurrent gubernatorial campaign, 0 = otherwise. *Presidential campaign* is a binary variable where 1 = presidential year, 0 = otherwise. *Endorsement* is an ordinal variable where 1 = incumbent/winner endorsed, 0 = no endorsement, −1 = challenger/loser endorsed. *Size of newspaper* is the number of column inches devoted to news. All p-values are two-tailed except in the following cases where our expectations are clearly directional: competition, gubernatorial campaign, presidential campaign, size of newspaper, endorsement.

[a]p < .01
[b]p < .05
[c]p < .10

Malcolm Wallop in the *Casper Star-Tribune* during his competitive campaign in 1988, while only eight unflattering traits were used to describe Senator Alan Simpson two years later during his low-key campaign.

As the findings in table 5.6 show, the closeness of the race influences the critical tone of coverage for both incumbents and challengers. When candidates are competing in the most competitive races (competition = 0), they can expect more than twenty additional negative traits describing their candidacies than candidates running in lopsided races (competition = 60).

In addition, spending by the challengers increases the number of negative traits published about the incumbents. This finding, coupled with the impact of challengers' spending described in table 5.4, suggests that challengers are successful in creating negative coverage of incumbents' traits when they expend more campaign resources. However, since we found that challengers' spending does not produce more criticisms (i.e., table 5.5) of incumbents in general, challengers cannot create negative coverage of incumbents on all topics, just on personal dimensions.

We also find that the newspaper's endorsement decision affects the tone of coverage. Candidates who are endorsed receive significantly fewer negative adjectives describing their candidacies, compared to candidates who are running against endorsed candidates. In this case, both incumbents and challengers enjoy more favorable coverage when they successfully secure a newspaper's endorsement.

Finally, this is the first analysis where the characteristics of the candidates affect the nature of trait coverage for challengers. In particular, more critical traits are used to describe inexperienced challengers. Every 1-point decline on the 9-point challenger quality scale is associated with one more negative trait published about the candidate.

Summary

The closeness of the campaign, the behavior of the candidates, competing news events, and the characteristics of the newspaper all affect the quality and quantity of information presented in the news, some more dramatically than others. First, as races become more competitive, more information is published in newspapers, and the information is presented more prominently. Furthermore, competitive races generate significantly more substantive news about the candidates' policy priorities and trait characteristics as well as more news about the horse race. Finally, the tone of the coverage given to the candidates varies with the closeness of the race. For instance, as races become more competitive, more critical comments about the candidates are presented in the news.

The behavior of the candidates also determines how much news coverage is allocated to the competing candidates. For example, incumbents who spend more money are successful in generating more coverage, more prominent coverage, and more issue attention for their own candidacies and for the candidacies of their opponents. Similarly, challengers who spend more money can produce more negative trait coverage of incumbents. Nevertheless, none of these effects approaches the magnitude of competition.

News personnel also consider the presence of competing news when allocating space for news about the Senate contest. When presidential and gubernatorial campaigns are waged, Senate candidates receive less news coverage, in general, and less attention to their personal qualities and policy views. Furthermore, when Senate candidates compete with other prominent politicians for news space, the quantity of news about campaign tactics and hoopla decreases, as does the number of criticisms published about these candidates.

Finally, newspapers give more favorable coverage to candidates they endorse. Consistent with Page's (1996) findings, we find that editorial decisions influence the substance of news stories. For example, incumbents who receive a newspaper endorsement receive more positive press attention, compared to incumbents who fail to impress a news organization. Fewer criticisms are published in general, and fewer negative personal traits in particular are used to describe endorsed incumbents. While many political observers have speculated about a "media bias," we have empirically validated this claim. The press alters coverage based on its preferences' for a candidate.[28]

While the analyses in this chapter suggest that the candidates' level of spending can affect the amount and the general content of news coverage, we still need to investigate the correspondence between the content of the candidates' messages and the specific substance of news coverage. In the next chapter, we explore this question by looking at the extent to which candidates are successful at controlling the substance and tone of the media's message. We also investigate whether the candidates' abilities to manipulate coverage vary with the competitiveness of the race and the content of the candidates' messages. Finally, by comparing the campaign messages of political rivals and the resulting news coverage, we look at which candidates are most effective at setting the news media's agenda.

[28] When newspapers choose to endorse a candidate, the incumbent is endorsed 82 percent of the time.

The Struggle for Control
over the News Media's Agenda

HOW CANDIDATES INFLUENCE THE CONTENT
AND TONE OF NEWS COVERAGE

THE GOAL of every candidate running for the U.S. Senate is to control the news media's agenda as a way of aiding electoral victory (Fenno, 1996). Candidates encourage coverage of certain topics while hoping to depress the amount of press attention devoted to other subjects. By shaping the news media's agenda, the candidates strive to control the content of coverage. To be sure, some candidates are successful at cajoling the press to focus on their choice of campaign messages, while others are not. An outstanding example of a successful candidate is Christine Todd Whitman. She focused her message on the economy in her bid to unseat U.S. senator Bill Bradley of New Jersey in 1990. Whitman tried to take advantage of voters' outrage with Democratic governor James J. Florio's $2.8 billion tax increase by linking a vote for Bradley with support for Florio. Whitman's campaign ran radio and television advertisements attacking Florio and produced bumper stickers with the slogan, "Get Florio, Dump Bradley." Whitman, along with her campaign staff, believed that an emphasis on the "Florio Factor" would encourage citizens to develop negative views of Bradley and more positive evaluations of Whitman.

The press responded. From October 1 to Election Day, 107 paragraphs were produced in the state's largest circulating newspaper connecting Bradley with economic matters. An additional 76 paragraphs linked Whitman with economic issues. This amount of coverage far exceeds the average amount of coverage that candidates garner regarding economic concerns. Incumbents receive thirty-four paragraphs, on average, while challengers typically manage only twenty-three across the same time frame.

Although Whitman was quite effective in setting the news media's agenda (even though she lost the election but later won the governorship in 1993), other candidates were far less successful. For example, Hubert Humphrey III, in his bid to unseat Senator David Durenberger of Minnesota, emphasized the need for a change in government with the tag line "A Change for the Better." However, his campaign theme was ignored by the *Minneapolis Star Tribune*; only one paragraph was devoted to Humphrey's theme during the course of the campaign.

Why was Whitman so successful at obtaining media attention for her chosen agenda while Humphrey failed so miserably? More generally, how do candidates cajole the news media to focus on their preferred campaign messages? Certainly all candidates would like voters to be inundated with their messages while their opponents' messages are relegated to obscurity. However, according to their campaign managers, most candidates believe that their messages are not covered extensively enough by the news media. Fifty percent of incumbents and 52 percent of challengers felt that there was a distinct "lack of coverage" of the main themes they presented to voters.

In this chapter, we examine the correspondence between the candidates' messages and the substance of campaign coverage. We are specifically interested in the extent to which candidates are successful at controlling the substance and tone of the media's message. We take a closer look at several policy domains, such as health care, the environment, and economic policy. We also assess the amount of news copy devoted to candidates' political experience, the trait most frequently stressed by candidates. Additionally, we look at whether candidates who conduct negative campaigns are more likely to generate critical coverage of their opponents. We also explore whether the candidates' abilities to manipulate coverage vary with the competitiveness of the race and the content of the candidates' messages. In other words, we investigate the forces that influence the news media's responsiveness to the candidates' messages. Finally, by comparing the campaign messages of political rivals and the resulting news coverage, we determine which candidates are most likely to win the "agenda-setting" battle.

Setting the Media's Agenda

Some of the most provocative and compelling research in recent years has demonstrated that voters routinely use information provided by the media when assessing the importance of policy matters and evaluating the performance of politicians (Iyengar and Kinder, 1989; Krosnick and Kinder, 1990). The media have the power, in many instances, to identify the topics individuals use to guide their evaluations of the competing candidates. This phenomenon, referred to as "priming," is a key reason why candidates strive diligently to shape the news media's agenda during the campaign.

While many researchers have examined the media's agenda-setting power, we are interested in moving one step back in the causal chain and examining how candidates influence the press's agenda. This link has not been investigated by scholars because of a dearth of data (two notable exceptions are Just et al., 1996, and Kahn, 1996). Investigators need both the candidates' messages as well as the media's coverage of the campaign to investigate this phenomenon. We are fortunate to have both these pieces of the puzzle. With this information in hand, we can explore the correspondence between what the candidates are talking about and what the press is actually reporting. Relying on our understanding of the nature of campaigns, we anticipate that the closeness of the race and the candidates' behavior will alter the correspondence between the candidates' messages and the media's agenda.

Setting the Media's Agenda: The Influence of Competition

Given what we know about how candidates develop their campaign messages and the norms that guide reporters and editors, we believe candidates' success at acquiring coverage of their chosen themes will increase with the closeness of the race. Candidates in competitive races, as was evident from the analyses in chapter 3, tend to present their messages more often, to discuss issues more frequently, and to articulate discernible positions on issues, compared to candidates in noncompetitive races.

Political dialogue focusing on salient issues and descriptions of the candidates' positions on issues provide valuable information for reporters and editors. Beyond the simple ease of writing stories about these messages, many members of the media believe it is their obligation to present voters with the information they need to make informed choices on election day (Bennett, 1996). This includes, among other things, the candidates' general campaign themes. Therefore, when candidates articulate a clear and meaningful message, typical of close contests, reporters will write and editors will approve stories about these messages. In this regard, competitive Senate campaigns resemble presidential campaigns where a certain amount of press coverage reports what the candidates are saying in their speeches and ads (Just et al., 1996; Page 1978; West, 1993).

The opposite is true in noncompetitive campaigns. Candidates produce fewer messages in general and fewer detailed messages in particular. In the case of the front-runner, the candidate is often presenting an amorphous message (e.g., "I take good care of the state," "My experience is invaluable for the state") that does not lend itself to exciting news copy. And, candidates who are trailing rarely have enough resources to disseminate their messages to a wide audience, even if the messages are clear. Reporters must expend considerable effort to identify the messages of these long-shot candidates.

Furthermore, journalists may assume that readers are not interested in digesting policy information about rivals in noncompetitive contests (Cook, 1996). Thus, reporters are unlikely to write thoroughly researched stories about the candidates' messages in lopsided campaigns. The end result is that few stories are reported, and those stories that are do not focus on the opponents' chosen messages. Subsequently, a close correspondence between what the candidates are saying and what the press is reporting is unlikely in non-competitive contests.

Setting the Media's Agenda: The Influence of Candidate Behavior

In addition to responding to the closeness of the race, reporters and editors also listen to the content and tone of candidates' messages when preparing articles about the campaign. Two examples from senatorial campaigns in West Virginia highlight how the press responds to what candidates are saying. Senator John D. Rockefeller IV made health care the centerpiece of his 1990 reelection campaign. As we discussed in chapter 3, Rockefeller highlighted his chairmanship of the Medicare and Long-Term Care finance subcommittee as well as his work on the Pepper Commission (a bipartisan group of health care policymakers) during his political speeches and political advertisements. In contrast, Senator Robert Byrd chose to emphasize his service to West Virginia in his 1988 reelection bid and avoided debates about policy. Given these differences in the senators' campaigns, we expect health issues to receive more press attention in 1990 than 1988. In fact, when we examined the *Charlottesville Daily Progress*, we found that West Virginia's largest circulating paper printed about five times more coverage about health care in Rockefeller's 1990 campaign than in Byrd's 1988 reelection contest (twenty-three paragraphs vs. five paragraphs).

More generally, we hypothesize that the status of the candidate (i.e., incumbent or challenger), the content of candidates' messages, and the tone of the campaign messages influence the likelihood of press coverage. If the candidate sending the message is a U.S. senator, the press may pay careful attention to the message when writing stories about the campaign. Reporters depend on U.S. senators as sources for a variety of news stories. These reporters may be likely to represent senators' messages faithfully as a way of maintaining their relationships with these important elected officials. Furthermore, the resources associated with the office of U.S. senator (e.g., professional staff with experience disseminating press releases and staging press conferences) enable incumbents to inform reporters when they are making news. Given these advantages of incumbency, sitting senators should be effective in encouraging coverage of their messages.

Challengers may also experience success in shaping the focus of news coverage. Ironically, challengers may be able to shape news coverage because they are not well-known political figures. Many challengers have never held public office and therefore do not have records that can be scrutinized by the press (Clarke and Evans, 1983). Even challengers with elective experience do not enjoy the same level of prominence as sitting senators. Since reporters are likely to be unfamiliar with the challengers' records and accomplishments, they may turn to the candidates directly for campaign information.

As Clarke and Evans (1983) explain, reporters covering congressional campaigns often shun more enterprising work such as the researching of public documents and prefer to rely on routine sources for news (e.g., news conferences, speeches, political advertisements). Since many political reporters simply do not have the time, resources, or inclination to engage in more time-consuming techniques, challengers may be able to focus media attention on the content of their agendas. Clarke and Evans (1983) find support for this contention when they report that journalists rely heavily on the challengers' speeches, interviews with the candidates, and news releases when covering the campaigns of U.S. House challengers. Reporters' dependence on information disseminated by the challengers' campaigns may increase the correspondence between the challengers' campaign themes and the substance of news coverage.

The content of the campaign messages, in addition to the status of the candidates, may affect whether the press is receptive to the candidates' messages. Prior scholarship (Kahn, 1991), as well as the findings in chapter 5, indicate that, when covering Senate elections, the press is more interested in presenting news stories about issues than about candidates' traits or a horse race. Thus, incumbents and challengers who discuss issues are more likely to experience a closer correlation between what they say and what the press is reporting than when they only discuss their traits or carry forth ambiguous themes such as "a time for a change."

Finally, we reason that the tone of messages is related to the correspondence between the candidates' agendas and the press's portrayal of the candidates' messages. Put simply, criticisms of the opponent attract attention from the media and the opponent (Cook, 1996). Harsh criticisms, supported with examples, embellished in ads, and repeated frequently are, if nothing else, "newsworthy." As Edelman (1988) explains, if a story develops into an attack of a candidate, so much the better. It is congruent with the economic norm of creating a large news audience by reporting a "political spectacle."

In summary, we contend that competition, the status of the candidates, and the content and tone of messages will influence the correlation between what the candidates want to communicate to voters and what the press believes is newsworthy. Messages involving issues and criticisms of the opponent are more likely to be covered by the press than self-congratulatory themes or messages that lack specificity. In addition, and deviating from the traditional belief that incumbents have advantages in nearly all aspects of campaigning, challengers may be just as adept as incumbents at influencing the media's coverage of their campaign themes. To generate stories about challengers, the press must rely on the challengers for information, since they often lack a prior voting record and a public history regarding political issues and policy debates.

The Correspondence between the Candidates' Themes and the Content of News Coverage

Our initial attempt to explain the correspondence between candidates' messages and news coverage focuses on "specific messages" emphasized by candidates, as opposed to the correspondence between media coverage and an overall "package of themes" stressed by candidates. In chapter 3 we provided evidence that candidates often focus on specific issues and traits; these themes constitute the heart and soul of their electoral campaigns. To measure candidates' core messages, we asked managers to identify the "main themes" of their campaigns.

In our first set of analyses, we explain the variance in the number of paragraphs that incumbents and challengers receive on four topics: health care, the economy, the environment, and personal experience. These four themes were the most common "main themes" emphasized by candidates and were often the themes that campaign managers mentioned first when asked to identify their candidates' main themes.

We examined media coverage from October 1 to Election Day. We chose to look at media coverage after October 1 because it is possible that it may influence the candidates' choice of main themes. For example, if reporters and editors decide early in the campaign that the election is fundamentally about the economy, then candidates may feel compelled to focus on economic issues. By examining media coverage late in the campaign, it is reasonable to assume that the agenda of the candidates is already in place. To measure whether candidates emphasized one of these topics, we simply included a binary variable measuring whether a manager mentioned the particular topic (e.g., health care) as a main theme of the campaign. In addition to measuring what the candidates wanted to emphasize, we also examined the influence of several rival factors that could alter the quantity of coverage given to these topics. First, we looked at whether the competitiveness of the race and the level of candidate spending enhances the amount of coverage devoted to each theme. Given our findings in chapter 5, we expected the amount of news attention given to these topics to increase with the closeness of the race. We also expected coverage of specific issues and traits to escalate when candidates are engaged in more active campaigns, as measured by levels of campaign expenditures.

In addition, we examined whether concurrent gubernatorial and presidential campaigns and the size of the state alter media coverage. Competing news events are likely to suppress coverage of Senate campaigns, including the amount of attention devoted to specific issues, traits, and criticisms. For example, a Senate challenger who is competing with presidential candidates for press attention may find it difficult to obtain coverage for the candidate's position on the environment. Similarly, larger states, with more competing news stories, may devote less coverage to the specific themes of a given campaign.

Finally, in some states, during certain years, the political climate may alter media coverage. For example, when a state is experiencing a profound economic recession, its leading newspaper may devote more coverage to economic issues when reporting on the Senate contest. To see whether a dominant issue in the state affects news coverage, we looked at the *Congressional Quarterly*'s discussion of the political climate as early as February for the upcoming senatorial campaign. This measure is preferable to other measures because it is temporally earlier than when candidates make decisions about strategies and occurs before the local media begin covering the campaign. In fact, the *CQ* measure predates the primary elections in all states.[1]

In table 6.1, we show whether candidates receive more coverage on health care, the economy, the environment, and their experience if they emphasized these topics as main themes during their campaigns, controlling for a variety of rival factors.[2]

The results presented here suggest that challengers who emphasize health care, the economy, the environment, and experience do receive more coverage compared to challengers who do not stress these themes. Across the four regression equations, the challengers' preferred campaign messages consistently influence patterns of press attention. In each model, the variable tapping the candidates' preferred messages easily defeats the null hypothesis. For example, challengers who focus on health care receive, on average, 11 more paragraphs discussing their views on health care than challengers who do not emphasize health care. The comparable paragraphs for the economy, the environment, and experience are approximately 15, 10, and 10, respectively.

Incumbents, in stark contrast, are less able to influence the amount of their news coverage on these topics. In each model, the variable representing the themes emphasized by the incumbents fails to reach statistical significance.

---

[1] In the statistical analyses in this chapter, we examined the impact of several other factors on coverage patterns (i.e., the size of the newspaper, type of race—incumbent or open race—the newspaper's endorsement decision, the opponent's level of spending, the seniority of the senator, the quality of the challenger, the gender of the candidate and whether the candidate was involved in a scandal). In virtually every case, these forces failed to influence the amount of coverage ($p < .10$). When these factors failed to reach statistical significance, we excluded these variables to increase the degrees of freedom in each analysis. Since we rely on the campaign manager interviews to ascertain the candidates' themes, the number of cases available for analyses is seventy-four for incumbents and seventy-two for challengers; this number is significantly smaller than the ninety-six cases available in the previous chapter.

[2] In this analysis, and in subsequent analyses, we examine incumbent and open winners together and challengers and open losers together since open candidates do not differ significantly from candidates contesting incumbent seats.

TABLE 6.1

OLS Regression Analysis Predicting Coverage of Specific Themes

A. Incumbent/Open Winner

	Health		Economy		Environment		Experience	
Candidate emphasized theme	.15	(4.7)	10.19	(9.93)	−2.64	(5.33)	1.37	(7.89)
Competition	−.43	(.10)[a]	−.54	(.17)[a]	−.39	(.10)[a]	−.43	(.20)[a]
Candidate spending	.84	(.81)	1.36	(1.48)	.78	(.87)	1.26	(1.68)
Gubernatorial campaign	−6.99	(3.99)[b]	−6.82	(6.58)	−6.52	(4.10)[c]	−10.16	(7.64)[c]
Presidential campaign	−4.86	(3.72)	−34.39	(6.77)[a]	−11.47	(4.08)[a]	−12.21	(7.72)[c]
Political climate	13.32	(10.08)	8.08	(9.25)	14.90	(5.30)[a]	—	
Population of state	1.16	(3.76)	4.30	(7.02)	2.02	(4.02)	−4.04	(8.0)
Constant	17.84	(24.21)	3.52	(44.57)	3.36	(25.98)	62.73	(51.83)
R^2	.32		.38		.33		.10	
N	74		74		74		74	

B. Challenger/Open Loser

	Health		Economy		Environment		Experience	
Candidate emphasized theme	11.31	(3.89)[a]	14.76	(8.78)[b]	9.85	(4.73)[b]	10.23	(5.42)[b]
Competition	−.29	(.08)[a]	−.70	(.17)[a]	.30	(.07)[a]	−.55	(.13)[a]
Candidate spending	.91	(.76)	.80	(1.57)	.37	(.59)	.16	(1.17)
Gubernatorial campaign	−1.55	(3.23)	.58	(6.38)	−4.03	(2.50)[c]	−1.23	(4.94)
Presidential campaign	−2.65	(3.24)	−16.22	(6.40)[a]	−3.36	(2.58)[c]	−5.03	(4.97)
Political climate	6.53	(8.64)	13.95	(8.19)[b]	−.59	(2.43)	—	
Population of state	−1.82	(3.11)	4.55	(6.53)	−.59	(2.58)	−3.75	(4.80)
Constant	24.07	(20.12)	1.61	(41.48)	17.27	(15.89)	50.39	(31.15)
R^2	.26		.26		.31		.27	
N	72		72		72		72	

Notes: The number in each cell is the unstandardized regression coefficient with the standard error in parentheses. The dependent variable is the number of paragraphs about each topic for the candidate. *Candidate emphasized theme* is a binary variable where 1 = candidate emphasized topic, 0 = otherwise. *Competition* ranges from 0 (0 points separating candidates in preelection polls) to 72 (72 points separating candidates). The following variables are logged to base 10: *incumbent spending, challenger spending, population of state*. *Gubernatorial campaign* is a binary variable where 1 = concurrent gubernatorial campaign, 0 = otherwise. *Presidential campaign* is a binary variable where 1 = presidential year, 0 = otherwise. *Political climate* is a binary variable where 1 = issue is important in state according to *CQ* February election report, 0 = otherwise. All p-values are two-tailed except in the following cases where our expectations are clearly directional: competition, gubernatorial campaign, presidential campaign, size of newspaper.
[a]$p < .01$
[b]$p < .05$
[c]$p < .10$

Incumbents who emphasize health issues, the economy, and the environment do not receive more coverage of these issues than senators who do not stress them. Similarly, incumbents focusing on their experience do not encourage reporters to focus more on their qualifications than incumbents who choose not to.

A. Incumbent/Open Winner

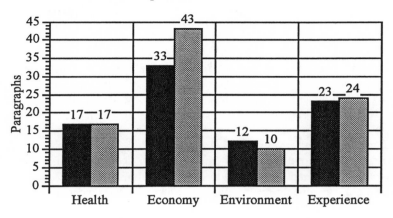

B. Challenger/Open Loser

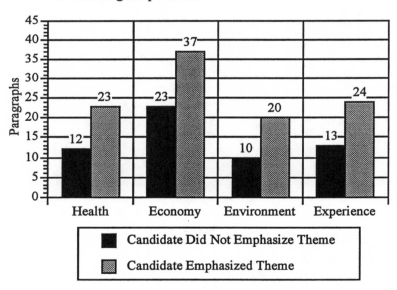

Figure 6.1. Differences in coverage of specific themes due to candidate's campaign emphasis. The point estimates are based on the unstandardized regression coefficients presented in table 6.1. We calculate the point estimates by varying the candidate's emphasis (i.e., emphasized theme; did not emphasize theme) while holding all remaining variables at their means (Lewis-Beck, 1980).

However, this does not mean that incumbents receive little coverage on these topics. In figure 6.1, we graphically represent the average number of paragraphs that candidates receive on health care, the economy, the environment, and experience when they emphasize these topics and when they do not stress these themes, holding all other factors in the model at their means. The figures reveal that incumbents often receive more coverage than challengers, irrespective of whether they stress these specific topics or not. This finding resonates with the general pattern of evidence from chapter 5. However, when a challenger targets a particular campaign theme, the challenger can reduce and, in some instances, eliminate the incumbency advantage in coverage. For example, when challengers highlight their experience, they almost double the number of paragraphs written about experience (i.e., 24 paragraphs, on average, compared to only 13), actually matching the amount of attention incumbents receive that is related to their experience. Incumbents, regardless of whether they emphasize their experience or not, receive about 24 paragraphs describing their electoral backgrounds. Similarly, when challengers stress the environment and health care, they are able to compete with incumbents for coverage on these issues.

In sum, the topics that challengers emphasize in their campaign messages influence the amount of press attention devoted to them. When challengers discuss certain topics in their campaign commercials and speeches, the press responds by covering these topics in more detail. It appears that the press is relying on the content of the challengers' messages to shape the content of stories about the challengers. Although incumbents often receive more news coverage than their opponents, they are less successful in determining the precise content of coverage. The campaign coverage devoted to incumbents does not vary with the emphases of their campaigns, at least on the topics we examined.

The remaining findings in table 6.1 reinforce the findings in chapter 5. For example, the closeness of the race always influences the amount of press attention given to specific issues and traits. The more competitive the race, the more coverage, irrespective of topic or candidate status. Similarly, the presence of competing campaigns often inhibits coverage of the Senate campaign, with the largest effect coming at the expense of incumbents.

Finally, to a limited extent, the political climate of the state alters the amount of coverage devoted to a particular issue. In the eight analyses presented in table 6.1 (four for the incumbent and four for the challenger), the variable tapping political climate was statistically significant twice. In both cases, once in the incumbents' model examining the environment and once in the economic model for the challengers, the size of the effects is approximately 14 paragraphs. That is, if these topics were mentioned as important issues in the state during the spring of the election year, then these issues were more likely to be covered during the fall campaign. Considering the total number of paragraphs presented in figure 6.1, fourteen paragraphs is a sizable amount of additional coverage on the environment, and a moderate amount of additional coverage about the economy.

Negative Campaigning and Patterns of News Coverage

In addition to controlling the content of press coverage, candidates also seek to alter the tone of the news. As discussed in chapter 4, candidates often engage in negative campaigning. When candidates decide to adopt a negative tone in their campaigns, they are choosing to "frame" their messages in order to produce critical impressions of their rivals. Researchers have determined that the "frame" of a message can alter people's views about public policy and politicians (Kahneman and Tversky, 1984; Iyengar, 1991; Tversky and Kahneman, 1981). In the context of our analysis, we adopt Kinder and Sanders's (1990: 74) definition of "frames" as "devices embedded in political discourse, invented and employed by political elites, often with an eye on advancing their own interests or ideologies." In a campaign setting, criticisms of opponents are frames used to advance the candidates' candidacies while hindering the opponents' chances of success.

When candidates focus on their opponents' weaknesses in their campaign communications, they hope to encourage the press to follow suit by publicizing these criticisms. Criticisms flowing from the media are virtually free for candidates, especially compared to commercials, and voters are more likely to view the criticisms as credible when they come from the media instead of emanating from candidates' ads (Graber, 1989).

Table 6.2 shows whether candidates can successfully generate criticisms of their opponents in the press when they engage in negative campaigns. To measure the candidates' efforts at framing, we relied on the description of each race in a preelection issue of *Congressional Quarterly*.[3] Since *CQ* reporters ascertained the tone of each race prior to the onset of coverage in October, we are confident that the candidates' campaign strategies precede coverage patterns.[4]

In this analysis, we examined the number of criticisms published about the opponent in the press. We were explicitly interested in whether candidates who wage negative campaigns cajole the press to publish more criticisms of their rivals. We controlled for several forces known to influence news coverage: competition, spending, concurrent campaigns, and characteristics of the newspaper.[5]

[3] To measure the tone of the candidates' campaigns, we create a binary variable where 1 = negative campaign as determined by *CQ*, and 0 = otherwise.

[4] As with all prior analyses in this book, we are concerned about the possibility of a reciprocal relationship. In this case, it is possible that criticisms reported in the press may influence candidate strategies and the closeness of the race, instead of vice versa. Thus, the data representing criticisms are taken from press coverage starting in October.

[5] See table 5.5 for a comparable analysis of press criticisms.

TABLE 6.2
Assessing the Relationship between Candidate Strategy and Number of Criticisms in the Press (OLS Regression Analysis)

	Criticisms about Incumbent/Open Winner			Criticisms about Challenger/Open Loser		
	Unstandardized Coefficient (standard error)		Beta	Unstandardized Coefficient (standard error)		Beta
Tone of challenger's campaign	8.04	(6.72)	.11	7.76	(4.95)	.15
Tone of incumbent's campaign	15.08	(6.87)ᵇ	.19	13.11	(5.06)ᵇ	.24
Competition	−.65	(.21)ᵃ	−.31	−.52	(.15)ᵃ	−.35
Challenger spending	1.21	(1.58)	.06	−1.05	(1.17)	−.08
Incumbent spending	1.46	(1.56)	.08	.54	(1.15)	.04
Gubernatorial campaign	−19.45	(6.43)ᵃ	−.27	−8.69	(4.74)ᶜ	−.17
Presidential campaign	3.86	(7.04)	.05	−.55	(5.19)	−.01
Endorsement	−12.32	(3.82)ᵃ	−.27	−2.10	(2.81)	−.06
Size of newspaper	.004	(.003)	.12	.004	(.002)	.17
Population of state	−2.48	(7.33)	−.03	.71	(5.4)	.01
Constant	51.63	(42.96)		20.55	(31.7)	
R^2	.52			.48		
N	96			96		

Notes: The dependent variable is the number of criticisms published about the candidate. Tone of *Candidates' campaign* is a binary variable where 1 = negative campaign, 0 = positive campaign. *Competition* ranges from 0 (0 points separating candidates in preelection polls) to 72 (72 points separating candidates). The following variables are logged to base 10: incumbent spending, challenger spending, population of state. *Gubernatorial campaign* is a binary variable where 1 = concurrent gubernatorial campaign, 0 = otherwise. *Presidential campaign* is a binary variable where 1 = presidential year, 0 = otherwise. *Endorsement* is an ordinal variable where 1 = incumbent/winner endorsed, 0 = no endorsement, −1 = challenger/loser endorsed. *Size of newspaper* is the number of column inches devoted to news. All p-values are two-tailed except in the following cases where our expectations are clearly directional: *competition, gubernatorial campaign, presidential campaign, size of newspaper, endorsement.*
ᵃp < .01
ᵇp < .05
ᶜp < .10

In addition, we examined the possibility that candidates who engage in negative campaigning may be criticized more frequently by the press. As we discussed in chapter 4, a negative strategy by candidates may create a backlash where attacking candidates incite more press criticisms of their own candidacies.

The results of the OLS regression analysis presented in table 6.2 reveal that incumbents are successful in encouraging criticisms of their opponents. Incumbents who decide to go negative create, on average, thirteen more criticisms of challengers in the newspaper, compared to incumbents who avoid orchestrating a negative campaign, *ceteris paribus*. However, challengers who wage a negative campaign do not generate more press criticisms of their opponents than challengers who decide to pursue a positive strategy.

We also found that a negative strategy can create a backlash by the press, but only among "attacking" incumbents. In particular, incumbents who run a negative campaign receive significantly more criticisms in the press than incumbents who run a primarily positive campaign. Holding everything else constant (e.g., competition, campaign spending, endorsement patterns), incumbents who run a negative campaign receive, on average, fifteen more criticisms in the newspaper than incumbents who refrain from an "attack" strategy. Challengers, on the other hand, do not risk such a backlash. Challengers running negative campaigns do not garner more criticisms than challengers who pursue a positive campaign strategy.

In addition to the impact of the candidates' strategies, the closeness of the race and the presence of a gubernatorial campaign also influence the number of criticisms reported in the press. Finally, we continue to find evidence, consistent with chapter 5, that newspapers publish significantly fewer criticisms of endorsed incumbents. Endorsed challengers, on the other hand, are unaffected by the editorial decisions of the papers. They do not enjoy fewer published criticisms, even if they receive a newspaper's endorsement.

In summary, the tone of the candidates' messages influences the messages produced by the media. While incumbents are not effective in altering the substance of their coverage, they can frame the tone of their opponents' coverage. When incumbents decide to incorporate criticisms in their messages, the press responds by reporting more of their attacks, compared to incumbents who decide to refrain from attacking their challengers. Challengers, unlike incumbents, are not able to generate negative coverage of their opponents when they run negative campaigns.[6] While challengers cannot affect the tone of their opponents' coverage, they do not suffer a backlash from the news media when they decide to "go negative." Incumbents, on the other hand, receive significantly more criticisms in the press when they engage in negative campaigning. These results show that the news media pay attention to the candidates' strategies when covering campaigns, and the tone of the incumbents' campaign is particularly consequential.

The Correspondence between Candidates' Campaign Packages and News Coverage

Up to here, we have provided evidence about how the press covers specific themes emphasized by candidates. In the present section, we look more holistically at campaign strategies adopted by incumbents and challengers. In-

---

[6] Consistent with the findings in chapter 5, candidates' spending is unrelated to the number of criticisms reported in the newspapers.

stead of examining coverage of specific themes, we look at how successful candidates are at securing press attention for their entire campaign agendas.

The interviews with campaign managers revealed that nearly all senatorial candidates emphasize several messages simultaneously.[7] In fact, when asked to identify "the main themes" of their campaigns, only 6 percent of managers responded with a single theme. One reason candidates emphasize a package of themes is so they will appeal to a multitude of constituencies. For example, Paul Wellstone stressed that his "independence" from corporate money would make him effective at fighting for a cleaner and safer "environment." Senator Tom Harkin emphasized that his "experience" in Washington would enable him to improve the lives of people tied to the "agricultural economy" in Iowa. In addition, certain themes can be readily assembled into a general rubric. For example, many Republicans emphasized "fiscal conservatism" and thus stressed issues such as "lower taxes," "smaller government," and a "balanced budget." Many incumbents emphasized a package of personality traits, such as "knowledge," "experience," "integrity," and "concern for the state."

In this analysis, we looked at the correspondence between media coverage and candidates' overall packages of themes. To identify the candidates' messages, we again relied on the campaign managers' answers to the open-ended question, "What were the main themes that you tried to stress in the campaign?" We then located the media coverage that matched these themes. For example, if a candidate mentioned health care, education, and experience in Washington, we located the number of paragraphs linking the candidate to these particular topics. As before, we matched managers' themes to the media coverage between October 1 and Election Day. Thus, we have a dependent variable that measures the number of news paragraphs that correspond with the candidates' main messages.

From October 1 to Election Day, the press reported, on average, 36 paragraphs corresponding with the incumbents' messages. The standard deviation is 39 paragraphs, suggesting that senators vary in their abilities to set the media's agenda. Senator David Karnes of Nebraska, for example, was quite adept at obtaining coverage for his chosen themes. He received a whopping 216 paragraphs of coverage devoted to the main messages of his campaign, from October 1 to Election Day. In contrast, 12 percent of senators received fewer than five paragraphs devoted to their main themes.

In the case of challengers, from the beginning of October to Election Day, the newspapers printed an average of 24 paragraphs reflecting their main messages. Similar to incumbents, the standard deviation of 33 paragraphs indicates substantial variation in challengers' abilities to influence media

[7] At the presidential level, Just et al. (1996) report that candidates' messages are almost always a mix of issue and character information.

coverage. Lynn Yeakel, in her attempt to unseat Senator Arlen Specter in Pennsylvania, garnered 162 paragraphs corresponding to her main themes. In contrast, 33 percent of challengers captured fewer than five paragraphs devoted to their main messages.

In the present section, we examine whether the candidates' choices of campaign strategies influence their ability to secure press attention for their campaign agendas.[8] As discussed in earlier chapters, candidates have at least three options available when deciding on campaign strategies. First, they can focus mainly on policy matters or more heavily on their personal characteristics. Second, if candidates decide to focus on policy, they need to choose the types of issues to emphasize. Finally, candidates have the choice of launching positive campaigns, focusing on their own strengths, or developing negative strategies where they attack their opponents on personal or policy grounds, or both.

We look at whether these three strategic decisions influence the candidates' abilities to obtain press attention for their agendas. Turning first to the trade-off between emphasizing traits or issues or both, we developed a scale ranging from 1 to 5, where 1 represents a candidate who focuses exclusively on traits, 3 represents an equal balance between traits and issues (i.e., a candidate who emphasizes experience and environmental issues), and 5 represents a candidate who focuses only on policy matters.

For incumbents, the average score on this trait-issue scale is 2.50, with a standard deviation of 1.55, while challengers score an average of 3.92, with a standard deviation of 1.43. These differences are consistent with our findings in chapter 3 where we report that incumbents are more likely than challengers to emphasize traits in their campaigns.

The choice between running a trait-oriented campaign versus an issue-dominated one may have important ramifications for press coverage. It could be the case that reporters prefer that candidates emphasize issues, since it may be easier to report issue priorities and positions than to discuss honesty or compassion. By focusing on issues, candidates may grab the attention of reporters who may then provide more press coverage for the candidates' remaining campaign themes.

While the choice between a trait-based and an issue-oriented campaign may alter coverage of a candidate's agenda, candidates who emphasize certain types of issues may be more successful in garnering coverage for their packages of themes. To explore this possibility, we developed a scale assessing whether the candidates focused on economic issues *or* on issues related to social policy and social programs.[9] We focused only on economic issues,

---

[8] To assess the candidates' choice of strategies, we rely on the campaign managers' description of the candidates' main themes.

[9] This scale ranges from -1 to 1, where 1 captures candidates who focus exclusively on

social issues, and issues related to social programs, since our analysis in chapter 3 indicated that these three policy areas make up the bulk of the issues emphasized by candidates. [10]

We expect that candidates who focus on economic issues will receive more coverage for their packages of themes. Reporters may view economic issues as more newsworthy, since many readers are interested in issues related to their pocketbook. Therefore, when candidates emphasize economic policy in their campaigns, reporters respond by focusing on these issues in their campaign coverage (Kahn, 1996). Furthermore, once reporters are paying attention to candidates who focus on economic issues, they may also attend to the other messages presented by these candidates.

Finally, we look at whether the tone of candidates' campaigns affects candidates' ability to generate coverage of their packages of campaign themes. We develop a binary measure where 1 indicates a predominantly negative campaign (i.e., a majority of a candidate's themes were negative); and 0 represents messages that are not generally negative.

While negative campaigns can generate exciting copy (Cook, 1996), negative campaigns may also distract reporters from candidates' other messages. In addition, some negative themes are difficult to cover, such as "time for a change in government." These messages, embraced by many challengers, are too amorphous to generate significant press coverage. While over one-third (38 percent) of the challengers' managers mentioned "time for a change" as a main theme of their campaigns, an average of only one paragraph was printed about this theme during the latter parts of the campaigns (October 1 to Election Day).

In the OLS analysis presented in table 6.3, we examine whether the choice of campaign strategies influences the candidates' abilities to secure news coverage for their overall agendas. Consistent with all prior analyses, we also examine how the competitiveness of the campaign, the candidates' level of spending, the population of the state, and the presence of gubernatorial and presidential campaigns influence coverage of the candidates' main themes. Finally, we include a measure assessing the number of themes emphasized by candidates, since candidates who focus on several topics may have a better chance of generating news coverage than candidates who emphasize a single theme.

The results suggest that the strategic decisions of challengers influence how the press covers the challengers' agendas. In contrast, incumbents' decisions about what information to stress in their campaigns do not appear to

---

economic issues; 0 represents candidates who emphasize a mix of economic and social/social program issues or candidates who chose not to emphasize these issues; and -1 indicates candidates emphasizing only social issues or social programs.

[10] See figure 3.1 for the relevant analysis as well as a definition of economic issues, social issues, and social program issues.

TABLE 6.3
OLS Regression Analysis Explaining Coverage of Candidates' Package of Themes

	Number of Paragraphs about Incumbents' Package	Number of Paragraphs about Challengers' Package
	Unstandardized Coefficient (standard error)	Unstandardized Coefficient (standard error)
Issue-trait scale	2.622 (3.06)	4.89 (2.32)[b]
Economic-social scale	11.57 (9.35)	15.47 (7.00)[b]
Tone of candidate's campaign	−21.83 (27.06)	−24.19 (8.22)[a]
Number of themes	0.39 (2.88)	5.42 (2.22)[b]
Competition	−0.75 (.26)[a]	−.76 (.19)[a]
Candidate spending	2.24 (2.22)	−.38 (1.76)
Gubernatorial campaign	−27.34 (11.22)[b]	2.54 (7.48)
Presidential campaign	−20.02 (10.35)[b]	−.72 (7.74)
Population of state	−3.37 (10.34)	.41 (7.58)
Constant	66.47 (66.82)	17.32 (48.44)
	$R^2 = .25$	$R^2 = .42$
	$N = 74$	$N = 72$

Notes: The dependent variable is the number of paragraphs published about the candidate's main messages. *Issue-trait scale* is an ordinal measure ranging from 1 (message exclusively about traits) to 5 (message exclusively about issues). *Economic-social scale* is an ordinal measure ranging from −1 (message exclusively about soical issues and social program issues to 1 (message exclusively about economic issues). *Tone of candidate's campaign* is a binary variable where 1 = predominantly negative campaign, 0 = predominantly positive campaign. The *Number of themes* ranges from 1 to 5. *Competition* ranges from 0 (0 points separating candidates in preelection polls) to 72 (72 points separating candidates). The following variables are logged to base 10: *incumbent spending, challenger spending, population of state. Gubernatorial campaign* is a binary variable where 1 = concurrent gubernatorial campaign, 0 = otherwise. *Presidential campaign* is a binary variable where 1 = presidential year, 0 = otherwise. *Endorsement* is an ordinal variable where 1 = incumbent/winner endorsed, 0 = no endorsement, −1 = challenger/loser endorsed. All p-values are two-tailed except in the following cases where our expectations are clearly directional: competition, gubernatorial campaign, presidential campaign, size of newspaper, endorsement.
[a] $p < .01$
[b] $p < .05$

have consequences for whether their themes are covered by the press. These results are consistent with our earlier analysis indicating that the substantive emphasis of challengers—and not incumbents—directly alters media coverage of specific campaign themes.

Challengers running issue-oriented campaigns capture more coverage for their chosen themes. In fact, challengers who focus exclusively on issues generate twenty more paragraphs of coverage than challengers who focus only on traits (i.e., 4.89 × 4-point change on the issue-trait scale). Similarly, the types of issues emphasized by challengers influence patterns of coverage. Candidates discussing only economic issues receive, on average, thirty-one more paragraphs describing their agendas than challengers who decide to stress social issues (i.e., 15.47 × 2-point change on economic-social scale).

In addition, the tone of challengers' campaigns has consequences for coverage of their main messages. Challengers who conduct negative campaigns are less effective in encouraging coverage of their packages of themes. Negative campaigns generate, on average, twenty-four fewer paragraphs devoted to the challengers' agendas. For incumbents, a negative strategy does not inhibit coverage of the senators' own themes.

The number of themes embraced by challengers also influences press patterns. Every additional theme articulated by a challenger produces, on average, five more press paragraphs about that candidate's agenda. In contrast, the number of topics emphasized by incumbents is not related to coverage of their agendas (i.e., the coefficient for the number of themes is small and statistically insignificant for incumbents).

While the challengers' campaign strategies are more consequential than the actions of incumbents, competing news events are more influential for incumbents. The presence of a gubernatorial contest and a presidential election produces fewer paragraphs about the incumbents' campaign themes. In contrast, these competing news events do not affect coverage of the challengers' agendas.

Finally, the level of competition in the race influences coverage of both the incumbent's *and* challenger's agendas. For incumbents and challengers, a one-point change in the closeness of the polls alters press coverage by approximately .75 paragraphs, all other things being equal. Thus, a 10-point change in poll standings is associated with about a 7.5 paragraph change in coverage of the candidates' main themes. Just as competition enhances press coverage in general, the closeness of the race leads reporters to spend more time discussing the specific themes embraced by the candidates.

In summary, candidates adopt particular strategies as a way of enhancing their own candidacies while creating doubts about their opponents' campaigns. The results presented in this chapter suggest that challengers' campaign tactics are more influential than the strategies used by sitting senators.[11] As discussed earlier, challengers may be successful in controlling news coverage because they are largely unknown to the press, and reporters must turn to these candidates for information about their campaigns. Incumbents, in contrast, have well-established records within their states, and these records

---

[11] Clarke and Evans (1983) report a similar finding when they show that candidate-initiated activities (e.g., speeches, interviews, news releases) produce more coverage for challengers than for incumbents in U.S. House races.

are likely to influence coverage of their current campaigns. News reporters, in covering incumbents' reelection campaigns, can turn to senators' legislative histories for information and insights when preparing stories (Clarke and Evans, 1983).

In addition, incumbents may have difficulty controlling media coverage of their campaigns because they are not only political candidates. Incumbents are sitting senators; consequently, news reporters rely on them as authoritative sources for news, whether campaigning or not. When a news event occurs, news personnel routinely turn to senators for their reaction and interpretation (Cook, 1989). Therefore, a senator's established record and the senator's status are important news sources that produce coverage for issues and events not embraced by the incumbent's own campaign.

Finally, the inability of incumbents to control their news coverage is consistent with Zaller's (1997) "rule of product substitution." Zaller (1997: 33) explains that reporters resist control by politicians and "seek to develop new and distinctive types of information that they can substitute for what politicians are providing." Journalists can resist control by incumbents because they have numerous other sources of information. With challengers, journalists are more dependent on the candidates themselves for news.

The Agenda-Setting Battle: Who Wins the Head-to-Head Competition

Reporters and editors have discrete amounts of space in which to cover campaigns. And, in theory, they receive two messages simultaneously, although one may be considerably louder than the other. They need to make important decisions about whether to provide equal time for the two messages or to give preferential coverage to one message over another. We are interested in understanding how reporters and editors make these decisions. In other words, for what reasons does one candidate's message receive more coverage than a rival's message?

To be sure, competing candidates vary dramatically in their ability to secure news space. For example, in his 1988 uphill battle against Senator Richard Lugar, Jack Wickes of Indiana attacked Lugar's record in the U.S. Senate and called for congressional term limits. Wickes's campaign agenda was ignored by the *Indianapolis Star*; he received a single paragraph devoted to his chosen themes. Meanwhile, thirty-six paragraphs focused on Senator Lugar's chosen campaign themes, which emphasized his qualifications and experience in the U.S. Senate.

Another challenger, Tom Tauke of Iowa, talked principally about the economy in his 1990 competitive battle against Senator Tom Harkin, and he was rewarded with ninety paragraphs focusing on his own agenda. Senator Harkin, in contrast, received little coverage of his major themes. Only thirty paragraphs focused on Harkin's effectiveness as a politician and his willingness to fight for the interests and values of Iowans.

These examples raise several questions. Why did one incumbent's message (i.e., Lugar's) receive thirty-six times more coverage than the challenger's, while another incumbent's message garnered only a third of the coverage that the challenger's message received? Was it because the challenger in Indiana adopted a negative message, while, in Iowa, Tauke's message focused on the economy? Or is it possible to explain the difference solely in terms of the levels of competition? After all, in Indiana the race was never close, while in Iowa it was competitive from the beginning. Much of what we have learned in chapter 5, and so far in chapter 6, helps us to answer these questions.

In terms of sheer amounts of coverage, the preponderance of evidence from chapters 5 and 6 suggests that incumbents receive more coverage than challengers. This advantage appears to be due primarily to incumbents' campaign activities and their status as U.S. senators. The content of their messages, on the other hand, appears to have little influence on the amount or content of their news stories. That is, if editors decide to print a story on the economy, they can glean information about the incumbent's economic record from past votes, or prior campaigns, irrespective of whether the incumbent is talking about the economy in the current campaign.

Challengers, in contrast, can increase coverage of their candidacies by structuring their messages around issues, especially economic policy. Thus, when faced with two competing messages and limited space, editors and reporters will likely print stories about the incumbents, almost reflexively, and will provide coverage for the challengers depending on the content of the messages.

Finally, evidence presented in chapters 5 and 6 suggests that candidates' messages have a higher likelihood of being presented as the election becomes more competitive. Indeed, the closeness of the race consistently and powerfully influences all aspects of campaign coverage. These findings generate some straightforward expectations regarding the outcome of the agenda-setting battle. Although incumbents will usually garner more coverage for their chosen themes compared to their challengers, the size of their advantage depends on the closeness of the race and the content and tone of the challengers' messages.

The data used in the forthcoming analyses come exclusively from races where both campaign managers were interviewed. This restriction, which is necessary because we need to measure the *two* competing messages, yields fifty-five races for analysis. Our first test examines media coverage when the candidates are emphasizing alternative messages (e.g., the incumbent is stressing one theme while the challenger is stressing a different one alto-

TABLE 6.4
OLS Regression Analysis Examining How Coverage of Themes Depends on
Opponent's Strategy

	Number of Paragraphs about Incumbents' Package	Number of Paragraphs about Challengers' Package
	Unstandardized Coefficient (standard error)	Unstandardized Coefficient (standard error)
Same/different theme	−6.8 (13.8)	−4.56 (9.03)
Issue-trait scale	7.42 (5.14)	5.36 (2.94)^c
Economic-social scale	1.54 (11.81)	11.89 (8.95)
Tone of candidate's campaign	−29.04 (30.16)	−33.05 (10.25)^a
Number of themes	−0.37 (4.7)	5.39 (3.66)
Competition	−0.48 (.31)^c	−.89 (.23)^a
Gubernatorial campaign	−26.10 (13.2)^b	−1.3 (9.4)
Presidential campaign	−19.12 (13.3)^c	−0.01 (.6)
Constant	43.97 (19.59)^b	23.26 (20.45)
	$R^2 = .23$	$R^2 = .43$
	N = 55	N = 55

Notes: The dependent variable is the number of paragraphs published about the candidate's main messages. *Same/different theme* is a binary variable where 1 = opponents emphasized same theme, 0 = opponents emphasized different themes. *Issue-trait scale* is an ordinal measure ranging from 1 (message exclusively about traits) to 5 (message exclusively about issues). *Economic-social scale* is an ordinal measure ranging from −1 (message exclusively about soical issues and social program issues to 1 (message exclusively about economic issues). *Tone of candidate's campaign* is a binary variable where 1 = predominantly negative campaign, 0 = predominantly positive campaign. The *Number of themes* ranges from 1 to 5. *Competition* ranges from 0 (0 points separating candidates in preelection polls) to 72 (72 points separating candidates). *Gubernatorial campaign* is a binary variable where 1 = concurrent gubernatorial campaign, 0 = otherwise. *Presidential campaign* is a binary variable where 1 = presidential year, 0 = otherwise. Endorsement is an ordinal variable where 1 = incumbent/winner endorsed, 0 = no endorsement, −1 = challenger/loser endorsed. All p-values are two-tailed except in the following cases where our expectations are clearly directional: competition, gubernatorial campaign, presidential campaign, size of newspaper, endorsement.
^{a}p < .01
^{b}p < .05
^{c}p < .10

gether). We use OLS regression to predict the amount of coverage devoted to each candidate's "package of themes," relying on the same model presented in table 6.3, with a few exceptions.[12] The results of this analysis are presented in table 6.4.

[12] This analysis is different from the analysis presented in table 6.3 in three ways. First, we restrict the analysis to cases where both campaign managers are interviewed. Second, we in-

Several findings emerge from the analyses in table 6.4. First, the variable measuring whether incumbents and challengers are stressing similar or different themes is statistically insignificant in both models. This suggests that the abilities of candidates to generate press coverage of their chosen themes do not depend on whether candidates are stressing similar or distinct themes. Second, competition influences the correspondence between candidate themes and press coverage. Third, challengers can influence the correspondence between coverage and their chosen messages by emphasizing issues instead of traits, whereas incumbents can do little to shape the content of their coverage. Fourth, challengers receive less coverage for their themes when they pursue a negative strategy. Finally, competing presidential and gubernatorial campaigns continue to rob coverage from the incumbents' themes while they have no impact on the challengers' coverage.

We use the regression coefficients from these explanatory models to make predictions about the amount of coverage devoted to the incumbents' and challengers' messages when the candidates are emphasizing different messages. We make an "average" prediction for challengers and incumbents, holding all of the remaining variables in the models at their means. In addition, we make several other predictions by manipulating the values of the theoretically important independent variables such as competition, the content of the candidates' messages, and the tone of the message, holding the remaining variables at their means. Through these various calculations, we shed some light on whether incumbents always have an advantage in the agenda-setting battle, or whether that advantage is related to the competing candidates' messages and the closeness of the race.

In all of the predictions presented in figure 6.2, candidates stress different themes. Turning to the general pattern of findings in the figure, we find that incumbents are slightly more successful than challengers in securing press attention for their agendas when the opponents focus on different messages. On average, 34 paragraphs are devoted to the incumbents' agendas, while only 28 paragraphs discuss the challengers' themes. Incumbents have an advantage when the race is not competitive; challengers receive virtually no coverage when polls in September signal lopsided elections, while incumbents manage to get 18 paragraphs on average. Incumbents also have an advantage when they stress either issues or traits, compared to when challengers emphasize these topics. Incumbents especially have an advantage if they are the only candidates stressing social issues, compared to when challengers are sending the only messages about social issues (33 paragraphs for the incumbents to 16 paragraphs for the challengers).

clude a variable assessing whether the opposing candidates' themes are similar or different. Third, given our limited degrees of freedom, we eliminate campaign spending and population from the models because these variables fail to reach significance in the incumbent *and* challenger models in tables 6.1, 6.2, and 6.3.

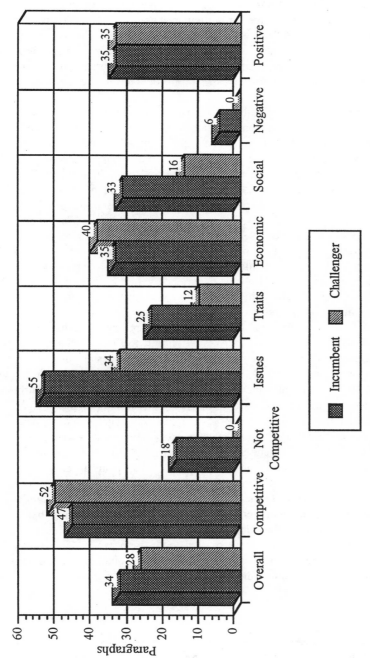

Figure 6.2. Who gets coverage when candidates emphasize different messages? The point estimates are based on the unstandardized regression coefficients presented in table 6.4. We calculate the point estimates by varying whether the candidates emphasized the same themes, the level of competition, the content of the candidates' messages, and the tone of the message while holding all remaining variables at their means (Lewis-Beck, 1980).

However, in some situations, challengers can actually overcome the incumbency advantage in coverage. In particular, when candidates compete in close races and when candidates emphasize economic issues, challengers are somewhat more successful than incumbents at capturing the media spotlight. For example, in the most competitive Senate contests, 47 paragraphs discuss the incumbents' campaign themes, while 52 are devoted to the themes emphasized by their challengers.

While competing candidates often articulate different themes in their campaigns, candidates also focus on the same topics in their electoral bids. However, once again, we find that the amount of attention devoted to these themes varies dramatically across different races. For example, in the 1992 campaign between Senator Christopher Dodd and Brook Johnson of Connecticut, both candidates focused on the economy and received the same amount of press attention: 63 paragraphs discussed economic issues for Dodd and 57 paragraphs discussed Johnson's economic proposals. In contrast, in the 1990 race between Senator Daniel Akaka and U.S. House representative Patricia Saiki, both candidates highlighted their electoral experience. However, Akaka was far more successful in securing coverage for his agenda: 62 paragraphs focused on his experience, while only 26 paragraphs discussed Saiki's qualifications in the *Honolulu Advertiser*.

We repeat the analysis presented in figure 6.2 for races where the candidates stressed the same themes. These findings are presented in figure 6.3. The general pattern of findings is strikingly similar to those in figure 6.2.[13] We once again see that incumbents are slightly more successful in securing coverage. This is true in six of the nine variations presented in figure 6.3. However, as before, the incumbency advantage in coverage depends on the competitiveness of the campaigns and on the choice of campaign messages. Incumbents maintain a slight overall advantage (27 paragraphs to 23 paragraphs), and this advantage increases in noncompetitive races, when both candidates stress the same general set of issues and when both candidates center on social issues. The incumbent advantage disappears in close races and when the two candidates compete directly for economic coverage.

In summary, regardless of whether opposing candidates articulate similar or divergent messages, incumbents often "win" the agenda-setting battle. However, the outcome of the battle depends on the candidates' choices of themes and on the competitiveness of the contests. When candidates are engaged in close races and focus on economic issues, challengers can successfully influence the news media's agenda.

---

[13] This is not surprising because the variable measuring whether incumbents or challengers are stressing similar or different themes is not statistically significant (see table 6.4).

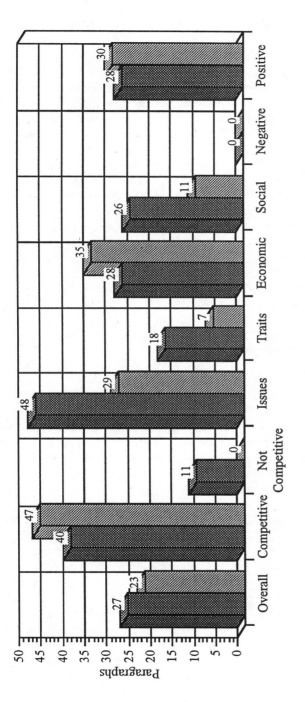

Figure 6.3. Who gets coverage when candidates emphasize similar messages? The point estimates are based on the unstandardized regression coefficients presented in table 6.4. We calculate the point estimates by varying whether the candidates emphasized the same themes, the level of competition, the content of the candidates' messages and the tone of the message while holding all remaining variables at their means (Lewis-Beck, 1980).

Summary

In this chapter we show that the challengers' choice of strategies consistently influences the substance of their news coverage. When challengers discuss certain topics in their campaigns, the press responds by covering these topics in more detail. Furthermore, the types of campaign strategies adopted by challengers influence the amount of press attention devoted to the candidates' "packages of themes." Challengers who run issue-oriented campaigns, for example, receive more coverage for their chosen themes.

Although incumbents typically receive more news coverage than challengers, they are less effective in shaping the content of their coverage. Press coverage of incumbents does not depend upon the senators' choices of campaign messages. Similarly, the types of campaign strategies employed by incumbents do not influence the amount of press coverage of their "packages of themes." Instead, the presence of a gubernatorial contest or a presidential election is much more likely to affect the incumbent's campaign agenda.

Incumbents are more successful at influencing coverage of their opponents. When incumbents pursue a negative campaign strategy, they generate more criticisms of their challenger. However, this strategy has its costs. Incumbents who decide to attack challengers are subject to a "backlash" of critical coverage in the press.

Finally, when we look at head-to-head competition for the news media's agenda, we find incumbents are often more effective at generating coverage. In most cases, whether incumbents and challengers are stressing different or similar themes, incumbents receive more coverage compared to challengers. The most notable exception is when candidates are engaged in competitive contests. In close races, the number of paragraphs printed about candidates' chosen themes are quite similar, irrespective of the status of the candidates, or whether the candidates are emphasizing similar or different messages.

After many pages and numerous analyses, this is an appropriate time to pause and reflect on where we have been and where we are going. First, we explored the forces that shape candidates' strategies. We spent a great deal of time examining how competition and media coverage affect how candidates craft their campaign messages. We have spent an equal amount of time locating the factors that influence how editors and reporters cover campaigns. We looked carefully at the role of competition and candidates' strategies for understanding patterns of campaign coverage. Our most consistent finding is that competition plays a powerful role in campaigns, shaping candidates' strategies and media coverage. The importance of competition is impressive. The closeness of the race affects the content and tone of the candidates' messages and the substance, quantity, and valence of news coverage.

But what of competition? We know it is not static across the life of campaigns. In fact, the level of competition changes notably from Labor Day to Election Day in most of the senate campaigns between 1988 and 1992. Indeed, one campaign manager told us that "any change in the polls, and there were many, for good or bad, caused our staff many headaches and hours of meetings." As we theorized in chapter 1, we do not believe that changes in competition are merely random fluctuations of voters. We argue that the level of competition in campaigns, best captured by public opinion polls, responds systematically to the actions of the candidates and the behavior of the press. In chapter 7, we will examine the validity of our claim by looking at whether coverage of campaigns in the news and the candidates' actions on the campaign trail affect the competitiveness of Senate races.

Part Four _____

CITIZENS' REACTIONS TO CAMPAIGNS

Seven

The Dynamics of Competition

THE IMPACT OF THE CANDIDATES AND THE NEWS MEDIA

IN THE FALL of 1988, Senator Dennis Deconcini, a Democrat, was seeking his third term as U.S. senator from Arizona. He was unopposed in the Democratic primary. His Republican opponent was earnest but inexperienced and lacking funds. In early October, Senator Deconcini was sitting atop a war chest in excess of $3 million while his challenger, Keith DeGreen, a financial planner by trade, had only $150,000 to spend, half of which was his own money. Polls in late September and early October indicated that Deconcini led by as much as 50 points. The stage was set for an easy Deconcini victory.

In mid-October, almost overnight, DeGreen's campaign caught fire. His new life was sparked by the revelation that Deconcini had acquired privileged "insider" information to purchase land in Arizona in the early 1980s that was sold to the federal government for large profits a few years later. The national GOP responded to the disclosure by funneling $212,000 into DeGreen's campaign; presidential GOP candidate George Bush pumped in an additional $5,000, and President Reagan taped an enthusiastic endorsement for DeGreen. DeGreen's campaign spent much of the incoming funds producing commercials that highlighted Deconcini's questionable good fortune in the world of real estate.

The largest circulating newspaper in the state, the *Arizona Republic*, suddenly became very interested in the campaign. The newspaper printed a dozen stories on the controversy in the last twelve days of the campaign, two of which were headlines on the front page of the paper, with an additional four articles making headlines in the "Valley and State" section of the paper.

Deconcini's comfortable lead evaporated. In a poll taken less than a week before Election Day, Deconcini was ahead by a mere 12 points, a change of a whopping 38 points. Deconcini fought back. He produced commercials and called press conferences to explain that his actions were not improper. Deconcini stressed that he did not profit as much as other investors and he did not use his position as a U.S. senator to obtain information about the real estate opportunity. He angrily criticized his challenger for misrepresenting his actions, stating that DeGreen was "an embarrassment to the Republican Party, because he's made this one of the dirtiest campaigns ever run" (*Arizona Republic*, November 9, 1988: 1).

In the end, on Election Day, the voters sided with their senator. Deconcini retained his seat with 57 percent of the vote. Nevertheless, the level of competition, measured by the polls, changed significantly from September to late October. It appeared that public opinion responded to the hint of a scandal, to the infusion of money into the challenger's campaign, and to the articles produced by the local press. By nearly all accounts, the level of competition in the race was affected by the actions of the candidates and the press.

Four years later, the citizens of Arizona were once again deciding whether they should reelect a U.S. senator. This time Senator John McCain, a Republican, was seeking reelection. McCain's campaign was far different than Deconcini's reelection bid. The hint of a scandal never materialized, the challenger received no eleventh-hour financial help, and the local press virtually ignored the contest for the duration of the campaign. McCain's early lead in the polls gradually drifted upward until Election Day, when he defeated his Democratic challenger by 24 points.

The biggest difference between the two campaigns is that Deconcini was unable to avoid the discussion of a scandal, while McCain's potential scandal passed him by. In the early 1990s, McCain, along with four other senators, was accused of pressuring federal regulators to ease their investigations into the business dealings of savings and loan financier Charles Keating. Keating had deep roots in Arizona and a long friendship with John McCain. He implored the senators to "call off" the regulators. Some senators were responsive (e.g., Senator Cranston from California) and attempted to pressure regulators to move their investigations elsewhere. The scandal became known in the popular press as the "Keating Five" scandal.

In due time, Keating's financial empire crumbled and U.S. citizens lost millions of dollars. However, the Ethics Committee in the Senate, examining the behavior of all five senators, exonerated McCain. The Committee declared that McCain had "exercised poor judgment" when he attended meetings where senators tried to convince federal regulators to avoid examining Keating's empire. But the Committee ruled that McCain did not improperly use the powers of his office.

McCain's challenger, Claire Sargent, made virtually no use of the Keating scandal. She lacked money, producing only one commercial, and her campaign never settled on a coherent message. The *Arizona Republic* printed less than one article per day from early September to Election Day about the campaign. The only media interest in the campaign came during the final ten days when President Bush named McCain to head a U.S. delegation to retrieve information from the Vietnamese government about U.S. soldiers missing in action during the Vietnam War. McCain, himself a POW for five years in Hanoi, was able to parlay this appointment into a solid stretch of positive media attention. The *Arizona Republic* produced seven positive articles in five days during the last week of October. One of the articles included photos released by the Vietnamese government of McCain injured and bed-ridden as a POW.

By Election Day, voters were presented with few reasons to oust McCain. The citizens of Arizona, already solidly supporting him, received only one set of messages throughout the campaign. They were witness to a continuous flow of media stories favorable to McCain during the final days of the campaign. In addition, many voters encountered a series of positive commercials stressing McCain's distinguished career in the Senate. Sargent, in contrast, was ignored by the news media and silenced by her lack of funds.

These two examples from Arizona serve to remind us that competition not only influences the behavior of the candidates and the media, but also responds to the actions of the candidates and the messages generated by reporters. The theory of campaigns outlined in chapter 1 also predicts that the activities of politicians and media elites influence levels of competition. That is, competition, as measured by aggregate polling numbers, is dynamic and regularly changes across the course of a campaign. Polls taken at different times during campaigns rarely exhibit a static pattern, much to the chagrin of leading candidates yet heartening for trailing ones.

In fact, an examination of the Senate races between 1988 and 1992 reveals that in a vast majority of campaigns, the polling numbers changed significantly between mid-September and the ten days preceding Election Day. In 61 percent of the races, polls became more competitive as campaigns progressed. In an additional 24 percent, the polls widened with the leader gaining strength as Election Day approached. Polls were static in only 15 percent of the campaigns, exhibiting insignificant change from mid-September to late October.

Undoubtedly, some of this fluctuation is the product of different samples and uninformed voter preferences measured early in the fall campaign. However, we believe that much of the volatility is systematic, where competition responds to the messages of the candidates and reporters. In chapter 1, we hypothesized a fully reciprocal relationship among candidates' strategies, media coverage, and competition. In this chapter, we complete this circle by examining how the campaign may change a candidate's standing in the polls.

Explaining the Dynamics of Competition

Polls that measure the competing candidates' support among the electorate are taken by senatorial candidates who can afford the cost and by most local newspapers and TV stations. Politicians, campaign strategists, financial contributors, editors, reporters, and many voters are interested in the candidates' positions in these preelection polls. Nearly all politicians who are ahead in the polls keep a close eye on them for any narrowing in their leads (Fenno,

1978, 1996), and "hope springs eternal" for those politicians who are behind. A common belief among candidates trailing in campaigns is that the polls could shift in their favor. Many losing campaign managers told us that the race would have tightened "if we had just a few more dollars," "if the media would have paid more attention to the behavior of the incumbent," "if the voters knew the truth about the senator," or "if the campaign had lasted a few more days." Put simply, the people who conduct and participate in campaigns believe that polls react to candidates' strategies and the actions of the press.

In the last third of the twentieth century, changes in the world of politics and campaigns help explain why polls taken in September may not resemble polls taken in late October. Today, voters' preferences are more fluid, especially in subpresidential campaigns. Compared to forty years ago, voters are less firmly attached to political parties (Miller and Shanks, 1996). Without a party affiliation to anchor preferences, citizens' evaluations of candidates are more malleable. The dramatic and rapid rise in split-ticket voting among individuals since the 1950s suggests that many voters are looking at the information disseminated during the campaign to guide their vote, rather then basing their decisions on a general set of ideological or partisan beliefs.

Coupled with the loosening of partisan ties, the dissemination of political information via computers, radio, and television has greatly accelerated, leading to potentially dramatic and sudden shifts in public opinion. Most senatorial candidates spend literally millions of dollars producing TV and radio commercials that have the potential of reaching nearly all voters in their homes and in their cars. The commercials can be created and spread to citizens in, at most, a few days. Likewise, the press has the ability to spread political information instantaneously throughout the state on several mediums at once. Stories about candidates appearing in morning newspapers, for example, may be repeated hourly on the radio throughout the day, and may finally appear on local TV news stations during the evening. As an example, the news of Deconcini's real estate troubles cropped up virtually overnight. Within a few days, hundreds of thousands of Arizonans were aware of his land deals. Thus, preferences that seem stable one day may indeed change markedly the next, reacting to the politics of the campaign.

To determine whether the candidate strategies and the news media's messages change the competitiveness of senate races, we rely on measures of candidate behavior and media coverage that *precede* changes in the closeness of the race. We use the final poll taken in each campaign to measure the competitiveness of the race at the end of the campaign; this serves as the dependent variable in our analysis.[1] To examine changes in competitiveness, polls taken early in the campaign are included as a crucial independent vari-

---

[1] These late polls were taken between October 26 and Election Day.

able.[2] The amount of change between these two sets of polls is the focus of our analysis.

We rely on two measures to tap messages disseminated by the media: the total amount of coverage about the race; and the total amount of criticisms generated about the candidates. The overall amount of media coverage represents the range of material that may change people's views about the candidates. We also included the measure of media criticisms because critical comments give voters explicit reasons for supporting one candidate over another.[3] We measure total media coverage and media criticisms for the October 1 and October 14 period. To capture candidate activity we use measures of campaign spending for incumbents and challengers between October 1 and October 14. Thus, the measures of candidate and press activity are situated squarely between the two measures of polls, providing us with an ideal opportunity to explain the changing levels of competition.

Besides the activities of the candidates and the media, there are other forces that may influence changes in public opinion from September to late October. Specifically, the characteristics of the candidates may alter poll standings (Fenno, 1996; Squire, 1992). For example, senior incumbents, unlike more junior colleagues, may be more adept at swinging polling numbers in their favor or thwarting a surge by a challenger. They have more experience running campaigns; they have a sense of when to release certain commercials, when to request more money from supporters, and when to criticize their opponents.

A second characteristic of candidates, the incumbent's involvement in a scandal, can also produce changes in the competitiveness of the race. Information about the scandal, disseminated during the campaign, may provide voters with compelling reasons to oust the sitting senator. As we saw with the examples from Arizona, some scandals alter public opinion very quickly.

Finally, quality challengers, similar to experienced incumbents, have orchestrated campaigns in the past. Experienced challengers, much more so than political neophytes, have a greater probability of altering the polls in their favor because of higher name recognition and their access to significantly greater resources.

We also include a variable that measures the size of the state. Prior research indicates that competition and the size of the state are positively related (Lee and Oppenheimer, 1997; Hibbing and Brandes, 1983). In a historical time-series analysis, Lee and Oppenheimer (1997: 13) conclude: "These

---

[2] These early polls appeared between September 16 and September 30.

[3] We did attempt to analyze the amount of coverage for challengers and incumbents separately. However, the correlation between incumbent and challenger coverage is .75 and the correlation between incumbent and challenger criticisms is .70, making it difficult to include separate measures of incumbent and challenger coverage in the analysis because of problems of multicollinearity.

results confirm some very old ideas about constituency size and political conflict . . . the politics of Senate elections in large states have, in fact, tended to be more competitive than those of small states." We control for the possibility that polls may be more dynamic in large states than in smaller ones.[4]

Similar to the dynamic analysis in chapter 3, the data used to examine changes in public opinion polls are analyzed in two ways. One set of parameter estimates are derived using Ordinary Least Squares Regression (OLS). A second set of coefficients are estimated with Two State Least Squares Regression (2SLS). The second analysis is necessary to correct for any autocorrelation that may affect the unbiased nature of the parameter estimates (Johnston, 1972; Markus, 1979).[5] The OLS and 2SLS findings are presented side by side in table 7.1 so that readers can compare the results directly.

The OLS and 2SLS findings are remarkably similar. The same three variables reach statistical significance in both analyses: media criticisms, challenger spending, and early polls.[6] Beginning with the amount of media criti-

---

[4] The size of the state also acts as a control for spending differences by candidates across states.

[5] The use of a lagged dependent variable (i.e., polls in September) is crucial to render the analysis dynamic. However, as discussed in chapter 3, inclusion of a lagged dependent variable may cause autocorrelation with the dependent variable, thereby biasing the estimators. Autocorrelation is quite possible when the amount of time between the measurement of dependent variable and the lagged variable is short, as in our analysis. As in chapter 3, we opt to use 2SLS to remedy the problem. It is necessary to "purge" the estimator of the covariations that result from the serially dependent error terms between early and late polls. We need a surrogate variable for the lagged variable that is correlated with the lagged variable but uncorrelated with the dependent variable. This "instrumental" variable can be substituted into the equation to predict the dependent variable.

To develop an instrumental or surrogate variable, we estimated early polls with all of the variables in the original model, plus some temporally determined variables. The temporally determined variables serve as exogenous variables because we can establish time order in each instance. The exogenous variables in the model included incumbent and challenger spending prior to early polls, total media coverage before early polls, media criticisms before early polls, the senator's share of the vote in the previous general election, and the "Cook Report," a prediction published by *CQ* in May concerning the likely competitiveness of the upcoming general election.

The model predicting early polls, the first-stage equation, produced an R^2 of .49. The following variables were statistically significant at the $p < .10$ level: early criticisms in the media, incumbent spending, the quality of the challenger, and the Cook predictions of competition.

[6] In estimating changes in polls, we also examined the impact of the candidates' choice of strategies. In particular, we looked at three hypotheses. First, do candidates who "go negative" affect the competitiveness of the race? Second, do candidates who focus mainly on issues affect the competitiveness of the race? Third, do candidates who focus mainly on traits affect the competitiveness of the race? In each case, the candidates' choice of strategy does not influence changes in polls ($p < .10$). As with all prior analyses in the book, we also included an open-race variable to see whether the type of race affects changes in the competitiveness of the campaign. The open-race variable failed to reach statistical significance ($p < .10$).

TABLE 7.1
Explaining Changes in Competition

	OLS	2SLS
	Unstandardized Coefficients (standard error)	Unstandardized Coefficients (standard error)
Total media coverage	.002 (.01)	−.0007 (.01)
Media criticisms	−.06 (.02)[a]	−.11 (.02)[b]
Incumbent spending	−.85 (1.33)	−.07 (1.71)
Challenger spending	−3.05 (1.13)[a]	−5.29 (1.42)[a]
Challenger quality	.004 (.38)	−.09 (.71)
Scandal	−1.11 (2.59)	−1.10 (3.58)
Seniority	.14 (.11)	.19 (.16)
Population size	2.04 (2.07)	4.28 (2.67)
Competition (lag)	.63 (.07)[a]	.42 (.20)[b]
Constant	16.48 (12.55)	17.75 (17.39)
N	97	97
R^2	.79	.65[c]

Notes: The dependent variable is competition October 22–Election Day. Competition ranges from 0 (0 points separating candidates in preelection polls) to 72 (72 points separating candidates). *Total media coverage* is the number of paragraphs about the race October 1 to October 14. *Media criticisms* is the number of criticisms about the race October 1 to October 14. *Incumbent spending* is measured in dollars and is taken from the October 1 to October 14 spending period. *Challenger spending* is measured in dollars and is taken from the October 1 to October 14 spending period. *Challenger quality* is the scale ranging from 1 to 9. *Scandal* is a binary variable. *Seniority* is measured by number of years in U.S. Senate. *Population size* is the size of the voting age population of the state. *Competition (lag)* is measured from poll results taken September 16 to September 30. The following variables are logged to base 10: incumbent spending, challenger spending, population of state.
[a] $p < .01$
[b] $p < .05$
[c] An R^2 derived from the second-stage equation should be interpreted with caution (Bartels, 1991).

cisms, the coefficients in both analyses indicate that as criticisms become more prevalent in the press, campaigns become more competitive. Focusing on the OLS unstandardized coefficient for interpretations, an increase of one criticism between the time of the early and late polls yields a change in competition of .06, on average, holding all other variables constant.

The second statistically significant variable in both analyses is spending by the challenger. The sign of the coefficients indicates that as the challengers spend more money during the first two weeks of October, the race tightens. This finding is consistent with a rich literature demonstrating that challengers can create a more competitive campaign by spending more money (Jacobson, 1980, 1997). The finding, of course, has face validity because early October is a critical time for challengers. During these weeks of the campaign, challengers must continue to improve their name recognition with voters while simultaneously building a case against incumbents. This requires money for commercials, appearances, fliers, and a staff to raise more money.

Using the unstandardized OLS coefficients presented in table 7.1, we illustrate how competition changes in response to changes in press criticisms and challenger spending.[7] The results of these calculations are displayed in figure 7.1. Turning first to media criticisms, the number of criticisms reported in the newspapers varied widely across this time period, ranging from 0 to 259, with a mean of 65 criticisms. As the data in figure 7.1 show, the level of competition in a campaign closes dramatically when the number of candidate criticisms increases. In campaigns where no criticisms are published about the candidates, we estimate that 29 points will separate the candidates in the polls. When papers publish 259 criticisms about the candidates, however, the race becomes much more competitive. In these campaigns, we estimate that 13 points will separate the two candidates in the polls. The change in competition, then, is 16 points (i.e., 29 − 13). This swing in the polls would make many races extremely competitive and would strike fear into the hearts of all leading candidates, irrespective of the actual size of their leads.

As with media criticisms, we use the unstandardized coefficients from the OLS analysis to provide a similar example for challenger spending. When challenger spending is at zero, we estimate a 40-point difference between the candidates in the polls. However, a tenfold increase in challenger spending produces a much closer race. With large increases in challenger spending, only 21 points are expected to separate the opposing candidates.[8] Thus, the change in competition generated by a tenfold change in challenger spending is 19 points (40 − 21). This change in competition, while dramatic, is not very likely to occur since challengers have a difficult time radically increasing their spending. Between 1988 and 1992, only two challengers were able to increase their spending by tenfold between the first two weeks of October and Election Day, while only four challengers more than doubled their spending across this period.

In the end, large increases in spending are not a viable way for most challengers to increase the competitiveness of their candidacies. Instead,

---

[7] In making these estimations, we hold all remaining variables at their means.

[8] The tenfold interpretation is necessary since campaign spending is logged to base 10 in these analyses.

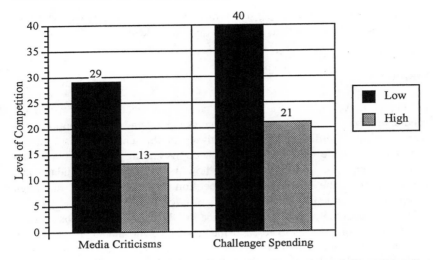

Figure 7.1. An examination of the impact of media criticisms and challenger spending on levels of competition. The point estimates are based on the OLS unstandardized regression coefficients presented in table 7.1. We calculate the point estimates by varying the level of media criticisms and the level of challenger spending while holding all remaining variables at their means (Lewis-Beck, 1980). The level of competition ranges from 0 (0 points separating candidates in pre-election polls) to 72 (72 points separating candidates in pre-election polls).

challengers are more likely to see the polls change if the news media decide to provide critical coverage of the campaign. However, challengers have a difficult time persuading the news media to criticize their opponents. As we saw in chapter 5, increases in challenger spending do not produce more criticisms of incumbents in the press (see table 5.5). Furthermore, the results presented in chapter 6 indicate that challengers who produce negative messages cannot generate more media criticisms of incumbents (see table 6.2).

If there is good news for the challengers, it resides in the fact that incumbents cannot widen their lead with a mere burst of spending. In both the OLS and 2SLS models, the spending variables for incumbents are far from statistically significant. This finding, too, conforms to an extant literature documenting that incumbent spending is less effective at influencing electoral outcomes in comparison with challenger spending (Jacobson, 1980, 1997).

In both analyses, the lagged dependent variables have a statistically significant and substantively important influence on the competitiveness of the race late in the campaign. Incumbents can take comfort in the amount of inertia that exists from one poll to another. Put simply, incumbents who lead in the polls in September are likely to continue to lead in late October.

Summary

In chapter 1, we presented a model of campaigns where the actions of the candidates, the stories presented by the news media, and public opinion polls were causally interdependent. The analyses in this chapter constitute our efforts to determine the final set of connections among these three key elements of campaigns. Indeed, explaining how the strategies of candidates and the activities of the media affect competition over the life of a campaign completes the circle of analyses that began in chapter 3.

We can conclude with some confidence that levels of competition react to the strategies of the candidates and the reports of the media. In particular, challengers that spend money between polls reported in the month of September and polls taken during the last week of the campaign can close the gap between themselves and incumbents. Although spending by challengers yields relatively modest changes in the polls, their spending is not in vain, especially when races are relatively competitive in September. In these campaigns, small changes in competition often make races extremely competitive where outcomes remain uncertain until the final ballots are tallied. In addition to the effects of spending, criticisms reported in the media produce quite dramatic changes in competition. The distance in the polls between front-runners and trailing candidates shrinks markedly when the media begin to criticize the candidates' policies and personal traits.

In summary, as we theorized many pages earlier, the actions of the candidates, the behavior of the news media, and public support for the candidates are interlocked. Our evidence reveals that the relationships among these forces are clearly dynamic and reciprocal, leading us to conclude that campaigns are best understood as a causal web. Early polls set in motion a series of activities by the candidates and the press. The actions of these key players not only affect one another, but ultimately change the competitive nature of the contest.

In the end, coming to grips with the nature of campaigns is only part of the story. In a representative democracy, we are interested in the consequences of campaigns. That is, how do campaigns affect voters? Do campaigns inform citizens? Do they clarify choices for potential voters? Do voters alter the criteria they use to evaluate candidates in response to what they see, hear, and read during campaigns? Put succinctly, do campaigns matter?

The conclusions from this chapter surely provide hints that voters respond to campaigns. The systematic reactions of polls to the activities of the candidates and the press provide clues that voters are influenced by campaigns.

Yet, the aggregate nature of the polls does not allow us to isolate how campaigns affect individual citizens. We must talk to voters directly to see exactly how and why they are influenced by campaigns. How do campaigns affect what voters know about candidates? And how do voters come to prefer one candidate over another? In the remainder of the book, we will explore these questions.

Eight

Citizens' Knowledge about U.S. Senate Campaigns

To DISCOVER how campaigns affect potential voters, we must examine individuals within their campaign environment. We know from the preceding pages that the campaign environment consists of the culmination of the interplay among competition, media coverage, and candidates' strategies. The confluence of these reciprocal and dynamic relationships defines the setting in which voters encounter candidates. Campaigns, then, vary along a continuum determined by the interaction among the candidates, the news media, and the competitive nature of the race. Campaigns at one end of the continuum consist of races where one candidate leads by a whopping amount in the polls, the candidates' messages are few in number and are mundane in content, and the media coverage is literally nonexistent. At the other end of the continuum, the polls indicate that races are extremely competitive, the candidates produce an abundance of interesting and useful messages, and the media cover the campaign daily. Because no two campaigns have the same configuration of these elements, voters' experience with campaigns varies greatly across states during the same election year and over time within the same state.

This continuum represents the intensity of campaigns. This intensity determines, in large part, the degree to which campaigns influence people's knowledge and attitudes about the competing candidates. Compared to political elites who earn their living creating, studying, and reacting to political events, voters are strikingly less attentive to politics. With the exception of political junkies, most citizens occupy their days with things apolitical. Americans, as Converse (1964) taught us several decades ago, are unabashedly disconnected from political discourse. Only intense campaigns are likely to avert people's attention away from the matters of home and work to matters of state and nation.

As campaigns increase in their intensity, voters have greater opportunities to bump into campaign information. Intense campaigns are a swirl of events, speeches, commercials, and debates. Voters are more likely to see a candidate's commercial on TV one day, read a headline about the campaign two days later, hear the latest poll results on the radio a week later, and overhear conversations at work somewhere in between.

When skilled candidates air clever and informative commercials, when the news media print numerous stories about the contests, and when the outcomes of the races are uncertain, voters have access to more information and are more motivated to process the information. Close races, because the outcomes are uncertain, heighten interest in campaigns and increase the probability that voters will watch entire commercials, read past headlines, or engage in conversations about the political campaigns. Therefore, as the intensity of campaigns increases, voters have more contact and connections with the candidates, gain more knowledge about the competing candidates, and, in the end, make more sophisticated decisions about the candidates.

Less intense campaigns are characterized by fewer messages, and the messages are often one-sided, uninteresting, and difficult to locate. In the lexicon of rational choice theory, information costs for finding candidate messages are high, maybe prohibitive, especially for voters trying to gather information about challengers. These low-intensity campaigns, either partially or completely, either intentionally or accidentally, are often ignored by voters.

Two campaigns from the Carolinas illustrate the dramatic differences in information and voter knowledge across campaigns. In 1990 voters in North Carolina were bombarded with information about the competitive contest between Senator Jesse Helms and Mayor Harvey Gantt. The polls indicated that the race was too close to call from beginning to end. Media coverage was extensive, with the *Raleigh News and Observer* publishing over three thousand paragraphs about the race. The competing candidates also provided citizens with their own messages, often focusing on controversial issues like affirmative action and abortion. The two contestants spent more than four dollars per citizen trying to reach potential supporters during the course of the campaign.

In dramatic contrast, just a few miles away in South Carolina, voters were living in a political vacuum. Senator Strom Thurmond, first elected in 1954, was challenged by a political neophyte who spent virtually nothing to unseat Thurmond. Campaign spending by both candidates averaged only 75 cents per potential voter. Thurmond was never seriously threatened during the course of the campaign, and the last poll of the campaign indicated that he was 50 points ahead of his challenger, Robert H. Cunningham. The media turned a deaf ear to the campaign, publishing only seventy-one paragraphs in the *Columbia State* paper during the entire campaign season.

Citizens residing in North Carolina were much more likely to be exposed to the candidates compared to their neighbors to the south. For instance, 60 percent of the respondents interviewed in North Carolina said they had seen Gantt on television and in the newspaper, *and* had heard him on the radio. In contrast, less than 10 percent of the respondents interviewed in South Carolina had seen Cunningham on these three medias. Furthermore, levels of information about the rivals in these two contests varied dramatically. While 51 percent of the respondents recalled Gantt's name, a meager 4 percent could recall Cunningham's name during postelection interviews.

In this chapter, we systematically explore how campaigns influence what citizens know about the competing senatorial candidates. We, of course, are not the first to attempt to assess the impact of campaigns. Nearly fifty years ago, Lazarsfeld and his colleagues (Lazarsfeld et al., 1944; Berelson et al., 1954) looked at whether campaigns influenced voters' evaluations of candidates. These studies uniformly pointed to the fact that campaigns played a minimal role in shaping voters' attitudes about the candidates. While the "minimal effects" conclusions of the Columbia studies discouraged research on campaigns for some time, there has recently been a revitalization of research aimed at isolating how campaigns affect voters' levels of information and attitudes about the candidates (e.g., Just et al., 1996; Delli Carpini and Keeter, 1993; Holbrook, 1996; Mondak, 1995; Krasno, 1994; Westlye, 1991; Bartels, 1988; Goldenberg and Traugott, 1984; Clarke and Evans, 1983; Patterson, 1980).

While the new wave of campaign research has uncovered more evidence for "campaign effects," these studies suffer from one of two limitations. On the one hand, scholars often neglect to document the campaign setting in sufficient detail. For example, some studies only examine political advertisements while ignoring press coverage, or vice versa. Other researchers, while adequately describing the campaign climate, study too few elections (e.g., one presidential election); therefore, their conclusions lack generalizability. In our study, we overcome these drawbacks by gathering an extensive amount of information about campaigns across a large number of elections.

Explaining Voter Information during Senate Campaigns

During campaigns, voters are presented with three general types of information by the candidates and the media. There is information available concerning the rudimentary facts about the candidates, such as their names and prior political experience. The central themes of the campaign, such as issues and the personal traits of candidates, are also discussed. Finally, critical information focusing on candidates' political decisions, policy positions, or personal behavior is often disseminated during campaigns. While these topics are touched on in nearly every electoral contest, as we have demonstrated, the relative amount of information on any one of these subjects varies dramatically across campaigns. We contend that the variance in information and competition during the campaign explains to a large extent what people know about the candidates.

While the context of the campaigns affects what people know about the candidates, the habits, preferences, and skills of citizens also influence their knowledge about campaigns. Just as no two campaigns are alike, no two voters are alike. People differ dramatically in their levels of political sophistication about politics (e.g., Converse, 1962, 1964; Dalager, 1996; Krosnick,

1990; Lodge and Hamill, 1986). Some citizens have an extensive understanding of politics and a great deal of stored information about policies and political candidates. Others know very little about political affairs. We expect people's levels of political expertise to affect what they know about the contestants in specific senatorial campaigns.

Similarly, citizens who rely heavily on the news media are likely to have more information about the competing Senate candidates. Prior research indicates that people who watch television news and regularly read the local newspaper are much more knowledgeable about political events and political figures (Brians and Wattenberg, 1990; Drew and Weaver, 1991; Larson, 1990; Zhao and Chaffee, 1995).

In addition, people who are more interested in politics will know more about specific Senate elections (Dalager, 1996; McLeod and McDonald, 1985; Robinson and Davis, 1990). These "political junkies" pride themselves on learning the most esoteric details about politicians. Beyond mere interest in politics, formal education also influences attention to and involvement in elections and politics generally (Rosenstone and Hansen, 1993). Schooling eases an individual's ability to acquire information about all topics, including campaigns. Voters also vary in the strengths of their attachments to political parties. Citizens with entrenched partisan beliefs routinely acquire news about political events and political figures (Miller and Shanks, 1996). Consequently, the partisan profiles of citizens are likely to influence voters' understanding of the candidates.

Although we need to be sensitive about the heterogeneity of the electorate when assessing the impact of political campaigns on voters' knowledge, the characteristics of the candidates may also influence people's understanding of the political contestants. People are likely to know more about senior senators as well as experienced challengers. Such candidates have simply been part of the political landscape longer, and citizens are more familiar with these figures. It is difficult to imagine someone in Massachusetts unfamiliar with Ted Kennedy. Likewise, voters have existing information about challengers who have been governors, such as Bob Kerrey of Nebraska, or mayors of major cities, such as Harvey Gantt of North Carolina, or members of the House, such as Les AuCoin of Oregon.

Candidates who are embroiled in scandals may be better known than candidates who have steered clear of such controversies. Since news organizations value conflict and controversy (Cook, 1996), candidates involved in scandals are likely to garner more media attention. For example, voters may be more familiar with U.S. Senate candidates who were implicated in the House "check kiting" scandal of the early 1990s.

Finally, the gender of the candidates may affect what people know about the Senate contestants. Even at this late date, eighty years after women's suffrage and thirty years after the "women's movement," women seeking high elective office are rare. The well-known discrepancy hypothesis (Lau, 1985; Reyes et al., 1980; Smith and Miller, 1979) suggests that people are likely to remember information that is unique or surprising. Voters unaccustomed to seeing women compete for the U.S. Senate will be more likely to take notice when the campaign is something other than the typical male versus male contest.

In the following section, we examine whether the intensity of the campaign, the skills, habits, and motivations of voters, as well as the characteristics of candidates influence voters' knowledge about senatorial candidates and campaigns.

Estimating the Relationship between Campaign Intensity and Voters' Knowledge about the Campaign

We rely on the National Election Study's Senate Election Study (NES/SES) to assess voters' levels of information concerning the candidates and campaigns. The NES/SES asked several questions inquiring about citizens' exposure to the campaigns, ascertaining whether voters had contact with candidates, probing respondents' levels of knowledge about the candidates, and wondering whether the messages conveyed during the campaigns found their way to the voters. We begin our analysis by looking at whether citizens were exposed to the campaigns and their contestants through the mass media.

Exposure to the Campaign

All candidates are concerned about whether citizens remember seeing, hearing, or reading about their candidacies. Candidates spend enormous sums of money generating publicity. Those lacking exposure are unable to educate voters about their qualifications or issue priorities. This is especially the case for challengers who typically begin their campaigns relatively unknown compared to incumbents. By looking at levels of exposure, we can establish whether voters had the opportunity to learn about the candidates during the campaign. If all things are equal, we expect voters' reports of exposure to increase monotonically with the intensity of the races.

The NES/SES asked respondents whether they saw the candidates on television, read about them in the newspaper, or heard about them on the radio (Jacobson, 1997; Krasno, 1994). We combined these three measures into indices of incumbent and challenger exposure ranging from zero to three, with zero indicating that a respondent was never exposed to the candidate across the three media, to three indicating that the respondent recalls seeing the candidate on television, hearing about the candidate on the radio, and reading about the candidate in the newspaper. The frequency distributions reveal that only 5 percent of the respondents report no exposure to the incumbents, while four times as many (20 percent) recall absolutely no exposure to the challengers.[1] At the other end of the continuum, nearly half of the respondents (i.e., 49 percent) report being exposed to the incumbents on all three media, while only approximately one-third of the respondents (i.e., 35 percent) say they learned about the challengers on all three.

To explain the variation across the indices of exposure, we operationalize the intensity of campaigns and the characteristics of voters and candidates. We turn first to campaign intensity. Since we conceptualize and have demonstrated empirically that campaign intensity is the product of an interwoven relationship among the activities of the candidates, the reports of the news media, and the closeness of the race, we create an index where each of these components is represented equally. One index is preferable to unique measures of competition, candidate behavior, and media coverage because these elements are causally interdependent. They form a constellation where each element is conditioned by the other two.

In addition, citizens are not exposed to each aspect of a campaign in isolation from the others. To begin, voters' understanding of candidates is affected simultaneously by both the candidates' and the news media's messages. As an example, by reading a profile of the candidate in the newspaper, a voter may learn that a candidate is opposed to tax increases. However, the voter's understanding of the candidate's stand may be influenced by negative commercials aired by the opponent highlighting the candidate's ethusiastic support for tax increases in the years before the current campaign. The voter's views of the candidate's stand on taxes may then be clarified (or muddled) by a political debate presented on a local television station. Finally, if the race is closely contested, the voter may spend more time and effort trying to figure out the candidate's true stand. In a low-intensity race, in contrast, the voter may have an opportunity only to see the first message about the candidate's tax stand.

In the end, we are interested in understanding how the campaign environment affects voters. We are not attempting to investigate the impact of a single speech, or an isolated commercial, or a particular media story. Instead, our goal is to examine how the campaign setting as an entity influences voters' understanding of campaigns. Indeed, given that the elements of intensity are interdependent, and since the interactions among these campaign actors affect people's understanding of the campaign, it is potentially misleading to estimate the independent impact of each element of intensity.

---

[1] As in earlier analysis, we analyze incumbents and winners in open races in one category and challengers and open-race losers in a second category. In each analysis, we include a measure for open races to see if the respondents' level of information about open candidates is different from their information about candidates contesting incumbent seats.

To measure competition, we use the last poll published before the election since respondents were interviewed after the campaign. To tap candidates' activities, we examine the total amount of money spent by the candidates.[2] Finally, we rely on the total number of paragraphs printed about the candidates during the campaigns as an indication of news content.[3] To achieve equal representation of the three elements of intensity, we normalize each component of the index and then sum the three scores.[4]

While we expect the intensity of campaigns to affect people's awareness of the electoral contests, we also understand that politically sophisticated citizens are likely to report more exposure to candidates. In developing a measure of political sophistication, we rely on research by political scientists and political psychologists that suggest the superiority of measures of political knowledge (e.g., Delli Carpini and Keeter, 1993, 1996; Krosnick, 1990; Zaller, 1990, 1992). For example, Fiske et al. (1990) look at how alternative measures of political expertise (i.e., media exposure, political interest, political activity, political self-schema, education, and political knowledge) predict political information processing and find that political knowledge is most important. Delli Carpini and Keeter (1993: 1180), reviewing this research, observe, "A common conclusion in an increasing number of studies is that factual knowledge is the best single indicator of sophistication."

In addition to the predictive power of political knowledge, this measure has other advantages. Questions assessing an individual's level of political knowledge are relatively immune to self-report biases, such as social desirability response sets or differences in "standards of self-description" (Fiske et al., 1990; Zaller, 1992). Also, this measure of political expertise requires no "judgment calls" from the researcher; each knowledge question has an objective and consensual answer (Fiske et al., 1990).

Since a standard definition of expertise represents accumulated knowledge in a particular domain (McGraw and Pinney, 1990), we operationalize political expertise as an individual's level of knowledge about politics. Specifically, we rely on six questions available in the NES/SES.[5] First, like Zaller

---

[2] For each state, we divide the amount of money spent by the voting-age population. Campaign spending for the 1988–1992 elections ranged from $0.15 to $8.87 per eligible voter, with a mean of $2.31 and a standard deviation of $1.75. We focus on spending to capture activity since the dependent variable is exposure to the campaign. Later in the chapter, when we ask respondents about specific topics of the campaign, we include measures of the candidates' messages, as well as measures of spending.

[3] We create separate indices for the incumbents and challengers. For incumbents, the index was comprised of competition, incumbent spending, and the total amount of media coverage devoted to the incumbent. For the challenger, the index of intensity contained competition, challenger spending, and the total amount of media coverage devoted to the challenger.

[4] To normalize, we rely on the following formula: $[(X_i - X_{mean})/X_{s.d.}]$. The normalization procedure produces a mean of zero and a standard deviation of one for each of the three components.

[5] The NES/SES does not include the standard knowledge questions included in the biennial NES

(1992), we examine "correct" placements of groups and candidates. We examine whether respondents can correctly place George Bush and the Democratic and Republican parties on the 7-point liberal/conservative continuum.[6] We also measure respondents' levels of information about the senators who are not up for reelection, since information about the those seeking reelection is contaminated by the intensity of the contests. We utilize the following three NES/SES measures to assess knowledge of a senator who is not seeking reelection: correct recognition of the senator's name, correct recall of the senator's name, correct ideological placement of the senator.[7] With these six questions, we created an index ranging from zero (the individual answered none of the questions correctly) to six (all questions were answered correctly).

Beyond voters' accumulated knowledge about politics, we assessed whether they pay attention to the news, whether they are interested in campaigns generally, what their level of education is, and what are their levels of partisan attachments. To assess attention to the news, we rely on the NES/SES questions asking voters how often during a week they watched a news program on TV or read a newspaper. We combined these two measures into one index tapping attention to the news.[8] In addition, the NES, as it has for nearly half a century, inquired about voters' levels of interest in politics, levels of education, and strength of partisan attachments.[9]

---

surveys (i.e., Which party controls the House of Representatives? Who is the vice-president of the United States?).

[6] We adopt a generous test when categorizing respondents' answers as correct. If a respondent said George Bush or the Republican party was moderate to extremely conservative, the respondent was coded as giving a correct response. Similarly, if the respondent said the Democratic party was moderate to extremely liberal, the answer was coded as correct.

[7] To measure correct ideological placement, we recoded ADA scores to range from 1 to 3 (1 = liberal, 2 = moderate, 3 = conservative) and averaged the scores for the two years prior to the respondent's interview date. Each respondent's answer to the ideological placement of the senator was also recoded from 1 to 3 (1 = liberal, 2 = moderate, 3 = conservative). If the difference between the respondent's recoded score and the recoded ADA score was 0, the respondent correctly identified the ideological placement of the senator. If the score was different from 0, the respondent incorrectly identified the ideological placement of the senator.

[8] The questions were: "How many days in the past week did you watch news programs on TV?" and "How many days in the past week did you read a daily newspaper?" Thus, the index ranges from 0 to 14 with 14 representing an individual who reports reading a newspaper and watching a news program every day.

[9] The measure of interest is the standard NES question, "Some people don't pay much attention to political campaigns. How about you? Would you say that you were very much interested, somewhat interested, or not much interested?" This was the very first question on the NES/SES survey and it does not refer to interest in the state's senatorial campaign. Thus, it is unlikely that respondents' answers were contaminated by later questions on the survey about the Senate campaign.

Education is measured as years of schooling. To measure strength of partisan attachment, we rely on the standard 7-point party identification scale. We folded the scale to create four categories: strong partisans, weak partisans, leaning partisans, and independents.

With the voters' characteristics accounted for, we turn to measuring the characteristics of the candidates. We employ measures to tap the seniority of the senators, the experience of the challengers, and any presence of scandals. The measurement of these concepts was introduced in chapter 3. To this trio of variables, we now add a measure of the candidate's gender.

The OLS models used to predict voters' levels of exposure are presented in table 8.1.[10] The variables capturing campaign intensity are statistically significant for both incumbents and challengers. In both models, the unstandardized coefficients for intensity are much larger than their respective standard errors. The substantive impact of intensity, however, is more than five times larger in the challenger model (i.e., .16 versus .03). The sizable difference highlights the importance of campaigns for introducing challengers to the voters.

To better understand the relationship between intensity and exposure, we use the unstandardized coefficients in table 8.1 to estimate the number of media outlets in which citizens report exposure to the candidates. In the case of challengers involved in low-intensity races (i.e., campaigns with the lowest score on the challenger intensity index), respondents recall being exposed to challengers on approximately one and a half media (i.e., the point estimate = 1.41).[11] In contrast, in high-intensity races, voters report exposure to the challenger on virtually every media (i.e., the point estimate = 3.00). People's exposure to the incumbents, on the other hand, is less responsive to the intensity of the races. Voters remember seeing incumbents on 2.2 media, on average, in low-intensity races, and on 2.5 media in high-intensity races.

Turning to the remaining variables in the model, both voters' and candidates' characteristics affect levels of exposure. The characteristics of voters, in particular, have an impressive bearing on whether people have been exposed to the campaigns. In the model for incumbents, each of the five personal characteristics reaches statistical significance, and in the challengers' model, four of the five characteristics statistically influence exposure levels. In both models, the beta coefficients suggest that voters' sophistication and attention to the news are quite important for understanding exposure to the campaign. In fact, in the incumbent model, both of these variables surpass the importance of the intensity of the campaign. This is not the case in the challenger model. The intensity of the campaign is the most important predictor of citizens' exposure to challengers.

---

[10] The variable measuring the type of race (i.e., open versus incumbent race) is only included in analyses in this chapter when it reached statistical significance at the p < .05 level. In the analyses presented in chapters 8 and 9 we rely on the p < .05 level to assess the statistical significance of coefficients. In the previous chapters, where the number of cases available for analysis was much smaller, we relied on the p < .10 level.

[11] In developing the point estimate, all remaining variables in the model are set to their means.

TABLE 8.1
OLS Analysis Explaining Exposure to Senate Candidates

	Exposure to Incumbent/Open Winner		Exposure to Challenger/Open Loser	
	Unstandardized Coefficient (standard error)	Beta	Unstandardized Coefficient (standard error)	Beta
Campaign Intensity	.03 (.005)[a]	.07	.16 (.006)[a]	.34
Respondent Characteristics				
Attention to news	.05 (.002)[a]	.24	.05 (.003)[a]	.19
Education	.007 (.003)[b]	.03	.01 (.004)[a]	.03
Interest	.04 (.007)[a]	.07	.07 (.009)[a]	.09
Political sophistication	.09 (.007)[a]	.17	.09 (.009)[a]	.13
Strength of party attachment	.02 (.01)[a]	.03	−.002 (.01)	−.001
Candidate Characteristics				
Challenger's experience	—	—	.02 (.005)[a]	.07
Gender	.02 (.02)	.008	.11 (.03)[a]	.04
Scandal	.02 (.03)	.005	—	—
Seniority	.008 (.001)[a]	.08	—	—
Constant	1.40 (.06)[a]		1.03 (.09)[a]	
R^2	.14		.23	
N	6,110		6,110	

Notes: Exposure is measured on a scale ranging from 0 to 3. *Campaign intensity* is an index comprised of competition, campaign spending, and media coverage (see text). *Attention to news* is measured on a 14-point scale. *Education* is measured by years of schooling. *Interest* is measured on a three-point scale. *Political sophistication* is based on a scale ranging from 0 to 6. *Strength of party attachment* is measured on a 4-point scale. *Challenger's experience* is measured on a 9-point scale. *Gender* is a binary variable where 1 = female candidate, 0 = male candidate. *Scandal* is a binary variable where 1 = candidate involved with a scandal, 0 = otherwise. *Seniority* is measured by years in the U.S. Senate. All p-values are based on two-sided tests.
[a]$p < .01$
[b]$p < .05$

Although not nearly as important as either campaign intensity or personal characteristics, the vitas of candidates also influence levels of exposure. The seniority of incumbent senators and the prior experience of challengers affect the probability of citizens' exposure to the candidates. Voters are more likely to remember seeing senators with long tenures in office than their more junior colleagues. Similarly, people are more likely to remember encountering women challengers with impressive political resumes than inexperienced male challengers.

Explaining something as simple as mere exposure to the candidates is a useful way to begin to gauge how campaigns influence voters' knowledge about the candidates. However, candidates have a greater opportunity of imparting information by personally contacting voters. In the next section, we look at whether personal contacts between candidates and potential supporters change with the intensity of the campaigns.

Contact with Voters

In a perfect world, candidates would continually contact voters during campaigns. Personal contact is controlled by the candidates and consequently is likely to generate positive impressions with voters. This is why candidates stand in front of factories shaking hands, make personal appearances at rallies, spend days on the telephone, and mail out letters and fliers to residents. For candidates, the personal touch in politics is ingratiating, even though time consuming and inefficient when compared to airing political commercials on television.

Contact between voters and candidates is not always initiated by the candidates. The skills, resources, and motivations of individuals lead them to write a letter to a legislator, or to call the office of a member of Congress, or to contribute money to a campaign (Miller and Shanks, 1996; Rosenstone and Hansen, 1993). Whether it is initiated by candidates or voters, we hypothesize that personal contact between citizens and candidates increases with the intensity of the campaign. As intensity increases, candidates dedicate more resources to contacting voters, because candidates cannot assume any voters are loyal supporters. Contacts and follow-up contacts help to solidify groups that have provided support in the past and to sway voters who are undecided. Likewise, voters are more likely to initiate contact in intense campaigns when information about the race is more prevalent and the outcome is uncertain.

To measure contact, we use the following five items from the NES/SES survey: met with the candidate, attended a meeting where the candidate spoke, talked to a member of the candidate's staff, received mail from the candidate, and knew someone who had contact with the candidate (Jacobson, 1997; Krasno, 1994). We employed all five measures to create indices of incumbent and challenger contacts ranging from zero (where an individual reports no contact with the candidate) to five (where the respondent reports contact with the candidate in all five situations).

The difference in the number of contacts between incumbents and challengers is dramatic. Twenty-three percent of the respondents report no contact whatsoever with incumbents, compared to a whopping 51 percent reporting no contact with challengers. Assuming that multiple contacts are more memorable and effective than simply one contact across an entire campaign, 38 percent of the sample report more than one contact with incumbents, compared to 16 percent reporting multiple types of contacts with challengers.

To explain this variance, we turn again to the intensity of the campaign, the characteristics of voters, and the backgrounds of the candidates. The OLS findings reported in table 8.2 demonstrate the importance of campaign intensity. However, as one might expect, the intensity of the race is much more important for explaining contact with challengers; the intensity coefficient in the challenger model is five times larger than the intensity coefficient in the

TABLE 8.2
OLS Analysis Explaining Contact with Senate Candidates

	Contact with Incumbent/ Open Winner		Contact with Challenger/ Open Loser	
	Unstandardized Coefficient (standard error)	Beta	Unstandardized Coefficient (standard error)	Beta
Campaign Intensity	.02 (.007)[a]	.04	.10 (.006)[a]	.23
Respondent Characteristics				
Attention to news	.04 (.004)[a]	.14	.02 (.003)[a]	.09
Education	.03 (.005)[a]	.08	.02 (.004)[a]	.05
Interest	.11 (.01)[a]	.12	.09 (.009)[a]	.12
Political sophistication	.16 (.01)[a]	.18	.07 (.008)[a]	.11
Strength of party attachment	.02 (.02)	.02	−.001 (.01)	.001
Candidate Characteristics				
Challenger's experience	—	—	.05 (.005)[a]	.12
Gender	−.003 (.04)	.001	.002 (.03)	.001
Scandal	−.24 (.05)[a]	−.05	—	—
Seniority	.02 (.002)[a]	.15	—	—
Constant	.11 (.10)		.12 (.08)	
R^2	.15		.16	
N	6,110		6,110	

Notes: Contact is measured on a scale ranging from 0 to 5. *Campaign intensity* is an index comprised of competition, campaign spending, and media coverage (see text). *Attention to news* is measured on a 14-point scale. *Education* is measured by years of schooling. *Interest* is measured on a 3-point scale. *Political sophistication* is based on a scale ranging from 0 to 6. *Strength of party attachment* is measured on a 4-point scale. *Challenger's experience* is measured on a 9-point scale. *Gender* is a binary variable where 1 = female candidate, 0 = male candidate. *Scandal* is a binary variable where 1 = candidate involved with a scandal, 0 = otherwise. *Seniority* is measured by years in the U.S. Senate. All p-values are based on two-sided tests.
[a]$p < .01$

incumbent model (.10 versus .02). Furthermore, the standardized coefficient in the challenger model (i.e., .23) indicates that the intensity of the campaign is by far the most influential factor in the model. Relying on the coefficients in the challenger model to calculate point estimates, we find that respondents residing in states with the least intense campaigns can expect, on average, .3 contacts with challengers. However, citizens observing the most intense campaigns will average about 1.5 contacts with challengers.

Campaign intensity is far less important for predicting contact with incumbents. The point estimates, derived from the OLS coefficients, show that individuals exposed to the least intense campaigns can expect, on average, 1.4 contacts with incumbents. In the most intense races, contact with incumbents increases slightly, with respondents averaging about 1.6 contacts with incumbents, all things equal. The betas in the incumbent model suggest that four of the five voter characteristics and two of the candidate characteristics are more consequential than campaign intensity. These findings make intuitive sense. Incumbents have a permanent staff set up to contact voters or to respond to voter-initiated contacts, irrespective of whether they are involved in a campaign (Fenno, 1978, 1996; Fiorina, 1977). Therefore, personal contact with the sitting senator is less dependent upon the intensity of the campaign.

Four of the five coefficients representing voter characteristics are influential in both of the contact models. As has been demonstrated in prior research, the skills and resources of individuals are related to whether voters reach out and contact candidates and legislators (Rosenstone and Hansen, 1993). Likewise, the experiences of candidates are significant predictors of contact. Senior senators, in particular, are adept at contacting or responding to voter-initiated contacts. The significant and negative coefficient for scandal suggests that those senators tainted with scandals have less contact with voters. This finding raises the question of whether the tainted senators initiated less contact with voters, or whether voters are less likely to contact a tainted senator, or maybe both. Finally, experienced challengers, many of whom have held elective office before and have had experience with the ritual of contacting voters, have more contact with voters than inexperienced challengers.

In sum, contact with voters, like exposure to voters, depends greatly on the intensity of the campaign and characteristics of voters and candidates. These findings generate other questions. If intensity is related to contact and exposure, is it also directly related to the information voters hold about the candidates? Does intensity educate voters about the competing candidates and the messages they are trying to convey? We press our analysis further in the remaining sections of the chapter.

Recognition and Recall of Candidates' Names

Some time ago, Tom Mann (1978) found that voters were quite adept at recognizing the names of U.S. House candidates when presented with a list of them, but they found it much more difficult to recall the names without the aid of a list. These patterns hold for the Senate races in our study. When presented with lists of candidates' names, 96 percent of respondents recognized the names of incumbent senators, while 77 percent recognized the names of the challengers. With regard to the tougher task of actually *recalling* the names of the candidates, 75 percent were able to recall the incumbents' names, while only 56 percent could do so with the challengers'.

These data are important given the notion that voters are uncomfortable supporting candidates they do not know. Fenno (1996) documents a strong desire among incumbents and challengers to increase name recognition among voters. Similarly, both Bartels's (1988) study of presidential primaries and Jacobson's (1997) analysis of congressional races demonstrate a correspondence between voters' knowledge of candidates and their willingness to support these candidates at the polls.

We expect the intensity of the campaign to be related to levels of recognition and recall, even controlling for voter and candidate characteristics. In table 8.3 we present logistic regression models aimed at explaining whether respondents recognized the names of the incumbents and challengers.[12] To assess recognition, respondents were asked to indicate whether they recognized the Senate candidates when they were read a list of names of people in politics. Respondents who recognized a candidate were coded 1, and those who failed to recognize a candidate were coded 0.

In table 8.3, the variables measuring the intensity of the campaign are statistically significant in both the incumbent and challenger analyses. The logit coefficient for intensity in the challenger model is three times larger than the coefficient in the incumbent model (i.e., .24 versus .06). The difference in the impact of intensity undoubtedly reflects the fact that many challengers enter campaigns relatively unknown, while this is not true for incumbents. In fact, with 96 percent of the respondents recognizing the incumbents' names, it is impressive that the intensity of the race is able to explain any of the variance in recognition, once candidate and voter characteristics are taken into account.

As expected, the characteristics of respondents are strongly related to whether people recognize the candidates' names. In both models, sophistication, attention to the news, interest, and education are all related to the voters' abilities to recognize the candidates, with political sophistication being

[12] Since the dependent variable is dichotomous, we used the more efficient logistic regression to estimate the model rather than OLS.

TABLE 8.3
Logit Analysis Explaining Recognition of the Candidates

	Recognition of Incumbent/Open Winner		Recognition of Challenger/Open Loser	
	Unstandardized Coefficient (standard error)	Beta	Unstandardized Coefficient (standard error)	Beta
Campaign Intensity	.06 (.02)[a]	.62	.24 (.01)[a]	1.39
Respondent Characteristics				
Attention to news	.03 (.007)[a]	.60	.02 (.004)[a]	.21
Education	.03 (.008)[a]	.44	.03 (.005)[a]	.23
Interest	.07 (.02)[a]	.48	.09 (.01)[a]	.32
Political sophistication	.23 (.02)[a]	1.73	.12 (.01)[a]	.46
Strength of party attachment	−.003 (.02)	.01	−.005 (.01)	.01
Candidate Characteristics				
Challenger's experience	—	—	.04 (.008)[a]	.27
Gender	−.007 (.07)	.01	.007 (.04)	.01
Scandal	.10 (.12)	.14	—	—
Seniority	.008 (.005)	.31	—	—
Open	.23 (.09)[a]	.42	.05 (.05)	.05
Constant	.14 (.16)		−.07 (.11)	
% correctly predicted	99%		80%	
N	6,110		6,110	

Notes: Recognition is a binary variable where 1 = respondent recognizes candidate, 0 = otherwise. *Campaign intensity* is an index comprised of competition, campaign spending, and media coverage (see text). *Attention to news* is measured on a 14-point scale. *Education* is measured by years of schooling. *Interest* is measured on a 3-point scale. *Political Sophistication* is based on a scale ranging from 0 to 6. *Strength of party attachment* is measured on a 4-point scale. *Challenger's experience* is measured on a nine-point scale. *Gender* is a binary variable where 1 = female candidate, 0 = male candidate. *Scandal* is a binary variable where 1 = candidate involved with a scandal, 0 = otherwise. *Seniority* is measured by years in the U.S. Senate. *Open is* a binary variable where 1 = incumbent race; 0 = open race. All p-values are based on two-sided tests.

[a] p<.01

the most consequential. Finally, strength of respondents' party attachment does not assist voters in recognizing the names of the candidates. In other words, strong Democrats and Republicans are no more likely to recognize the names of the candidates than Independents, once the other forces in the models are taken into account.

As to candidate characteristics, the quality of the challenger is related to the recognition of the challenger. This finding matches a long line of research demonstrating that challengers with prior political experience are bet-

ter candidates and more readily recognized by voters (Abramowitz and Segal, 1992; Jacobson, 1997; Squire, 1992). Neither seniority, scandal, nor
gender is related to rates of recognition.

The findings in table 8.3 once again highlight the importance of campaign
intensity and voter characteristics when it comes to understanding who is
able to recognize the candidates. Do these patterns persist when the task is
more difficult, that is, when voters are asked to recall the candidates' names?
To measure recall, we rely on the NES/SES question asking respondents to
name the candidates in their state's U.S. Senate race. Respondents who correctly recall the candidates' names are coded 1, and those unable to recall
the candidates' names are coded 0.

Models estimating the voters' likelihood of recalling the candidates' names
are presented in table 8.4. The intensity of the campaign predicts strongly
the voters' likelihood of recalling the candidates' names. In both the incumbent and challenger models, the logit coefficients for intensity are much
larger than the corresponding standard errors. As with the prior analyses of
exposure, contact, and recognition, the intensity of the campaign is particularly important for predicting recall of the challenger's name. A comparison
of the unstandardized logit coefficients in the incumbent and challenger
models shows that intensity is three times as important for challenger recall
compared to incumbent recall (.15 versus .05).

We also find that sophisticated, interested, educated, and attentive respondents are more likely to recall the candidates' names, compared to other
respondents. Finally, the results in table 8.4 suggest that women candidates,
experienced challengers, and senior senators are more memorable to respondents than male candidates, inexperienced challengers, and junior senators.
We graphically illustrate the impact of intensity by converting the logit coefficients in tables 8.3 and table 8.4 to probabilities.[13] In figure 8.1a we show
that individuals have a .89 probability of recognizing the incumbent's name
in a low-intensity race and a .92 probability in a high-intensity race, when all
other things are equal. In the challenger model, the corresponding change in
probability is much more dramatic. In the low-intensity campaign, there is
only a .57 chance that a respondent would be able to recognize the challenger's name. In contrast, in a highly intense campaign, the likelihood of a
respondent's recognizing the challenger's name is a whopping .96 percent.

Turning to the impact of intensity on people's abilities to recall the candidates' names (see fig. 8.1b), voters have a .51 probability of recalling the
incumbents' names in low-intensity races and a .64 probability in highly
intense races. The same calculation for challengers reveals that respondents
have a .22 probability of remembering the challengers' names in races where

---

[13] In calculating these probabilities, we rely on the procedure described in King (1989) by
varying the level of campaign intensity and holding all the remaining variables in the model at
their means.

TABLE 8.4
Logit Analysis Explaining Recall of the Candidates

	Recall of Incumbent/ Open Winner		Recall of Challenger/ Open Loser	
	Unstandardized Coefficient (standard error)	Beta	Unstandardized Coefficient (standard error)	Beta
Campaign Intensity	.05 (.006)[a]	.22	.15 (.008)[a]	.81
Respondent Characteristics				
Attention to News	.03 (.003)[a]	.25	.03 (.004)[a]	.28
Education	.04 (.003)[a]	.25	.05 (.006)[a]	.36
Interest	.11 (.01)[a]	.32	.12 (.01)[a]	.40
Political Sophistication	.22 (.01)[a]	.69	.23 (.01)[a]	.82
Strength of Party Attachment	.01 (.01)	.02	.01 (.01)	.02
Candidate Characteristics				
Challenger's Experience	—	—	.02 (.006)[a]	.12
Gender	.09 (.03)[a]	.07	.16 (.04)[a]	.14
Scandal	.06 (.05)	.03	—	—
Seniority	.01 (.002)[a]	.16	—	—
Open	− .10 (.04)[a]	.09	− .07 (.04)	.06
Constant	− 1.65 (.10)[a]		− 2.73 (.13)[a]	
Percent correctly predicted	70%		79%	
N	6,110		6,110	

Notes: Recall is a binary variable where 1 = respondent recalls the candidate's name, 0 = otherwise. *Campaign intensity* is an index comprised of competition, campaign spending, and media coverage (see text). *Attention to news* is measure on a 14-point scale. *Education* is measured by years of schooling. *Interest* is measured on a 3-point scale. *Political sophistication* is based on a scale ranging from 0 to 6. *Strength of party attachment* is based on the 7-point party identification scale. *Challenger's experience* is measured on a 9-point scale. *Gender* is a binary variable where 1 = female candidate, 0 = male candidate. *Scandal* is a binary variable where 1 = candidate involved with a scandal, 0 = otherwise. *Seniority* is measured by years in the U.S. Senate. *Open* is a binary variable where 1 = incumbent race, 0 = open race. All p-values are based on two-sided tests.

[a] $p < .01$

intensity is at its lowest compared to a .61 probability during extremely intense campaigns. Thus, campaign intensity is consistently more important for learning about challengers compared to learning about sitting senators.

An Examination of How Intensity Affects Voters' Knowledge of Campaign Themes

Thus far, we have shown that people have more interactions with candidates and know more about candidates when they witness intense campaigns.

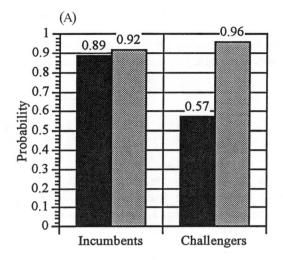

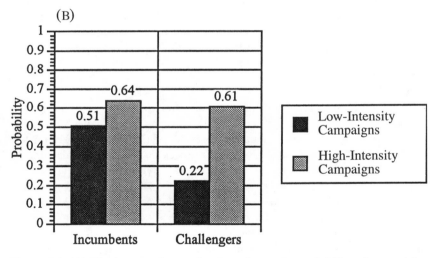

Figure 8.1. (A) The impact of campaign intensity on the probability of recognizing the candidate's name. (B) The impact of campaign intensity on the probability of recalling the candidate's name. These probabilities are based on the unstandardized estimates presented in tables 8.3 and 8.4. We calculate the probabilities by varying the level of competition in the race while holding all remaining variables at their means (see King, 1989: 105).

They develop a more extensive understanding of political contestants when candidates spend more money, when the news media devote more coverage to the race, and when polls indicate a "horse race." In the present section, we look at whether intensity affects the specific information voters have available about candidates.

Issue Awareness

To assess what voters know about specific campaign themes, we rely on the following open-ended question included in the NES/SES survey: "In your state, what issue did the candidates talk about the most during the campaign for the Senate?"[14] We expect citizens to know more about the issues of the campaign when the candidates spend a great deal of money emphasizing their issue positions and priorities and when the news media focus extensively on policies in their coverage of the competitive contests.

We begin by investigating whether an individual's likelihood of mentioning an issue, any issue, varies with the intensity of the campaign. The case of the Carolinas suggests that the campaign setting is consequential. Almost two-thirds of the respondents (64 percent) from North Carolina in 1990 volunteered an answer to the campaign-issue question, while only one-third of their neighbors in South Carolina were able to respond to this same open-ended question.

To examine the campaign context more systematically, we modify our measure of intensity to reflect the candidates' emphases on policy, the news media's coverage of issues, and the closeness of the race. We rely on the issue-trait scale introduced in chapter 6 to measure the attention candidates give to issues. Remember that this scale is derived from answers to the campaign managers' survey and ranges from 1 to 5, where 5 represents a candidate who focuses exclusively on issues, 3 represents an equal balance between traits and issues, and 1 represents a candidate who focuses only on traits.[15] We multiply each candidate's score with the amount of money spent to capture the substance and potential reach of the candidate's message. To assess the attention the news media give to issues, we measure the number of paragraphs published about issues during the campaign. Finally, as al-

---

[14] It is important to note that the question does not single out issues according to incumbents or challengers, but rather treats the candidates together. Thus, none of the analyses that rely on this question compare campaign effects by the status of the candidate. Nevertheless, the question provides a rich source of data about whether voters were able to learn information about the campaign.

[15] Given our reliance on the campaign manager data, we look only at Senate races where interviews were completed with the Senate candidates.

ways, we include a measure of poll standings to assess the closeness of the race.[16]

In addition to the measure of campaign intensity, we also include the measures of respondents' and candidates' characteristics employed in previous models. Thus, we can determine whether differences in the campaign setting affect people's willingness to mention an issue as a major theme of the campaign. As the findings in table 8.5 suggest, the campaign is indeed

TABLE 8.5
Logit Analysis Examining Identification of Issues of the Campaign

	Unstandardized Coefficient (standard error)	Beta
Campaign Intensity	.02 (.008)[a]	.10
Respondent Characteristics		
Attention to news	.01 (.004)[a]	.08
Education	.03 (.006)[a]	.16
Interest	.10 (.01)[a]	.30
Political sophistication	.05 (.01)[a]	.16
Strength of party attachment	.05 (.02)[a]	.10
Candidate Characteristics		
Challenger's experience	.02 (.007)[a]	.11
Gender	.12 (.04)[a]	.09
Scandal	−.08 (.05)	.05
Seniority	−.004 (.003)	.06
Constant	−.45 (.12)[a]	
% correctly predicted	60%	
N	3,653	

Notes: The dependent variable is a binary variable where 1 = respondent mentions an issue of the campaign, 0 = otherwise. *Campaign intensity* is an index comprised of (1) competition, (2) campaign spending and candidates' issue emphasis, and (3) media coverage of issues (see text). *Attention to news* is measured on a 14-point scale. *Education* is measured by years of schooling. *Interest* is measured on a 3-point scale. *Political sophistication* is based on a scale ranging from 0 to 6. *Strength of party attachment* is measured on a 4-point scale. *Challenger's experience* is measured on a 9-point scale. *Gender* is a binary variable where 1 = female candidate, 0 = male candidate. *Scandal* is a binary variable where 1 = candidate involved with a scandal, 0 = otherwise. *Seniority* is measured by years in the U.S. Senate. All p-values are based on two-sided tests.

[a] $p < .01$

[16] The modified index of intensity has the following components: (1) (incumbent campaign message*incumbent spending) + (challenger campaign message*challenger spending), (2) number of paragraphs published about incumbent's issue priorities + number of paragraphs published about challenger's issue priorities, (3) difference in incumbent and challenger's poll standings. Each of the components is normalized and then the three are summed to create the modified index.

influential. The unstandardized coefficient for intensity easily surpasses its standard error. In close races, when candidates focus exclusively on issues and the news media present an abundance of issue coverage, individuals respond by mentioning issues in response to the campaign question. On the other hand, in lopsided races when candidates ignore issues in favor of traits and when the news media spend little time focusing on policy, respondents are less willing to identify issues of the campaign.

In addition to the political setting, the characteristics of respondents continue to be important for understanding what individuals know about candidates and campaigns.[17] Answering open-ended queries about a campaign can be daunting for respondents. Each of the measures of voter characteristics influences the respondent's likelihood of identifying an issue, with interest in campaigns leading the way.

The strong influence of voters' characteristics somewhat dwarfs the impact of candidates' characteristics. Only two of the candidate coefficients are statistically significant: challenger quality and gender.[18] Taken as a whole, the intensity of the campaign and the interests, talents, and habits of voters are better predictors of issue knowledge than the characteristics of the candidates.

These results demonstrate convincingly that the messages presented during campaigns, as well as citizens' own predispositions, affect what people know about electoral contests. Hard-fought campaigns focusing on policy encourage people to identify issues discussed in the campaigns, especially individuals with the requisite political skills and motivation. We now present voters with a more challenging task. We examine whether respondents are able to identify correctly the specific issues disseminated during the campaign, and whether their correct answers covary with the intensity of the race.

Correctly Identifying Campaign Themes

Fenno (1978, 1996) discovered that candidates worry about whether voters listen to their messages. They constantly wonder whether their commercials were effective. And, were the pamphlets easy to read? Did the audience pay attention to the speech? Although we are less worried than the candidates, we are curious about whether voters are able to identify the themes for

---

[17] Consistent with prior analyses in this chapter, the variable measuring the type of race (i.e., open vs. incumbent race) is not included in table 8.5, because the variable failed to reach statistical significance (p < .05) in the incumbent and challenger models.

[18] As we have seen in prior analyses, voters appear to be more informed when a woman is in the race, compared to the typical male-versus-male contest.

which candidates spend millions upon millions of dollars while trying to communicate them to the electorate.

We use the campaign manager surveys to identify the candidates' main themes,[19] and then check whether respondents name correctly any of these themes when asked about the main issues of the campaign.[20] Overall, only 19 percent of the respondents were able to correctly name one of the main issues of the Senate campaign in their state. In South Carolina, where the issues of the campaign were barely audible, only 3 percent of the respondents correctly identified an issue of the campaign. The rate of success almost quadrupled in North Carolina, where 15 percent of the respondents were able to name the main issues of the race.

To determine whether citizens' answers were related to the campaign context, we developed an index of intensity that included the amount of candidate spending, the amount of news coverage devoted to each candidate's agenda, and the closeness of the race. The remainder of the model remains the same as in table 8.5. The findings are presented in table 8.6.

The intensity of the campaign is the most important variable predicting voters' abilities to identify the main themes of campaigns. The beta coefficient is nearly twice as large as any other standardized coefficients. In figure 8.2, we graphically illustrate the importance of the campaign context. We use the coefficients presented in table 8.6 to estimate people's knowledge of the campaign themes in low- and high-intensity races. In the most hard-fought races where candidates are spending a great deal of money disseminating their messages and where there is an abundance of news attention devoted to the candidates' agenda, an individual has a .65 probability of correctly identifying the candidates' major themes. On the other hand, when one candidate has a substantial lead in the polls, when the candidates are not campaigning aggressively, and when the press ignores the candidates' messages, people are much less informed about the content of the campaign. In

---

[19] Given our reliance on the campaign manager data, we only look at Senate races where interviews were completed with the Senate candidates.

[20] Although the test is simple, there is a potential measurement problem that we want readers to recognize. Since the NES question inquired explicitly about issue themes, respondents may not respond when their campaign focused primarily on candidates' personal traits. For example, when candidates focused only on traits, and respondents failed to answer the issue question, their answers may be correct since no issues were discussed by the candidates. Or, it is also possible that respondents who fail to give a response to this question have no idea what the main themes of the campaign were. We were faced with two options. One, restrict the analysis to only those campaigns where the candidates' main themes focused on issues. Two, include all campaigns because many citizens mentioned themes other than issues. That is, voters mentioned personal traits, ideology, and general themes, such as "time for a change," when responding to the campaign issue question. We analyzed the data both ways and found no substantive differences in the analyses. Thus, we include all races so as not to lose those voters who, irrespective of the question, readily responded with the correct theme of the campaign, even if it was not an issue.

TABLE 8.6
Logit Analysis Examining Correct Identification of Campaign Themes

	Unstandardized Coefficient (standard error)	Beta
Campaign Intensity	.07 (.006)[a]	.59
Respondent Characteristics		
Attention to news	.03 (.005)[a]	.29
Education	.01 (.007)[a]	.07
Interest	.07 (.02)[a]	.23
Political sophistication	.08 (.01)[a]	.29
Strength of party attachment	−.004 (.02)	−.009
Candidate Characteristics		
Challenger's experience	−.04 (.008)[a]	−.26
Gender	.16 (.08)[a]	.15
Scandal	.12 (.06)[a]	.08
Seniority	−.02 (.003)[a]	−.36
Open	.12 (.06)[a]	.11
Constant	−.89 (.14)[a]	
% correctly predicted	81%	
N	3,653	

Notes: The dependent variable is a binary variable where 1 = respondent correctly identifies a campaign theme, 0 = otherwise. *Campaign intensity* is an index comprised of (1) competition, (2) campaign spending, and (3) amount of media coverage given to candidates' themes (see text). *Attention to news* is measured on a 14-point scale. *Education* is measured by years of schooling. *Interest* is measured on a 3-point scale. *Political sophistication* is based on a scale ranging from 0 to 6. *Strength of party attachment* is measured on a 4-point scale. *Challenger's experience* is measured on a 9-point scale. *Gender* is a binary variable where 1 = female candidate, 0 = male candidate. *Scandal* is a binary variable where 1 = candidate involved with a scandal, 0 = otherwise. *Seniority* is measured by years in the U.S. Senate. *Open* is a binary variable where 1 = incumbent race, 0 = open race. All p-values are based on two-sided tests.
[a]p < .01

these least intense races, individuals have only a .35 probability of correctly identifying the major issues.

We also find that respondents with more political sophistication, education, and interest are better able to identify the main themes of campaigns. In addition, people who follow the news media more regularly are quite adept at identifying the themes disseminated by the candidates.

Finally, the characteristics of the candidates affect a respondent's likelihood of recalling the main themes of the campaign. Seniority is the most influential. The negative sign suggests voters are less likely to identify the themes of senior senators. This is understandable given our findings in chapter 3 where we reported that incumbents tend to shy away from clear-cut policy themes.

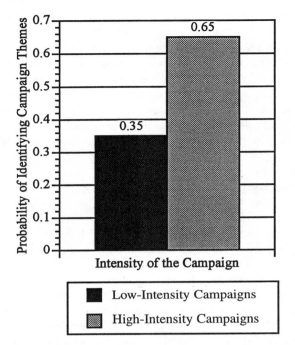

Figure 8.2. The relationship between the intensity of the campaign and correctly identifying the main themes of the campaign. These probabilities are based on the unstandardized estimates presented in table 8.6. We calculate the probabilities by varying the level of competition in the race while holding all remaining variables at their means (see King, 1989: 105).

In sum, candidates, in concert with the news media, can determine what people know about the main themes of campaigns. During intense races when candidates allocate extensive resources to spread their messages and when the news media focus attention on these messages, voters respond by correctly identifying these themes. People can recognize campaign themes that are articulated by candidates and presented in the media if the messages are loud enough and if the voters are sufficiently interested in them to listen. The next time Fenno hits the campaign trail he can reassure candidates that, under certain conditions, voters are able to identify candidates' messages.

Evaluating the Candidates

Assessing what voters know about the candidates is only the beginning of the story. An important next step is discovering whether voters use what they learn to evaluate the competing candidates. Does the campaign environment independently affect citizens' feelings toward the candidates? To answer this question, we turn to measures designed to tap voters' impressions of candidates. One of the most productive ways to assess evaluations of candidates is to ask individuals what they like and dislike about the candidates. The main strength of this approach is that respondents use their own words, mentioning any dimension that comes to mind. As Stokes et al. (1958: 369) explain, since respondents provide their own answers to these questions, these questions tap the "diversity [and] relative frequency of ideas." Because these questions are open-ended, they impose virtually no constraints on what respondents can say.[21]

The NES/SES asked all respondents to identify what they liked and disliked about each of the candidates. Nearly half of the respondents (49 percent) reported that they liked at least one thing about the incumbent, while only half as many people (25 percent) stated they liked something about the challenger. When asked to identify something they disliked about the candidates, respondents were about equally likely to criticize incumbents as well as challengers (28 percent and 25 percent, respectively).

In the present analysis, we are interested in seeing whether variances in the campaign setting affect people's evaluations of the candidates. We examine whether respondents are more likely to talk about issues as a reason for liking a candidate when the campaign is characterized by substantial policy discussion. The case of the Carolinas suggests that citizens' evaluations of the candidates are responsive to the campaign climate. In the low-intensity race in South Carolina, a meager 3 percent of the respondents mentioned an issue when describing what they liked about Democratic challenger Robert Cunningham. However, in North Carolina where Harvey Gantt was engaged in a lively policy exchange with Senator Jesse Helms, eight times as many respondents (24 percent) offered an issue as a reason for liking Gantt.

To explain the likelihood of mentioning an issue when evaluating the candidates, we look at the context of the campaign, the characteristics of the voters, and the characteristics of the candidates.[22] Respondents who stated an

---

[21] The main problem with the likes/dislikes questions is that respondents who are more articulate are more likely to answer than those who feel uncomfortable expressing their thoughts to virtual strangers. Respondents are much more likely to assess candidates when confronted with closed-ended questions, like the classic 100-point feeling thermometer. While open-ended questions are susceptible to an "articulation bias," we attempt to control for this problem by including voter characteristics (e.g., sophistication) that covary with articulation skills. We use the likes/dislikes questions here because we are interested in examining specific comments related to campaigns. We cannot detect this level of specificity with the feeling-thermometer measure.

[22] We measure voter characteristics and candidate characteristics as we have earlier in this chapter, with two exceptions. First, we have recoded party to capture the direction of partisanship as well as the strength of attachment. For instance, respondents who are strongly attached to the party of the candidate they are evaluating receive the highest score on a 5-point scale,

issue as a reason for liking the candidate are coded 1; all other respondents are scored 0.[23]

To assess systematically the impact of the campaign setting, we rely on an index reflecting the amount of issue information presented by the candidates and the media as well as a measure of the closeness of the race.[24] With this measure of intensity, we can see whether "likes" related to issues are directly affected by the context of the campaign. In addition, we look at whether exposure, contact, and knowledge of the candidates (i.e., recall and recognition) influence people's likelihood of mentioning an issue as a reason for liking the candidates. By including these measures, we can see how exposure and contact with the candidates as well as knowledge of the candidates affect evaluations.

The results of the logistic regression analyses are presented in table 8.7.[25] The intensity of the campaign is strongly related to voters' likelihood of mentioning an issue in response to the "likes" question. As races become more competitive and the amount of issue discussion increases, so does the probability that citizens will mention an issue when stating what they like about incumbents and challengers.

In figure 8.3, we illustrate the importance of the campaign setting by relying on the logit coefficients in table 8.7 to graph specific probabilities. As the figure shows, the impact of the campaign environment is more consequential for challengers. In a noncompetitive race devoid of issue discussion, an individual has only a .11 probability of mentioning an issue as a reason for liking the challenger. However, when policy debate is prevalent in a very intense race, the likelihood of mentioning an issue more than doubles. In intense races characterized by an extensive issue dialogue by the challenger and the media, a respondent has a .27 probability of mentioning an issue as a reason for liking the challenger. The campaign environment also increases

---

while respondents who are strongly attached to the party of the candidate's opponent are given the lowest score. We have also included a 7-point scale measuring ideological attachment. With this scale, an extremely conservative respondent will be given the highest score on the ideological scale when rating a Republican candidate and the lowest score when rating a Democrat. The gender of the candidate was removed from these analyses because it did not reach statistical (p < .05) nor substantive significance.

[23] Eleven percent of the respondents offered an issue as a reason for liking the incumbent, and 6 percent offered an issue as a reason for liking the challenger.

[24] The index used here is the same as the campaign intensity index employed to examine answers to the open-ended questions inquiring about the campaign themes, except we develop separate indices for incumbents and challengers. Since we rely on the campaign manager data to develop the index, we only look at Senate races where interviews were completed with the Senate candidates.

[25] The variable measuring the type of race (i.e., open versus incumbent race) is not included in table 8.7 because it failed to reach statistical significance in the incumbent and challenger models.

TABLE 8.7

Logit Analysis Examining Issues as a Reason for Liking the Candidate

	Incumbent/Open Winner		Challenger/Open Loser	
	Unstandardized Coefficient (standard error)	Beta	Unstandardized Coefficient (standard error)	Beta
Campaign Characteristics				
Campaign intensity	.05 (.01)ᵃ	.21	.12 (.03)ᵃ	.42
Exposure	.05 (.04)	.09	.15 (.05)ᵃ	.48
Contact	.09 (.02)ᵃ	.25	.12 (.03)ᵃ	.36
Recognition	1.10 (.50)ᵇ	.48	1.46 (.51)ᵃ	.36
Recall	.06 (.06)	.01	.32 (.08)ᵃ	.40
Respondent Characteristics				
Attention to news	.01 (.008)	.09	−.009 (.01)	−.11
Education	.0001 (.01)	.001	.04 (.01)ᵃ	.36
Interest	.04 (.02)ᵃ	.12	.04 (.03)	.17
Political sophistication	.06 (.02)ᵃ	.20	.01 (.03)	.04
Party attachment	.13 (.02)ᵃ	.35	.18 (.03)ᵃ	.67
Ideology	.03 (.01)ᵇ	.11	.05 (.02)	.25
Candidate Characteristics				
Challenger's experience	—	—	−.009 (.01)	.05
Scandal	−.16 (.10)	−.10	—	—
Seniority	.01 (.03)	.02	—	—
Constant	−2.70 (.53)ᵃ		−3.43 (.56)ᵃ	
% correctly predicted	89%		93%	
N	3,653		3,653	

Notes: Mentioning an issue is a binary variable where 1 = mentions an issue as a response to the open-ended "likes" question, 0 = otherwise. *Campaign intensity* is an index comprised of (1) competition, (2) campaign spending and candidates' issue emphasis, and (3) media coverage of issues (see text). *Exposure* is measured on a scale ranging from 0 to 3. *Contact* is measured on a scale ranging from 0 to 5. *Recognition* is a binary variable where 1 = respondent recognizes candidate, 0 = otherwise. *Recall* is a binary variable where 1 = respondent recalls the candidate's name, 0 = otherwise. *Attention to news* is measured on a 14-point scale. *Education* is measured by years of schooling. *Interest* is measured on a 3–point scale. *Political sophistication* is based on a scale ranging from 0 to 6. *Strength of party attachment* is measured on a 4-point scale. *Ideology* is a 7-point scale measuring strength and direction of ideological position. *Challenger's experience* is measured on a 9-point scale. *Scandal* is a binary variable where 1 = candidate involved with a scandal, 0 = otherwise. *Seniority* is measured by years in the U.S. Senate. All p-values are based on two-sided tests.

ᵃ $p < .01$

ᵇ $p < .05$

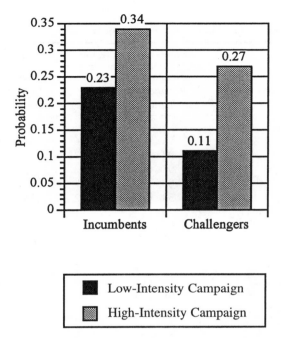

Figure 8.3. The impact of campaign intensity on the probability of mentioning an issue as a reason for liking the candidate. These probabilities are based on the unstandardized estimates presented in table 8.7. We calculate the probabilities by varying the level of competition in the race while holding all remaining variables at their means (see King, 1989: 105).

the likelihood that people will offer issues as reasons for liking the incumbent, but the impact of the campaign setting is somewhat less powerful for sitting senators.

The remaining measures of the campaign (i.e., exposure, contact, recognition, and recall) are particularly important for evaluations of challengers. Respondents who have had more contact with challengers, personally and via the media, as well as respondents who can recognize and recall the challengers' names are much more likely to offer issues as a reason for liking the challengers.

Certain types of citizens are more likely to offer issues when asked to describe what they like about the Senate contestants. Of particular importance is the party of the respondents. Citizens who share the candidate's party are much more likely to comment positively about issues when describing the candidate, compared to respondents who identify with the party of the candidate's opponent. Finally, the characteristics of the candidates do

TABLE 8.8
Logit Analysis Examining Issues as a Reason for Disliking the Candidate

	Incumbent/Open Winner		Challenger/Open Loser	
	Unstandardized Coefficient (standard error)	Beta	Unstandardized Coefficient (standard error)	Beta
Campaign Characteristics				
Campaign Intensity	.08 (.01)[a]	.36	.11 (.02)[a]	.31
Exposure	.07 (.03)[b]	.13	.20 (.03)[a]	.52
Contact	.04 (.02)[b]	.12	.03 (.02)	.07
Recognition	.88 (.26)[a]	.41	.83 (.12)[a]	.79
Recall	.38 (.04)[a]	.42	.33 (.05)[a]	.31
Respondent Characteristics				
Attention to news	.003 (.005)	.03	−.006 (.006)	−.06
Education	.03 (.008)[a]	.20	.04 (.008)[a]	.29
Interest	.07 (.02)[a]	.23	.07 (.02)[a]	.24
Political sophistication	.12 (.02)[a]	.42	.09 (.02)[a]	.33
Party attachment	−.19 (.01)[a]	.61	−.12 (.01)[a]	−.36
Ideology	−.01 (.01)	.01	−.02 (.01)[b]	−.08
Candidate Characteristics				
Challenger's experience	—	—	−.01 (.01)	−.06
Scandal	.26 (.06)[a]	.17	—	—
Seniority	.01 (.003)[a]	.18	—	—
Open	−.31 (.06)[a]	−.26	−.07 (.05)	−.06
Constant	−2.36 (.29)[a]		−2.27 (1.9)[a]	
% correctly predicted	76%		77%	
N	3,653		3,653	

Notes: Mentioning an issue is a binary variable where 1 = mentions an issue as a response to the open-ended "dislikes" question, 0 = otherwise. *Campaign intensity* is an index comprised of (1) competition, (2) campaign spending and candidates' issue emphasis, and (3) media coverage of issues (see text). *Exposure* is measured on a scale ranging from 0 to 3. *Contact* is measured on a scale ranging from 0 to 5. *Recognition* is a binary variable where 1 = respondent recognizes candidate, 0 = otherwise. *Recall* is a binary variable where 1 = respondent recalls the candidate's name, 0 = otherwise. *Attention to news* is measured on a 14-point scale. *Education* is measured by years of schooling. *Interest* is measured on a 3-point scale. *Political sophistication* is based on a scale ranging from 0 to 6. *Strength of party attachment* is measured on a 4-point scale. *Ideology* is a 7-point scale measuring strength and direction of ideological position. *Challenger's experience* is measured on a 9-point scale. *Scandal* is a binary variable where 1 = candidate involved with a scandal, 0 = otherwise. *Seniority* is measured by years in the U.S. Senate. *Open* is a binary variable where 1 = incumbent race, 0 = open race. All p-values are based on two-sided tests.

[a] p < .01
[b] p < .05

not influence the likelihood of mentioning issues in response to the "likes" question.

As Jacobson (1997) has discovered, when voters come to know candidates, they inevitably learn things they like *and* dislike about them. We find evidence that supports Jacobson's contention. In table 8.8 we examine the likelihood that respodents will mention an issue when talking about what they *dislike* about the candidates. If voters provide an issue as a reason for disliking a candidate, they were coded 1; all others were coded 0.[26]

In both the incumbent and challenger models, the campaign intensity measure is statistically significant. These results indicate that as the amount of issue discussion and the competitiveness of the race increases, citizens are more likely to offer issues as reasons for disliking the candidates. In figure 8.4, we graph the logit coefficients from table 8.8. These results indicate that the probability of mentioning an issue as a reason for disliking the incumbent is one and a half times greater as one moves from a noncompetitive campaign to an extremely competitive campaign. For challengers, the pattern is similar.

In addition, the remaining campaign variables are also vitally important predictors of negative issue comments. The importance of these factors demonstrates that a voter who is more familiar with the candidates is more likely to find something to dislike about the candidates' policy orientations.

The characteristics of the voters also play an important role in predicting who will state a negative comment based on an issue. The party attachment of citizens powerfully influences their evaluation of the candidates. In addition, the significance of voter sophistication suggests that people are more likely to offer comments when they know more about politics and feel comfortable articulating their comments to interviewers.

Finally, unlike positive comments based on issues, the seniority of the senator as well as the taint of scandal are related to negative comments. The importance of seniority suggests that as people learn more about their senators, they eventually learn something about the senators' views on public policy that they dislike. The statistical significance of scandal indicates that voters are able to draw connections between scandals and issues rather than simply linking scandals to personal traits.

Summary

By placing citizens in their campaign setting, we have clearly demonstrated that "campaigns matter." The variation in the competitiveness of Senate races as well as the vast differences in the substance and tone of the cam-

---

[26] As mentioned earlier, 28 percent of the respondents offered an issue as a reason for disliking the incumbent, and 25 percent offered an issue as a reason for disliking the challenger.

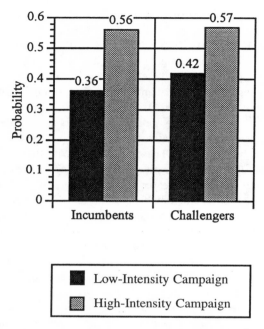

Figure 8.4. The impact of the campaign intensity on the probability of mentioning an issue as a reason for disliking the candidate. These probabilities are based on the unstandardized estimates presented in table 8.8. We calculate the probabilities by varying the level of competition in the race while holding all remaining variables at their means (see King, 1989: 105).

paign dialogue allow us to document voters' responsiveness to the campaign, controlling for a host of rival explanations. As races become more intense, people's exposure to and contact with the candidates increases, as does recognition and recall of the candidates' names. The electoral setting is particularly important for challengers where variations in the campaign setting powerfully affect people's interaction and knowledge of these candidates.

We also find that citizens can learn the themes disseminated by candidates when the race is competitive and the candidates' messages are presented repeatedly by the candidates and the news media. People's ability to identify issues and the candidates' specific themes are significantly affected by the campaign setting. Finally, people consider the context of the campaign when developing impressions of the candidates. When issue information is prevalent in closely contested races, citizens respond by offering issues as a reason for liking *and* disliking the candidates.

The analyses in this chapter demonstrate consistently that the campaign setting influences voters' interactions with the candidates, knowledge of the candidates, and evaluations of the candidates. In the next chapter, we investigate whether the intensity of the campaign influences the criteria voters use when evaluating candidates. In low-intensity races, where information is scarce and the campaigns are uninteresting, voters may rely on simple heuristics, such as partisanship. However, when the intensity of the races increases, people may begin to rely more heavily on sophisticated criteria, such as ideology and issues.

Nine

How Voters Make Decisions
in U.S. Senate Campaigns

THE 1988 SENATE race between Connie Mack and Buddy MacKay of Florida was a donnybrook. Never mind that George Bush coasted easily to a victory over Michael Dukakis in the Sunshine State and that only a handful of the state's nineteen congressional races were competitive that year. Floridians from Miami Beach to the panhandle were directly or incidentally exposed to the intense senatorial campaign between the two former House members. The two rivals spent nearly $9 million, with Mack leading the way by expending more than $5 million during the general election campaign. The polls suggested the race was very close during the final weeks of the campaign. Ultimately, Mack won by a mere 33,000 votes out of more than four million cast.

By the end of the campaign, Mack and MacKay were widely known by the Florida electorate; less than 10 percent of Florida respondents failed to recognize both candidates' names when queried by the NES/SES interviewers. Over 90 percent of respondents remembered seeing, hearing, or reading about the candidates on television, on the radio, or in the newspaper. Although the candidates' messages touched on numerous issues, Mack tried to define the race as an ideological battle between himself, a "time-tested conservative," and his opponent, a "Dukakis liberal." Likening MacKay to the liberal Massachusetts governor was a serious charge in Florida, one requiring a counterattack. MacKay fought back, reminding voters of his moderate voting record in the House and stressing that the campaign was indeed an ideological choice. However, the choice was between an "extreme conservative" and a "mainstream" centrist. The candidates' commercials and speeches, as well as the newspaper coverage of the campaign, centered on the ideological differences between the candidates.

The intense ideological campaign was not lost on the citizens of Florida. A full 50 percent of the NES/SES sample responded that Mack was a conservative when asked to place him on the ideological continuum. Furthermore, 50 percent of the sample viewed MacKay as a moderate, much to his liking. An additional 10 percent saw MacKay as a liberal, much to Mack's liking. To be sure, these are impressive numbers given that both candidates began the race as U.S. House members representing together only approximately 11 percent of the Florida electorate. The candidates' messages were received across Florida, from the Gulf to the Atlantic, from the Keys to the Georgia border.

In striking contrast, four years later the same electorate struggled when asked to place two different U.S. Senate candidates on the same ideological scale. In 1992, Democratic senator Bob Graham was seeking his second term as a U.S. senator. He had served the people of Florida in one capacity or another since 1966. He had been governor from 1978 to 1986. And in 1986, he defeated the incumbent senator, Republican Paula Hawkins, in an expensive hard-fought campaign.

The election of 1992 was quite different for Graham. It was an easy victory. He defeated his opponent, Bill Grant, by 30 points, outspending him by a margin of twelve to one. Grant was a former U.S. House member and a former Democrat. Grant was without money and a coherent message, and was best known for his 106 overdrafts at the House bank. Although policy discussion appeared in an isolated speech or in an occasional newspaper article, the campaign could not be characterized as an ideological or issue debate between the contestants.

The very same electorate that appeared alert and knowledgeable in 1988 struggled with the NES/SES questions in 1992. Although approximately 90 percent of Floridians recognized their former governor and current senator's name, fewer than 20 percent could correctly place him on the ideological scale, a full 30 percent below MacKay and Mack. Citizens were much less familiar with Grant. Only about 50 percent recognized Grant's name, and less than 20 percent of the NES/SES respondents could accurately place him on the ideological scale. In fact, more than 40 percent of the Florida respondents did not answer the ideological question when queried about Grant.

These two campaigns raise interesting questions about how the intensity of the campaign affects the criteria voters use to evaluate candidates. It is hard to imagine that Florida voters in 1988 ignored the candidates' ideological positions when deciding between Mack and MacKay. It is also hard to imagine that many voters considered Graham's and Grant's ideological views when choosing between these two opponents. While the electorate was virtually identical across these four years, the nature of the campaigns varied dramatically.

In this chapter we investigate whether citizens weigh certain considerations more carefully than others when they arrive at their local libraries, grammar schools, or community centers to cast their ballots for U.S. senator. We believe voters respond to the campaign by considering the information discussed by the candidates and disseminated by the news media. In particular, we expect the intensity of the campaign to condition the criteria voters use to evaluate candidates.

While we expect the campaign environment to affect how voters make decisions about candidates, people will differ in their susceptibility to campaign information. In particular, voters vary dramatically in their attention to politics, in their general understanding of political phenomena, in their ability to synthesize new political information, and in the cohesiveness and persistence of their political predispositions (Converse, 1962, 1964; Converse and Markus, 1979; Delli Carpini and Keeter, 1996; Krosnick, 1990; Lodge and Hamill, 1986; Luskin, 1987; Sniderman et al., 1990; Zaller, 1992). Converse (1990: 372), reflecting recently on the differing levels of political awareness among the electorate, noted "The two simple truths I know about the distribution of political information in modern electorates are that the mean is low and the variance is high." Indeed, in chapter 8 we demonstrated that voters with different political backgrounds vary dramatically in their knowledge about candidates and the campaigns.

This heterogeneity in people's understanding of politics suggests that different types of voters will employ different criteria when evaluating candidates (Otatti and Wyer, 1990; Rivers, 1988; Sniderman et al., 1990; Zaller, 1990). Sniderman et al. (1990) demonstrate that informed voters (i.e., political experts) are more likely to compare candidates' ideological predispositions and issue positions, while people with less information (i.e., political novices) rely on retrospective evaluations of the incumbents when making decisions during elections.

These findings raise important questions about the influence of the electoral setting on people's evaluations of candidates. For example, does the impact of campaign intensity depend on an individual's level of political expertise? Do informed voters always focus on sophisticated comparisons of the candidates, even in low-intensity races? Is it possible to entice political novices to employ more complicated criteria when the campaign intensifies?

To answer these questions, we need to understand how political experts and political novices think about politics. Political psychologists, relying on both experimental and survey data, find that political experts possess a tightly connected cognitive structure that organizes their political beliefs and attitudes (Krosnick, 1990; McGraw and Pinney, 1990; Kinder and Sanders, 1990; Lusk and Judd, 1988). These cognitive structures tend to be organized around abstract ideological principles and to produce attitudes that are more cohesive and interconnected than the cognitive structure of political novices (Converse, 1964; Nie et al., 1976; Judd and Milburn, 1980).

People with high levels of political expertise routinely rely on complicated decision rules. Regardless of the campaign setting, political experts consider ideological and issue differences when evaluating candidates. However, as the intensity of a campaign increases and more information becomes available about the candidates, political experts will rely *more* heavily on these sophisticated criteria when evaluating candidates.

Political novices, on the other hand, customarily think about politics in simple terms and rarely rely on abstract principles (Converse, 1964; Krosnick,

1990). Only in intense races, when information is plentiful, will novices begin to use sophisticated criteria when assessing the candidates. When the political environment provides a plethora of news about the candidates' policies and ideological views in an exciting setting, novices will respond by considering this complicated information when making judgments about the candidates. In other words, as the intensity of a campaign increases, novices will begin to use a greater number of criteria (i.e., simple and complicated decision rules) when judging candidates.

We turn now to an empirical examination of whether campaigns influence the decision criteria that voters employ when evaluating candidates and whether the effects of campaign intensity vary according to how sophisticated voters are about politics.

Does Campaign Intensity Influence How Citizens Evaluate Candidates?

To measure how citizens evaluate competing candidates, we rely on the NES/SES feeling thermometer ratings of the candidates.[1] In particular, we create a variable measuring comparative candidate evaluations. In races involving an incumbent, we calculate the arithmetic difference between the incumbent and challenger scores on the standard NES feeling thermometer scales (incumbent scores minus challenger scores). In races without an incumbent (i.e., open races), we calculated the arithmetic difference between the winning and losing candidate scores on the standard NES feeling thermometer score (winner scores minus loser scores).[2]

To capture the campaign setting, we construct the campaign intensity index employed in chapter 8. It consists of the activities of the candidates as measured by campaign spending, the number of newspaper paragraphs devoted to the race, and the closeness of the contest, as indicated by the final preelection poll.[3] As we have done previously, we normalize each component to achieve equal weighting.

To develop a model that captures the criteria that voters use to evaluate

---

[1] Comparative feeling-thermometer scores are excellent predictors of respondents' votes. In fact, prior research shows that the comparative feeling-thermometer scores predict 90 percent of respondents' votes correctly (e.g., Kenney and Rice, 1988; Markus and Converse, 1979). We find the same pattern for the NES/SES sample.

[2] As in earlier analyses, we analyze incumbents and winners in open races in one category and challengers and open-race losers in a second category. Some respondents did not rate the candidates on the feeling thermometer; we place them at 50 so as not to lose them from the analysis.

[3] The index of intensity has the following components: (1) incumbent spending + challenger spending, (2) number of paragraphs published about incumbent + number of paragraphs published about challenger, (3) difference in incumbent and challenger's poll standings.

candidates, we turn to a wealth of research findings in the field of voting behavior. Scholars examining presidential, House, and Senate elections have identified a number of factors that citizens consider when making their decisions at the ballot box. These forces can be divided into four categories: the citizens' political attitudes (e.g., party attachment, ideology, issue preferences), the prevailing national conditions (e.g., economic assessments, presidential approval), campaign activity (e.g., personal contact, media exposure), and familiarity with the candidates. We begin by discussing citizens' political attitudes.

Political Attitudes of Citizens

The most durable and well-established predictor of candidate evaluations, regardless of the electoral contest, is party identification (e.g., Campbell et al., 1960; Markus and Converse, 1979: Miller and Shanks, 1996). Studies of Senate elections have documented the importance of party identification in predicting the vote (Abramowitz, 1980; Abramowitz and Segal, 1990; Hinckley, 1980; Jacobson and Wolfinger, 1989; Smith and Squire, 1991; Wright and Berkman, 1986). We employ the standard 7-point scale to measure the impact of party identification in the 1988, 1990, and 1992 Senate elections.[4]

In addition to party identification, there is evidence from aggregate and individual analyses that ideology is related to how citizens assess senatorial candidates (Abramowitz, 1980; Abramowitz, 1988; Abramowitz and Segal, 1992; Westlye, 1991; Wright and Berkman, 1986). To measure ideology we constructed a variable that captures the "comparative ideological distances" between each respondent and the two candidates. First, respondents were asked to place themselves on the standard 7-point ideological scale.[5] Second, we developed an estimate of each candidate's actual position on the same 7-point ideological scale.[6] We calculated the absolute distance between re-

---

[4] We recode party identification so that respondents who strongly identify with the party of the incumbent (or open winner) are given the highest score ($+3$), while respondents who strongly identify with the party of the challenger (or open loser) are given the lowest score (-3). Respondents who did not answer the party identification question were recoded to the middle of the scale.

[5] In addition to the self-placement question, the NES/SES asked respondents to place the candidates on the ideological scale. However, these assessments may be affected by projection (e.g., Conover and Feldman, 1989). To further complicate matters, the process of projection may covary with intensity. In particular, voters may become more motivated to project their views on candidates as the race intensifies (Bartels, 1988). Given these potential problems, we prefer to rely on a more objective measure of the candidates' ideological position.

[6] To estimate the ideological position of the candidates, we relied on the campaign manager survey, where managers were asked to place their candidates on the 7-point ideological scale.

spondents' self-placement on the ideological scale and the position of each candidate. Next, the respondents' distance from the challenger or open loser was subtracted from their distance from the incumbent or open winner, with the resulting figure indicating which candidate the respondents are closer to ideologically.

Although a relationship between ideology and the senatorial vote has been established, an examination of the role of issues has proven to be more difficult (Jacobson and Wolfinger, 1989; Whitby and Bledsoe, 1986; Westlye, 1991; Wright and Berkman, 1986). It is not easy to isolate the important issues in all Senate contests in a given year, since some of the salient issues in Senate campaigns vary from state to state. In addition, to measure accurately the degree of issue voting, one needs to assess the respondents' position on an issue, the candidates' position on the issue, and the importance of the issue to the respondents.

Unfortunately, the NES/SES does not provide all the information necessary to measure issue voting in senatorial elections directly. Therefore, we needed to improvise and looked to Rahn's (1993: 482–483) efforts to study issue voting. First, we relied on a series of items asking respondents to identify their spending preferences for six federal programs.[7] Second, to assess candidates' positions on these six issues, we estimated a mean position for the Democratic and Republican candidates running for the U.S. Senate between 1988 through 1992 on these same issues.[8] We then matched the respondents' positions with the candidates' positions on each issue. For example, if a respondent's position on the environment was identical to the mean Democratic position, the respondent was scored $+1$. Conversely, if the respondent's position on the environment was congruent with the Republican mean position on this issue, the individual received a score of -1. This calculation was conducted for each issue, creating a scale ranging from -6 (i.e., the respondent and the Republican candidate held identical positions on each

---

We obtained ideological positions for 76 percent of the candidates. Where survey data were not available for an incumbent or nonincumbent who had served in the House of Representatives, we calculated the candidate's average ADA scores for the two years preceding the election. These ADA scores were used to place the candidates on the ideological scale. Finally, survey data and ADA scores were not available for 11 percent of the candidates. For these cases, we relied on an average ideological score, based on candidates in the sample who shared the party and status of the missing candidates.

[7] Questions about the environment, education, welfare, health care, child care, and defense were asked in 1988, 1990, and 1992. The questions take the following form: "Should federal spending [on improving and protecting the environment] be increased, decreased, or kept about the same."

[8] The mean position of the candidates was determined by examining descriptions of the candidates' positions on these issues from the content analysis of the state's largest newspaper. We calculated mean positions for Democratic and Republicans instead of scores for individual candidates because coverage of some candidates' positions was sparse.

issue) to +6 (i.e., the respondent and the Democratic candidate held identical positions on each issue). Finally, we recoded the issue scale so that respondents who held identical positions to that of the incumbent or open winner were given the highest score, while respondents sharing the exact same positions as the challenger or open loser were given the lowest score.[9]

We believe this scale allows us to examine how issue preferences influence comparative evaluations of the candidates for at least three reasons. First, the spending questions allow us to assess the respondents' actual positions on six distinct issues. Second, since these questions tap issues that often top the public agenda, the issues are likely to be salient to respondents. Finally, because we know the average Republican and Democratic positions on these issues, we can estimate the positions of each candidate contesting a Senate seat.[10]

Perceptions of National Conditions

Voters may consider the prevailing national conditions when casting their ballots (e.g., Ferejohn and Calvert, 1984; Hetherington, 1996; Jacobson, 1987; Jacobson and Kernell, 1983; Miller and Shanks, 1996; Tufte, 1975). Although aggregate and individual level studies show that economic conditions influence congressional outcomes, it is not clear whether voters evaluate the economy according to their "pocketbook" or "sociotropically" (e.g., Hibbing and Alford, 1981; Kinder and Kiewiet, 1979; Kramer, 1983; Tufte, 1975). Given the availability of the appropriate questions in the NES/SES, we can test whether personal or national economic conditions influence people's evaluations of Senate candidates.[11]

In addition to the debate over *which* economic situation (national or personal) influences voters, scholars have also tried to isolate whom voters hold

[9] To enhance manageability, the thirteen-point scale was collapsed into five categories (i.e., -4 through $-6 = -2$; -1 through $-2 = -1$; $0=0$; 1 through 2 = 1; 3 through 4 = 2).

[10] Our model of comparative candidate evaluations does not include a measure of respondents' assessments of the candidates' personality characteristics. While recent work has shown that evaluations of the candidates' personalities affect voters' decisions (Goldenberg et al., 1988; Kinder, 1986; Miller, 1990; Rahn et al., 1990), the NES/SES does not include an adequate measure of trait assessments. For example, the battery of closed-ended trait measures routinely asked by the NES during presidential years is not included in the NES/SES.

[11] The wording of the sociotropic economic question is: "Now, thinking about the country as a whole, would you say that over the past year, the nation's economy has gotten better, stayed about the same, or gotten worse?" The wording of the pocketbook economic question is: "We are interested in how people are getting along financially these days. Would you say that you and your family living here are better off, or worse off financially than you were a year ago?" For each question, we use the 5-point summary measure which ranges from "much better off" to "much worse off." People who did not answer the questions were treated as if they saw no change in the economic situation.

responsible for the state of the economy. Kramer (1971) and Stein (1990) suggest that voters hold all members of the president's political party responsible for the state of the economy, while Hibbing and Alford (1981) suggest that only incumbents of the president's party are held responsible. With the 1988–1992 data, we can sort out whom voters hold responsible for the state of the economy.[12]

Similarly, there is the possibility that attitudes about the president influence evaluations of Senate candidates. First, the "coattail effect" suggests that voters simply use their vote for the president as a guide in their choice of Senate candidates (Calvert and Ferejohn, 1983; Ferejohn and Calvert, 1984; Campbell and Sumners, 1990). We test for the coattail effect in 1988 and 1992.[13] Second, "referendum voting" suggests that voters may support the Senate candidate of the president's party if they approve of his job performance (Jacobson, 1992, Kernell, 1977; Tufte, 1975). We test for referendum voting by examining whether approval of the president is related to overall evaluations of the Senate candidates in 1988, 1990, and 1992. The presidential approval measure ranges from strongly approve to strongly disapprove.[14]

Campaign Activity

The activities of the candidates are likely to influence people's impressions of Senate candidates. An important activity that affects people's views of the candidates is contact with voters, both personal and via the mass media (Goldenberg and Traugott, 1987; Jacobson, 1987). We distinguish between personal and media contact because the impact of these activities is likely to differ. As discussed in chapter 8, since the candidate controls personal contact, such contact is likely to generate positive impressions. Media exposure, on the other hand, is influenced by reporters, the candidate, and the candidate's opponent. Therefore, this information is likely to be more critical

---

[12] Given the "sociotropic/pocketbook" distinction and the "across-the-board/incumbent only" distinction, we specify four competing hypotheses. First, the "sociotropic/across-the-board" hypothesis suggests that voters who believe that the national economic situation is getting worse will blame all candidates of the president's party. Second, the "sociotropic/incumbent only" hypothesis predicts that voters who believe that the national economic situation is getting worse will blame only the incumbents of the president's party. Third, the "pocketbook/across-the-board" hypothesis suggests that voters who believe their personal economic situation is getting worse will blame all candidates of the president's party. Fourth, the "pocketbook/incumbent only" hypothesis predicts that voters who believe their personal economic situation is getting worse will blame only the incumbents of the president's party. Each of the economic variables ranges from -2 to $+2$.

[13] The coattail measure ranges from -1 to 1. Respondents in 1990 and respondents who failed to cast a vote for the president are recoded to the middle of the scale.

[14] The approval measure ranges from -2 to $+2$.

than the information provided exclusively by the candidate. To assess personal contact and media exposure, we rely on the measures introduced in chapter 8.[15]

Candidate Familiarity

According to Jacobson (1997: 92), "Among the most consistent findings produced by studies of congressional voters over the past generation is that simple knowledge of who the candidates are is strongly connected to voting behavior." In both House and Senate elections, the more familiar voters are with a candidate, the more likely they are to support the candidate at the polls. To assess respondents' familiarity with Senate candidates, we develop an index ranging from 0 to 2 for each candidate. Respondents who can recall and recognize the candidate's name are given a score of 2, respondents who can only accomplish one of these tasks are given a score of 1, and respondents who cannot recognize or recall the candidate's name are given a score of 0.

Expectations about How Campaign Intensity Conditions Voters' Decisions

We have five general expectations about how intensity affects decision making in Senate elections. First, sophisticated criteria will become increasingly important as the intensity of the race escalates. Relying on a rich literature, we consider ideology and issue judgments to be representative of sophisticated criteria (e.g., Converse, 1964; Kinder, 1983; Sniderman et al., 1990). These decision rules require citizens to possess a great deal of information, which may be unavailable in low-intensity contests. In addition, citizens must be willing and able to integrate ideological and issue information when forming impressions of the candidates. Thus, we expect that as races become more intense, citizens will be more likely to draw connections between their own ideological and issue positions and their overall evaluations of the candidates.

A second hypothesis focuses on the use of simpler cues, such as party identification, economic assessments, referendum voting, and presidential coattails. The information necessary to rely on these heuristics is available in all types of Senate contests. For example, citizens should be able to ascertain

---

[15] Instead of creating comparative measures of contact and exposure, we have developed distinct measures for the competing candidates since we believe the impact of contact and exposure is likely to differ with the candidate's status (i.e., personal contact may be more powerful for incumbents and winners in open races than for challengers and open-race losers).

the candidates' party affiliation in virtually every electoral setting. Similarly, voters will be able to assess the state of the economy, regardless of the intensity of the Senate campaign. And, voters do not need much information from the campaign in order to link their vote for president to their vote for U.S. senator. Therefore, we expect these easy cues to be influential in even the most lopsided contests. However, even these heuristics may gain importance as the intensity of the campaign increases. Information about each candidate's party, the president's performance, and the health of the economy will be more plentiful in hard-fought campaigns. And, since competitive campaigns are more exciting, people may spend more time thinking about these criteria. Consequently, as campaigns intensify, even these easy voting cues may become more important.

Our third expectation deals with familiarity with the candidates. In low-intensity campaigns, simply knowing the candidates' names may generate positive impressions of the candidate. However, as the intensity of the campaign increases and people develop a more extensive understanding of the candidates' qualifications, ideological positions, and policy preferences, merely knowing the candidates' names may not translate into positive views of the candidates. As campaigns become more competitive, we expect that sheer familiarity with candidates will no longer act as a resource for the candidates.

Campaign activity is the focus of our fourth hypothesis. Competitive campaigns are inherently more interesting than low-key contests; therefore, as campaigns increase in their intensity, we expect the impact of media exposure and personal contact to increase. For example, people witnessing competitive campaigns are more likely to pay attention to the candidates' advertisements on television and to consider impressions formed during personal contacts with the candidates. Therefore, as races become more intense, campaign activities will have a more powerful influence on overall evaluations of the candidates.

Finally, we expect that people will differ in their susceptibility to changes in the campaign setting. Political novices routinely rely on simple cues, like retrospective evaluations of the incumbent, when drawing distinctions between competing candidates. We expect that when campaigns become more intense and more information is available in a more interesting setting, novices may respond by employing more sophisticated decision rules. Political experts will rely on sophisticated decision rules even in low-intensity races. However, experts will place more weight on these sophisticated criteria in intense races when ideological and issue information is more prevalent. In sum, novices will rely on sophisticated criteria only in intense races. Experts will use complicated decision rules in all campaign settings. However, as the intensity of the race increases, the impact of these criteria on overall evaluations will increase.

Testing the Impact of Campaign Intensity
on People's Voting Decisions

We interact the index of intensity with the independent variables to determine whether campaign intensity conditions the impact of these explanatory variables on people's assessments of candidates.[16] Specifically, we estimate a multiplicative model using OLS regression analysis. The results, presented in table 9.1, demonstrate convincingly that the campaign setting influences the criteria that voters use to assess candidates. First, the baseline coefficients indicate that citizens rely on a variety of different criteria in even the most mundane settings.[17] Nine of the twelve coefficients are statistically significant at the p < .01 level or better. Second, the impressive number of statistically significant interaction coefficients indicates that campaign intensity dramatically conditions the criteria that people use to form impressions about candidates.

To understand more fully how campaign intensity influences citizens' evaluations of candidates, we examine the effect of each independent variable at different levels of campaign intensity.[18] We calculate the slopes of the explanatory variables for three levels of intensity: the effect of an explanatory variable when campaign intensity is at its lowest level; the effect of an explanatory variable when intensity is moderate; and the effect of an explanatory variable when intensity is at its peak. These results are presented in table 9.2.

These calculations demonstrate that the effect of the campaign setting on voters' assessments of candidates is pervasive. Virtually all of the criteria change with the intensity of the race: complicated decision rules (e.g., ideology and issues), simple cues (e.g., party identification and presidential approval), contact with the candidates, and knowledge of the candidates.

[16] To estimate whether respondents rate open-race candidates differently than candidates running in incumbent races, we included a binary variable for open races (i.e., 0 = open race; 1 = incumbent race). This analysis revealed that the variable measuring open races was statistically insignificant (.14 with a standard error of .16). We also interacted the open-race variable with intensity since it is possible that differences between open races and incumbent races change with the intensity of the contest. However, neither the baseline coefficient (1.33 with a standard error of 1.19) nor the interaction coefficient (− .06 with a standard error of .65) was statistically significant. Therefore, we removed these variables from the model. The exclusion of these variables does not change the substantive nor statistical significance of any of the remaining variables.

[17] The baseline coefficient indicates the slope of the independent variables when campaign intensity equals zero (Friedrich 1982). These coefficients show the impact of the independent variables at the lowest level of campaign intensity.

[18] Friedrich (1982) shows that information is lost by only examining the average effect of the interaction coefficients (i.e., the interaction coefficients reported in table 9.1). Therefore, he recommends calculating "conditional slopes" to examine the effects of the independent variables across multiple levels of the conditioning variable. We calculate the conditional slopes of the independent variables at different levels of intensity by following the steps described in Friedrich (1982: 805–809).

TABLE 9.1
Comparative Evaluations of Senatorial Candidates:
A Multiplicative Model

Variable		
Baseline Effects		
Ideology	.12	(.18)
Issues	1.66	(.35)[a]
Coattail voting	6.18	(.86)[a]
Party identification	5.13	(.36)[a]
Presidential approval	1.95	(.29)[a]
Sociotropic/across-the-board	1.01	(.35)[a]
Incumbent/winner exposure	2.55	(.55)[a]
Challenger/loser exposure	.03	(.47)
Incumbent/winner contact	4.99	(.32)[a]
Challenger/loser contact	−5.11	(.48)[a]
Incumbent/winner familiarity	3.91	(.83)[a]
Challenger/loser familiarity	−1.49	(.78)
Intensity	.58	(.44)
Interaction Effects		
Ideology*Intensity	.31	(.06)[a]
Issues*Intensity	.31	(.12)[a]
Coattail voting*Intensity	.07	(.32)
Party ID*Intensity	.35	(.12)[a]
Presidential approval*Intensity	.44	(.10)[a]
Sociotropic*Intensity	.06	(.13)
Inc/winner exposure*Intensity	−.35	(.10)[a]
Chall/loser exposure*Intensity	.15	(.16)
Inc/winner contact*Intensity	.31	(.11)[a]
Chall/loser contact*Intensity	−.32	(.15)[a]
Inc/winner familiarity*Intensity	−1.10	(.30)[a]
Chall/loser familiarity*Intensity	.77	(.27)[a]
Constant	−.98	(1.23)
R^2	.26	
N	6,110	

Notes: See text for a discussion of how each variable is operationalized. All coefficients are OLS unstandardized coefficients with standard errors in parentheses. All p-values are based on two-tailed tests.
[a]$p < .01$

Beginning with the sophisticated criteria, we see that the impact of issues and ideological evaluations becomes more powerful as races become more intense. These decision rules require citizens to assemble and integrate complicated campaign information. Since citizens observing highly competitive campaigns are more likely to be exposed to this type of information, it makes sense that these complicated criteria become more important.

TABLE 9.2
The Impact of the Independent Variables on Comparative Evaluations of Senatorial
Candidates at Three Levels of Campaign Intensity

Variable	Low Intensity	Moderate Intensity	High Intensity
Ideology	.12 (.17)	2.29 (.41)[a]	4.15 (.71)[a]
Issues	1.66 (.35)[a]	3.83 (.73)[a]	5.69 (1.29)[a]
Coattail voting	6.18 (.87)[a]	6.67 (1.09)[a]	7.09 (1.54)[a]
Party identification	5.13 (.36)[a]	7.58 (1.03)[a]	9.68 (1.85)[a]
Presidential approval	1.95 (.28)[a]	5.03 (.73)[a]	7.67 (1.3)[a]
Sociotropic/across-the-Board	1.00 (.36)[a]	1.42 (1.03)	1.78 (1.85)
Incumbent/winner exposure	2.55 (.55)[a]	.10 (1.51)	−2.00 (2.70)
Challenger/loser exposure	.03 (.47)	1.08 (1.79)	1.98 (2.33)
Incumbent/winner contact	4.99 (.23)[a]	7.16 (.68)[a]	9.02 (1.84)[a]
Challenger/loser contact	−5.11 (.47)[a]	−7.35 (.88)[a]	−9.27 (1.68)[a]
Incumbent/winner familiarity	3.91 (.82)[a]	−3.51 (2.19)	−9.87 (3.91)[a]
Challenger/loser familiarity	−1.49 (.77)	3.90 (1.94)[a]	8.52 (3.60)[a]

Notes: The figures in this table are derived from the OLS estimates in table 9.1. The coefficients are OLS unstandardized coefficients with standard errors in parentheses. All p-values are based on two-tailed tests.
[a]$p < .01$

To illustrate the power of campaign intensity, we examine the variable measuring ideological evaluations at each level of intensity. The coefficient of .12 in low-intensity races (first column of table 9.2) indicates that a one-unit change on the ideological scale (which ranges from −3 to +3) yields only a .12 change in relative candidate evaluations. This slope estimate is not significantly different from zero, indicating that ideological assessments do not affect overall evaluations in low-intensity contests. In a moderately intense campaign (second column of table 9.2), a one-unit change on the scale is associated with a 2.29 change in relative candidate evaluations. Finally, in a very intense campaign (third column of table 9.2), the same one-unit increase yields more than a 4-point change in relative candidate evaluations. The magnitude of this effect is underscored with a simple example. In a low-intensity race, two individuals at opposite ends of the ideological scale would score the candidates less than one point differently on the comparative feeling thermometer, all other things being equal. In contrast, the same respondents in an intense race, holding everything else constant, would score the candidates 25 points differently on the feeling thermometer.

The strong effect of campaign intensity is also evident for issues. The impact of issues on feeling-thermometer scores more than triples from low-intensity to high-intensity elections. In low-intensity races, every 1-point movement on the issue scale produces less than a 2-point movement on the comparative feeling thermometer. In high-intensity campaigns, the same 1-point movement is associated with more than a 5-point change in feeling-thermometer scores.

Campaign intensity, in addition to influencing people's reliance on complex decision rules, also affects the importance of some simple cues. In particular, the impact of party identification and referendum voting changes markedly with the context of the race. For example, the significant interaction coefficient presented in table 9.1 and the conditional slopes in table 9.2 show that party identification becomes much more influential as races become more intense. Party attachment may become more consequential in competitive contests because people are more likely to acquire party information in hard-fought races. In lopsided races, news about the candidates is scarce, and people may be unfamiliar with a candidate's party affiliation (especially that of the challenger). However, as intensity increases, the sheer amount of news generated by candidates and the press escalates dramatically, thereby increasing the probability of citizens recognizing a candidate's party affiliation.

Similarly, referendum voting gains importance as races become more hard-fought. In competitive races, candidates' messages about the success or failure of the president and his programs may be more likely to reach potential citizens. In addition, people may be more interested in these races and, hence, more willing to draw connections between the president's performance and the evaluations they make of the Senate candidates. The conditional slopes for presidential approval, presented in table 9.2, almost quadruple in size from the most lopsided races to the most competitive. In low-intensity races, when respondents change from disapproval of the president's performance to approval (i.e., a movement of 2 points on the approval scale), their evaluations of the candidates change approximately 4 points on the comparative feeling thermometer. However, in high-intensity campaigns, the same movement on the approval scale produces more than a 15-point change on the feeling thermometer.

The importance of other heuristics, coattail voting, and economic assessments is not affected by the context of the campaign, as indicated by the insignificant interaction coefficients in table 9.1.[19] The campaign climate may

[19] In our initial analyses, we tested the four rival hypotheses described in note 12. We tested the "sociotropic/across-the-board" and the "pocketbook/across-the-board" hypothesis with the full sample of races, while we tested the "sociotropic/incumbent only" hypothesis and the "pocketbook/incumbent only" hypothesis with incumbent races since these later hypotheses predict that only incumbents will be held responsible for the economy. These analyses showed that only the sociotropic/across-the-board hypothesis received empirical support. Given these findings, and following the rule of parsimony, we reestimated the multiplicative model including only the sociotropic/across-the-board variable.

be less powerful here because these particular decision rules do not require voters to process much campaign-related information. This is most likely the case for coattail voting where citizens simply let their vote for president determine how they will vote in the Senate contest.

Campaign intensity also influences the impact of candidate familiarity. In low-intensity races, simply knowing the name of the candidate produces favorable impressions. However, as the intensity of the race escalates, familiarity no longer breeds favorability. In the most intense contests, the respondent who recognizes and recalls the candidate actually rates the candidate lower on the feeling thermometer.

In low-intensity races, where little information is available, respondents seem to rely on simple familiarity as a favorable heuristic. If they know the candidate, they give the candidate high scores on the feeling thermometer. This resonates with Stokes and Miller's (1966: 205) finding regarding U.S. House races where they conclude that, "in the main, to be perceived at all is to be perceived favorably." Familiarity, however, fails to be a resource in intense races. As races increase in their competitiveness, respondents receive both positive and negative news about the candidates. In this setting, what respondents know about the candidates is more extensive, more negative, and leads to more critical evaluations.

Turning to exposure and contact with the candidates, we find that the intensity of the campaign does not always affect the impact of campaign activity. More specifically, personal contact is more likely to enhance citizens' impressions of candidates as races become more intense, while the influence of media exposure is less conditioned by intensity.

The positive impact of personal contact can be seen by examining the significant interaction coefficients for incumbent contact and challenger contact in table 9.1. To illustrate, the data in table 9.2 indicate that in low-intensity races, a respondent with three contacts with the incumbent (the middle of the contact index) will rate the incumbent about 15 points higher on the comparative evaluations scale. In the most intense races, the same three contacts will produce more than a 27-point change on the feeling-thermometer scores. We find the same pattern for challengers. As races become more intense, challengers receive the same type of benefit from personal contact with potential supporters.

In competitive races, personal contact probably becomes more important because people are paying closer attention to the campaign. Indeed, some of the contact in intense races may be initiated by the citizens themselves. In these races, citizens may be more willing to tie positive feelings generated by personal contact to their overall evaluations of the political contestants.

Media exposure, unlike personal contact, is not controlled by the candidate. Therefore, exposure to the candidates does not necessarily produce positive impressions. The results displayed in tables 9.1 and 9.2 illustrate the point. Exposure to incumbents in low-intensity races is positive and significant. In these campaigns, sitting senators are portrayed more positively on the airwaves since the challenger is largely invisible. However, the negative and significant interaction coefficient for incumbent exposure suggests that as the intensity of the race increases, exposure to the incumbent no longer produces positive impressions. For example, in low-intensity races, every increase in media exposure produces a 2.55 advantage for incumbents on the comparative feeling thermometers. However, in more competitive races (i.e., races with moderate to high levels of intensity), incumbents receive no benefit from media exposure, as indicated by the statistically insignificant conditional slopes.

For challengers, media exposure is never significantly related to comparative evaluations. As the data in table 9.1 indicate, neither the baseline slope nor the interaction coefficient reaches statistical significance for challenger exposure. Regardless of the level of campaign intensity, exposure to the challenger does not noticeably affect people's evaluations of the candidates.

To summarize our findings thus far, we present three graphs in figure 9.1. The first graph (a) shows how the intensity of the race affects people's reliance on one sophisticated criteria: issue assessments. As the figure illustrates, the slope of the line representing the impact of issues on overall evaluations becomes significantly steeper as races increase in their intensity. In low-intensity races, the difference in comparative thermometer scores for respondents at opposite ends of the issue scale is only 7 points. In contrast, in high-intensity races, respondents at opposite ends of the issue scale differ much more dramatically in their assessments of the candidates. A respondent with the same policy views as the incumbent has a comparative thermometer score of 23 points, a strong preference for the incumbent.[20] The respondents who share the challenger's views on issues, on the other hand, do not differ in their assessments of the candidates (i.e., a score of 0 on the comparative feeling thermometer).

The next graph (b) in figure 9.1 reveals that not all criteria are sensitive to the intensity of the race. The simplest cue—presidential vote—has the same impact on comparative evaluations, regardless of the intensity of the race. The three lines, representing races with different levels of campaign intensity, overlap and are barely distinguishable from one another.

Finally, the third figure (c) suggests that the impact of certain campaign activities is affected by the context of the campaign. While personal contact with the incumbent is always helpful, the consequences of contact are most rewarding in high-intensity races. In these competitive races, respondents

---

[20] Prior work employing comparative feeling thermometers reveals that when respondents give one candidate an advantage on the feeling thermometers, even as small as one point, they are considerably more likely to vote for the candidate (e.g., Markus and Converse, 1979).

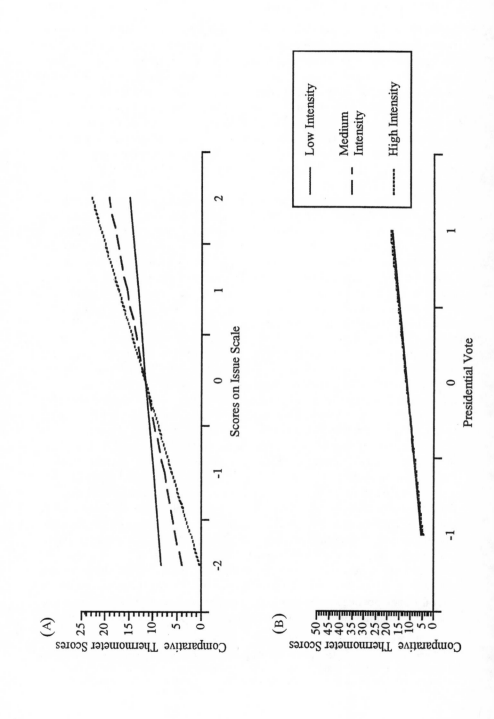

Low Intensity

Medium
Intensity

High Intensity

(A)

Comparative Thermometer Scores

Scores on Issue Scale

(B)

Comparative Thermometer Scores

Presidential Vote

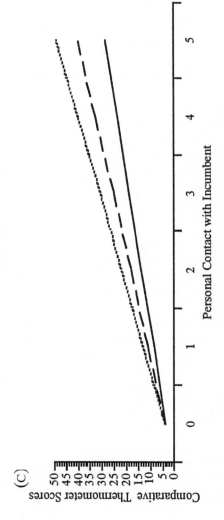

(C)

Comparative Thermometer Scores

Personal Contact with Incumbent

Figure 9.1. The conditioning impact of intensity on comparative thermometer scores. (A) The effect of issues on evaluations of Senate candidates for different levels of intensity. (B) The effect of presidential vote on evaluations of Senate candidates for different levels of intensity. (C) The effect of incumbent contact on evaluations of senate candidates for different levels of intensity. We relied on the coefficients in table 9.1 to calculate the point estimates in these graphs. We varied the independent variable of interest (e.g., issue scores) while keeping all the remaining variables at their means.

with the highest contact scores rate the incumbent almost 50 points higher than respondents who have had no personal contact with the incumbent.

An Additive Model of Candidate Evaluations: A Comparison

To examine further the influence of the campaign environment on voters' decision-making processes, we compare the results of our multiplicative model with a traditional additive model of comparative candidate evaluations. The additive model, by definition, is devoid of the campaign setting; all campaigns for the U.S. Senate are considered identical. The results of the additive model (see table 9.3), which include all the independent variables from the multiplicative model, differ markedly from the findings discussed above.[21]

A comparison of the coefficients in the two models (additive vs. multiplicative) demonstrates that the additive model misrepresents how people evaluate candidates in U.S. Senate campaigns. Beginning with people's reliance on sophisticated decision rules, the results of the additive model underestimate the impact of ideology and issues in moderate and intense Senate campaigns. For example, the additive model indicates that every 1-point change in ideological-proximity scores is associated with a .35 change in feeling-thermometer scores. This estimated impact of ideology is accurate only for people in low-intensity races.[22] In moderately intense races and intense races, the coefficient for ideology is much larger.[23] In fact, in high-intensity contests, the coefficient is almost twelve times larger than the coefficient estimated in the additive model, indicating that every 1-point change in ideological scores is associated with a 4.15 change in feeling-thermometer scores.

The results of the additive model also underestimate the impact of simple cues, such as party identification and referendum voting. Once again, the coefficients from the additive model represent low-intensity races more accurately than competitive campaigns. As an illustration, the additive results

---

[21] In an initial estimation of the additive model, we included a binary variable for open race (i.e., open race = 0; incumbent race = 1). However, the binary variable failed to reach statistical significance and was dropped from the model. The unstandardized coefficient was .50, with a standard error of 1.23.

[22] The coefficient for ideology fails to reach statistical significance (p < .05) in the additive model, and in low-intensity contests in the multiplicative model (see table 9.2).

[23] The additive model more accurately represents low-intensity campaigns than competitive campaigns because low-intensity contests are most common in Senate races. For example, 30 percent of the respondents in the NES/SES sample were exposed to races that received a score of three or less on the campaign intensity index, while less than 10 percent of the sample was exposed to races receiving a score of ten or higher on the intensity index. The intensity index ranges from 0 to 13.

TABLE 9.3

Comparative Evaluations of Senatorial Candidates: An Additive Model

Variable	Unstandardized Coefficient (standard errors)
Ideology	.35 (.18)
Issues	1.78 (.35)[a]
Coattail voting	6.76 (.86)[a]
Party identification	5.00 (.36)[a]
Presidential approval	2.01 (.29)[a]
Sociotropic/across-the-board	1.03 (.36)[a]
Incumbent/winner exposure	2.51 (.55)[a]
Challenger/loser exposure	−.29 (.45)
Incumbent/winner contact	5.30 (.33)[a]
Challenger/loser contact	−6.20 (.43)[a]
Incumbent/winner familiarity	3.86 (.82)[a]
Challenger/loser familiarity	−2.42 (.74)[a]
Constant	−.07 (1.23)
R^2	.23
N	6,110

Notes: All coefficients are OLS unstandardized coefficients with standard errors in parentheses. All p-values are based on two-tailed tests.

[a] $p < .01$

indicate that as a respondent moves 3 points on the party identification scale (e.g., from the end of the scale to the middle), the respondent's comparative feeling-thermometer ratings change approximately 15 points. However, in intense races the same 3-point change in party identification produces almost a 30-point change in comparative feeling-thermometer scores.

Finally, by looking only at the additive model of comparative candidate evaluations, we glean an incomplete picture of the role of media exposure, familiarity, and personal contact in Senate campaigns. The additive model indicates that media exposure leads people to develop positive images of incumbents. However, the multiplicative model shows that media exposure is helpful only in low-intensity races. As races become more competitive, incumbents receive no benefit whatsoever from media exposure.

Similarly, the data in table 9.3 indicate that familiarity with the candidate produces more positive impressions. Again, this is not uniformly true in senatorial contests. The results of the multiplicative model show that greater familiarity actually leads to more negative feelings for the candidates as races increase in their intensity.

The impact of personal contact is also distorted in the additive model. The additive coefficient for incumbent and challenger contact is most accurate for citizens witnessing low to moderately intense races. However, the additive results do not hold for intense races where personal contact with the candidate is significantly more powerful. For example, the additive coefficient for incumbent contact indicates that every 1-point increase in personal contact produces about a 5-point change in feeling-thermometer scores. In the most intense races, the same 1-point increase is associated with about a 9-point change in comparative evaluations.

In summary, these findings reveal that the average estimates produced by a traditional additive model of comparative candidate evaluations conceal important differences in how voters assess candidates. Since Senate races vary markedly in their intensity, and because people respond to changes in intensity by altering their decision rules, a model incorporating variations in the campaign context provides a more accurate picture of how people develop impressions of U.S. Senate candidates. By assessing the impact of the campaign climate, a multiplicative analysis of comparative candidate evaluations provides important clues about how citizens form impressions of candidates.[24]

Even though these findings indicate that the context of the race alters respondents' decision-making processes, it seems unlikely that every respondent would be affected equally by the stimuli present in the campaign environment. We turn now to an examination of how an individual's level of political expertise conditions the impact of campaign intensity.

How Political Expertise Mediates the Impact of Campaign Intensity

To analyze how different individuals react to the intensity of the campaign, we divide respondents into two categories based on their level of political knowledge (see the political-sophistication index introduced in chapter 8). We consider people to be political novices if they correctly answered fewer than five of the questions included in the political-sophistication index, and we classified people as political experts if they correctly answered five or six of the questions tapping political knowledge.[25]

We reestimate the multiplicative equation presented in table 9.1 for novices and experts. We present the baseline and interaction coefficients for both groups of respondents in table 9.4. The data in the table illustrate three important differences between experts and novices. First, the larger baseline coefficients for experts suggest that in the least intense races, knowledgeable

---

[24] We also estimated the multiplicative and additive models for respondents who said they had cast a vote for U.S. senator. The results are substantively similar when comparing the voting sample with the full sample (see Kahn and Kenney, 1997).

[25] Based on this categorization, 68 percent of the sample was labeled as political novices, and 32 percent was labeled as political experts. The relatively large number of political novices compared to political elites is consistent with prior work examining levels of political sophistication among the electorate (e.g., Converse, 1964). We divide the measure of political knowledge into two categories to ease the interpretation of the results.

TABLE 9.4

A Multiplicative Model of Comparative Evaluations of Senatorial Candidates:
A Comparison of Novices and Experts

Variable	Novices		Experts	
Baseline Effects				
Ideology	.19	(.21)	.28	(.36)
Issues	.68	(.41)	2.96	(.66)[a]
Coattail voting	5.18	(1.04)[a]	7.69	(1.53)[a]
Party identification	4.02	(.42)[a]	7.13	(.69)[a]
Presidential approval	1.47	(.33)[a]	2.35	(.59)[a]
Sociotropic/across-the-board	.60	(.42)	2.13	(.67)[a]
Incumbent/winner exposure	3.00	(.61)[a]	1.55	(1.19)
Challenger/loser exposure	−.29	(.54)	.88	(.93)
Incumbent/winner contact	5.06	(.41)[a]	4.47	(.54)[a]
Challenger/loser contact	−5.21	(.61)[a]	−4.63	(.76)[a]
Incumbent/winner familiarity	3.17	(.96)[a]	6.11	(1.68)[a]
Challenger/loser familiarity	−.91	(.93)	−3.15	(1.43)[b]
Intensity	.61	(.48)	−.34	(1.17)
Interaction Effects				
Ideology*Intensity	.18	(.07)[b]	.63	(.12)[a]
Issues*Intensity	.29	(.14)[b]	.47	(.23)[b]
Coattail voting*Intensity	.24	(.39)	−.10	(.56)
Party ID*Intensity	.27	(.15)	.43	(.24)
Presidential approval*Intensity	.32	(.12)[a]	.73	(.20)[a]
Sociotropic*Intensity	.14	(.15)	−.17	(.24)
Inc/winner exposure*Intensity	−.25	(.21)	−.44	(.41)
Chall/loser exposure*Intensity	.22	(.19)	−.002	(.32)
Inc/winner contact*Intensity	.33	(.14)[b]	.16	(.18)
Chall/loser contact*Intensity	−.68	(.19)[a]	.40	(.25)
Inc/winner familiarity*Intensity	−1.17	(.37)[a]	−.47	(.56)
Chall/loser familiarity*Intensity	.78	(.33)[a]	.82	(.48)
Constant	−.83 (−1.33)		−1.77 (3.32)	
R^2	.20		.38	
N	4,163		1,947	

Notes: All coefficients are OLS unstandardized coefficients with standard errors in parentheses. All p-values are based on two-tailed tests.

[a] $p < .01$

[b] $p < .05$

respondents rely more heavily than novices on attitudinal decision rules such as issues, coattail voting, party identification, presidential approval, and sociotropic assessments. For each of these variables, the unstandardized coefficients are substantially larger for experts than novices. These differences imply that people with higher levels of political expertise are better equipped to make attitudinal judgments about the candidates, even when the electoral contest is unexciting and little information is available about the candidates.

A second difference between experts and novices can be seen by examining the size of the interaction coefficients for the attitudinal variables. While the impact of ideology, issues, and presidential approval is conditioned by the intensity of the race for both experts and novices (as indicated by the statistically significant interaction coefficients), the electoral climate is more consequential for experts. For each of these attitudinal criteria, the interaction coefficient is considerably larger for the politically knowledgeable respondents. In the case of ideology, the coefficient for experts is over three times larger than the coefficient for novices (.63 versus .18).

To illustrate that experts' reliance on attitudinal calculi are more sensitive to the campaign climate, we examine the importance of issue assessments. When novices change from completely agreeing with one candidate on the issues to completely agreeing with the opponent (i.e., a movement of 5 points on the issue scale), evaluations of the candidates change about 3 points in low-intensity races and 22 points in the most intense races (i.e., a difference of 19 points). For experts, the same movement on the issue scale produces about a 15-point change in evaluations in low-intensity races and a 45-point change in the most intense races (i.e., a difference of 30 points).

The third difference between experts and novices centers on the influence of campaign contact and candidate familiarity. The impact of personal contact and the importance of candidate familiarity are conditioned by the intensity of the race for novices, but not for experts. In other words, novices' reliance on these criteria depends upon the context of the election. For experts, the importance of contact and familiarity does not vary with changes in the campaign climate. The interaction coefficients for contact and familiarity for incumbents and challengers are always statistically significant for novices, but these same interaction coefficients never reach statistical significance for experts.

To summarize, we present four graphs in figure 9.2. The first two graphs (a and b) illustrate how campaign intensity affects how novices and experts weigh ideological matters. The graphs show that the impact of intensity is more powerful for experts. In low-intensity campaigns, novices at opposite ends of the ideological scale rate the candidates 2 points differently on the feeling thermometer. In the most intense races, evaluations differ by 25 points. In contrast, in low-intensity races, experts at opposite ends of the ideological scale evaluate the candidates less than 3 points differently on the feeling thermometer. In comparison, in high-intensity races, these experts rate the candidates more than 80 points differently on the same scale.

The next two graphs (c and d) demonstrate that the impact of personal contact is conditioned by intensity more powerfully for novices than for experts. For instance, in low-intensity races, novices who have experienced

Figure 9.2

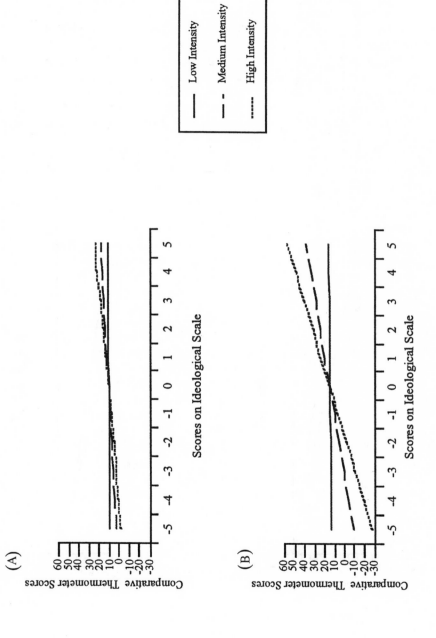

Figure 9.2. The conditioning impact of intensity on comparative thermometer scores for political novices and political experts. (A) The effect of ideology on evaluations of Senate candidates for different levels of intensity for political novices. (B) The effect of ideology on evaluations of Senate candidates for different levels of intensity for political experts. (C) The effect of incumbent contact on evaluations of Senate candidates for different levels of intensity for political novices. (D) The effect of incumbent contact on evaluations of Senate candidates for different levels of intensity for political experts. We relied on the cofficients in table 9.4 to calculate the point estimates in these graphs. We varied the independent variable of interest (i.e., ideological scale scores and incumbent contact) while keeping all the remaining variables at their means.

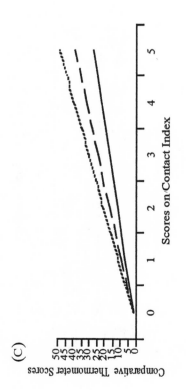

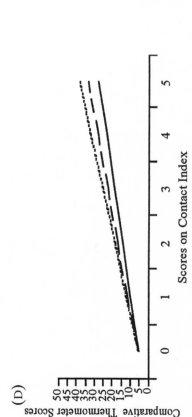

five types of contact with incumbents score incumbents 25 points higher on the feeling thermometers, compared to novices who have experienced no contact with incumbents. In high-intensity races, the incumbency advantage in evaluations increases significantly. Novices at opposite ends of the contact index evaluate the candidates more than 45 points differently on the thermometer scale. Among experts, on the other hand, the importance of personal contact is less affected by the intensity of the race. The closeness of the three lines in figure 9.2D shows that for experts the importance of contact is not strongly conditioned by the intensity of the race.

Summary

In this chapter, we find people are responsive to their campaign environments. Competitive campaigns encourage individuals to rely more heavily on both sophisticated criteria and simple decision rules when forming impressions of candidates. Citizens witnessing a competitive campaign resemble thoughtful voters who weigh ideology, issues, and assessments of the president's performance when making decisions. This mixture of policy, party, and referendum is an impressive array of criteria for citizens to use when making judgments about competing candidates.

This is certainly not the case in noncompetitive campaigns where one candidate is virtually certain of victory, where campaign activities are diminished, and where media coverage is minimal. In these campaigns, overall evaluations of the candidates are not tightly tied to a clear set of decision rules. Citizens rely less heavily on policy (e.g., issues, ideology), presidential assessments, and personal contact when distinguishing between political rivals.

While the campaign setting is clearly consequential, we also need to consider the characteristics of the voters when examining how people make decisions in Senate elections. In low-intensity contests, attitudinal calculi are less powerful for novices than experts. However, as races become more competitive, these attitudinal calculi become more important for all citizens. When it comes to the impact of personal contact and candidate familiarity, novices are clearly more responsive to changes in the campaign setting. Overall, our findings suggest that the context of the campaign and the characteristics of citizens significantly influence how people make decisions about candidates. Incorporating the diversity of the electorate as well as the heterogeneity of the political context enriches our understanding of how "voters decide."

Part Five

CONCLUSIONS

Ten

Conclusions and Implications

AN ESSENTIAL characteristic of a representative democracy is the presence of ongoing, uncensored, reasoned, and reflective discussions of problems facing the citizenry and the potential solutions to these problems. In large-scale democracies with millions of citizens, a common setting for these civic conversations is the campaign period preceding elections. Campaigns act as catalysts for the creation of political discourse focused squarely on the great issues of the moment. Only through campaigns can large numbers of citizens be exposed to political dialogue for a modicum of costs.

The conversations emanating from political campaigns yield, at least, three distinct benefits for representative governments. The first asset is that campaign discourse may broaden citizens' perspectives on the complex challenges facing the nation. Discussions may captivate people's interests and encourage them to entertain new ideas and to reexamine established beliefs and attitudes. Ideally, civic conversations may move citizens past their own self-interest, introducing them to concepts and ideas beyond their own purview. We are encouraged by Mill's (1991: 255) optimistic view in "Considerations on Representative Government:"

> Still more salutary is the moral part of the instruction afforded by the participation of the private citizen, if even rarely, in public functions. He is called upon, while so engaged, to weigh interests not his own; to be guided, in case of conflicting claims, by another rule than his private partialities; to apply, at every turn, principles and maxims which have their reason of existence the common good: and he usually finds associated with him in the same work minds more familiarized than his own with these ideas and operations, whose study it will be to supply reasons to his understanding, and stimulation to his feeling for the general interest. He is made to feel himself one of the public, and whatever is for their benefit to be for his benefit.

The idea that the convictions of citizens may be enlightened, or altered, or at least reflected upon by the simple act of participation in political dialogue is as relevant today as at any time in history. Currently, the United States is a nation comprised of a heterogeneous population with strikingly divergent interests. Disagreements can be located on a myriad of social, economic, moral, and philosophical issues (Page and Shapiro, 1992). Individuals' attitudes on the defining issues of our times are shaped by numerous cross-cutting forces such as religious convictions, political predispositions, and racial and ethnic characteristics (Miller and Shanks, 1996). Finding common ground among disparate citizens on issues such as abortion, the death penalty, affirmative action, prayer in schools, the rights of the accused, environmental regulation, and education, to name just a few, is difficult. Citizens need help understanding where the intersection of common beliefs may lie. Campaigns could be a place where political elites model for citizens how to listen to opposing views, afford respect for emotionally held attitudes, and identify goals and priorities that can be embraced by the many rather than the few.

The discussions emanating from campaigns play yet another role in a representative democracy. They help to create and facilitate important links of communication between representatives and those they are sworn to represent. These links are essential for the nature of the representative process. For example, linkages are important so that representatives have the information necessary to, in Madison's view (*Federalist*, no. 10), "refine and enlarge the public views by passing them through the medium of a chosen body of citizens." These connections are equally important because they allow legislators to "explain Washington activity." Candidates often use the campaign period to take stock of their activities during the previous legislative session. Fenno (1978: 136) discovered, "When House members are at home. . . . They explain what they have done while they have been away from home. By explaining we mean to include the description, the interpretation, and the justification of their behavior." Describing, interpreting, and justifying behavior is crucial in order for legislators to establish and maintain their legitimacy as representatives. This is especially important if they have not acted in the general interest of those they represent. Pitkin (1967: 209–210) stipulated that "representatives must not be found persistently at odds with the wishes of the represented without good reason in terms of their interest, without a good explanation of why their wishes are not in accord with their interests."

Finally, conversations during campaigns should serve as a medium where competing policy initiatives are presented to the citizenry for review. Campaigns are the only place in our representative democracy where time is allotted for hundreds of candidates and thousands of media elites to discuss and present to the people the policies that will most directly affect the course of their lives. We return once again to the insights of Mill (1991: 282) in "Considerations on Representative Government." Relying on Mill's words, we envision the role of campaigns as

> an arena in which not only the general opinion of the nation, but that of every section of it, and as far possible of every eminent individual whom it contains, can produce itself in full light and challenge discussion; where every person in the country may count upon finding somebody who speaks his mind, as well or better

than he could speak it himself—not to friends and partisans exclusively, but in the face of opponents, to be tested by adverse controversy; where those whose opinion is overruled, feel satisfied that it is heard, and set aside not by a mere act of will, but for what are thought superior reasons, and commend themselves as such to the representatives of the majority of the nation.[1]

The discussions of policy proposals require a great deal of time and effort by candidates and citizens. Candidates need to reveal their policy prescriptions for improving the nation in sufficient detail so that voters are able to weigh competing visions for the future. Citizens' decisions on the proper course for welfare, health care, or child care, for example, require a great deal of comparative reflections. Dahl (1956: 56–57) observed: "Advocates of democracy have generally supposed that the majority choice ought to be a reflective one; rational choice requires knowledge of one's own values, technical knowledge about the alternatives, and knowledge about the probable consequences of each alternative. Such knowledge, it has traditionally been held, requires time for debate, discussion, hearings, and other time-consuming devices."

Page (1996), writing forty years after Dahl and knowing full well that voters are not armed with the type of information Dahl required, argued that public deliberations are possible as long as political elites generate issue discussions that are germane to the lives of their constituents. Page (1996: 8) writes: "The crucial factors, according to classical liberals, are competition and diversity. Let opposing views contend vigorously in the marketplace of ideas; the true will defeat the false. So long as there exists some competing elites who share the values of various groups of citizens, the citizens can rely on cues from those they trust and form sensible judgments, even if the contents of the media are somewhat unbalanced and unrepresentative."

Public deliberation can take place in many different forums. Campaigns are ideal settings since they have the potential to reach millions of citizens at once, especially at the dawn of the twenty-first century when the capability of sending and receiving information continues to improve. In the end, campaigns should be an "arena" where a multiplicity of viewpoints is heard. They should serve as a "marketplace" where candidates propose solutions to current problems while opponents and the media critique the proposals in the full light of day. The quality of discussion should be open, amicable, and trusting; but at the same time, it needs to be reflective and critical. Campaigns should elevate the awareness and tolerance of citizens toward the views and beliefs of neighbors not of similar religion, or party, or ethnicity,

[1] In this passage Mill was referring to a committee in Parliament named the "Committee on Grievances" where all citizens could be heard. In a representative democracy of more than 260 million constituents, such as the United States, we envision campaigns as providing a similar role as Mill's committee.

or ideology. Campaigns should afford citizens chances to contact candidates, to shake their hands, to make connections with their representatives. But, do campaigns fulfill these demanding ideals? Do they invigorate and breathe vitality into our democratic process?

The Candidates

Our examination of U.S. Senate campaigns affords us some important insights and analytical leverage to answer these questions. We turn first to the behavior of candidates for initiating civic conversations in contemporary America. Do candidates instigate discussions on a wide range of topics? Do they describe pressing national problems and present potential solutions? Do they take clear stands on the issues, indicating how they might govern if elected? As a general rule, candidates do not engage in an extensive dialogue about public policy. In fact, the dearth of issue discussion by senatorial candidates is quite dramatic. The evidence is compelling. On average, candidates make issues the fundamental focus of their advertisements only 36 percent of the time; they typically discuss only two issues during a campaign. When candidates do focus on an issue in one of their ads, they declare a clear position only half of the time. They discuss controversial issues, those representing the most intractable problems facing our nation, less than a third of the time.

In addition, candidates are rarely prodded into the discussion of policy imperatives by the media, nor are they typically cajoled by their opponents. When the media focus on particular topics in their campaign coverage, candidates often choose to ignore these topics. Likewise, candidates are rarely coerced into a dialogue on specific issues by their opponents.

Candidates do not like to initiate policy dialogue unless forced to do so by public opinion polls indicating that the outcome of the campaign is uncertain. Almost magically, the likelihood of candidates' mentioning an issue in advertisements increases as the outcome of the campaign becomes more uncertain. In the most competitive elections, a candidate has a .71 chance of mentioning an issue during a commercial. In addition, in highly competitive races, there is slightly over a 50 percent probability that candidates will actually articulate clear positions on issues in their advertisements. These commercials, although only 30 seconds long, provide valuable insights into the expressed plans of candidates. Finally, in competitive races, candidates begin to discuss some of the most controversial issues facing the nation, issues such as abortion, death penalty, school prayer, and gun control.

Only the level of competition in the race consistently induces candidates to focus more time on policy matters. There is little support for the lore that challengers, although dramatically underfunded, are wide-eyed idealists bringing matters of public policy to the forefront of campaigns. In addition, we find no evidence to suggest that Democratic and Republican candidates work diligently and passionately on issues salient to their most loyal constituencies. For example, Democrats, typically assumed to be the guardians of the rights of America's poorest citizens, do not, as a matter of practice, generate discussions about the failure of America's health care system to reach those who cannot pay, at least in the three senatorial periods we examined. Similarly, the voices of Republican candidates were usually silent about reducing the tax burden on middle-income Americans, citizens believed to be squarely entrenched in the Republican fold.

The effects of competition go beyond cajoling the candidates to address issues. Competitive elections encourage candidates to engage in a critical dialogue about the future of the country. Such critical commentary is an integral part of any representative democracy since political conversations require debate, disagreement, and conflict in order to be thorough, balanced, and insightful. Competing views, by necessity, cannot be fully debated without pointed and sometimes harsh criticism. For compelling ideas to flourish, they must be tested before hostile audiences.

As races become more competitive, candidates are more likely to attack their opponents. Such attacks include critiques of the opponent's policy agenda, criticisms of the rival's issue positions, attacks of the candidate's personal traits, and the assignment of blame for unpopular policy outcomes. Incumbents, in particular, are sensitive to the closeness of their contests. When incumbents are virtually guaranteed of reelection, they rarely speak ill of their opponents. However, when the outcome of their race is unclear, incumbents have approximately a .50 probability of attacking their challengers. If candidates provide policy discussion and critical commentary only in the closest of races, do the media fill the void?

The Media

Do the media discuss the "state of the union" during campaigns, even if candidates opt out of the debate? As with candidates, the answer depends. A crucial criterion for coverage is an uncertain outcome. If it appears that the race is competitive, then the campaign is deemed newsworthy by people who have the power to allocate news space. Without competition, media coverage of senatorial races is largely nonexistent, turning to other political races and events.

Citizens searching for coverage of senatorial campaigns will often have a difficult time. From Labor Day to Election Day, potential voters reading their local paper will find fewer than ten stories on the front page and fewer than ten headlines about the senatorial contestants. Spread across nearly twelve weeks of a campaign, they will have the chance to read only 154 paragraphs about the issues, fewer than two paragraphs per day. Even less still, only 54 paragraphs will be published describing the characteristics of the candidates, strikingly less than one paragraph per day from Labor Day to the end of the campaign.

The media elites, lacking time and resources, routinely report what is given to them by candidates. True investigative reporting is typically too time consuming. These constraints on the press tend to provide a modicum of advantages to challengers. Lacking prior information about most challengers, reporters tend to rely on the information disseminated by the challengers' campaigns when covering these candidates. While incumbents receive more overall coverage than challengers, the challengers' messages are reported more faithfully than the messages of incumbents.

The nature of campaign coverage changes dramatically when races are more competitive. In fact, compared to noncompetitive races, the number of stories appearing on the front pages of local newspapers and the number of times candidates' names appear in headlines triples and quadruples, respectively, in races where the outcome is too close to call. The number of paragraphs allocated to the coverage of issues in competitive races, compared to noncompetitive races, can increase over five times in the same newspapers covering elections only two years apart. Finally, the correspondence between what the candidates are discussing and what the press is reporting increases with competition. For example, when candidates discuss issues, the press reports this discussion more faithfully when competition is at its peak.

Finally, in close races the media begin to critique the candidates and their proposals. The amount of critical commentary in the press increases dramatically as races become more competitive; and, in turn, competition increases in response to the media's willingness to criticize candidates' records, their proposals, and their backgrounds. On average, candidates are criticized in the press less than once a day. In contrast, in the most competitive races, nearly three criticisms a day are written about each candidate, and these criticisms become more frequent as Election Day approaches. The types of criticisms range from questioning the candidate's issue priorities, critiquing the candidate's policy positions and background, attacking the candidate's campaign strategy, and relying on unflattering adjectives to describe the candidate.

The Citizens

The foregoing pages illustrate how competition alters the political discussion flowing from elections. Competitive elections bear no resemblance to those where one candidate leads by large margins across the entire campaign. Perhaps our most compelling finding is that citizens respond powerfully to the nature of the political dialogue. Civic conversations, ensconced in a competitive setting, invigorate citizens. People are more likely to be exposed to candidates' messages, to have personal contact with candidates, and to know the candidates' names when they are witnessing a hard-fought campaign. Beyond mere familiarity, citizens are more likely to identify the issues in hard-fought campaigns, to identify the themes disseminated by competitive candidates, and to cite issues as reasons for liking and disliking candidates who are engaged in close contests. Although these patterns are true for all candidates, they are most dramatic for challengers.

The effects of campaigns reach further still. Voters actually adjust the criteria they use to evaluate candidates as races become more intense. When information is plentiful and people are interested in the campaign, they respond by relying more heavily on sophisticated criteria, in addition to simple decision rules, when evaluating candidates. When campaigns focus on issues and national policies, voters consider the candidates' ideological and issue positions, along with their assessments of the president's performance, when making decisions about Senate contestants.

The campaign setting can empower even the least politically sophisticated voters, leading them to employ more complicated concepts when evaluating candidates. A competitive campaign environment, characterized by a plethora of information about the competing candidates, can encourage political novices to consider the candidates' ideological and issue positions when making decisions at the ballot box. Such sophisticated decisions by political novices are simply not possible in less competitive settings. Alterations in the political setting powerfully influence what people know about the political contestants and how they choose between competitors. We provide the clearest evidence to date documenting Key's (1966; 2–3) notion of the "echo chamber":

> The voice of the people is but an echo. The output of an echo chamber bears an inevitable and invariable relation to the input. As candidates and parties clamor for attention and vie for popular support, the people's verdict can be no more than a selective reflection from among the alternatives and outlooks presented to them. Even the most discriminating popular judgment can reflect only ambiguity, or even foolishness if those are the qualities of the input into the echo chamber. A candidate may win despite his tactics and appeals rather than because of them.

The transcendent importance of competition for improving the quality of campaigns raises questions about how to increase levels of competition in U.S. legislative elections. This is not an idle concern. In the Senate elections in our study, the final polls in more than one-third of the races indicated that the competing candidates were separated by 30 points or more. These findings are not unique to the Senate races in our study. Prior researchers have discovered similar patterns in other senatorial campaigns (Kahn, 1996; West-lye, 1991; Abramowitz and Segal, 1992). In House elections, competitive elections are even less common (Jacobson, 1997; Krasno, 1994).

However, competitive elections do exist. In our study, polls taken during the final week of campaigns indicated that candidates were separated by 10 points or less in one-fourth of the races. And, in more than one-third (i.e., 35 percent) of the races, the candidates were separated by fewer than 15 points in the final preelection poll. Thus, a swing of a mere 2 or 3 points would make any of these elections dramatically closer, and in many cases, the lead would actually change hands.

Speculating on ways to create more competitive campaigns forces us to consider ways of reforming the electoral process. Although noting Fiorina's (1996: 4) observation that "the best of intentions . . . can 'reform' one imperfect state into another even more imperfect [state]," we feel that the ill-effects of noncompetitive elections are pernicious enough to warrant a national dialogue on ways to encourage competition.

A list of topics comes to mind. First, since the spending patterns of challengers often influence the competitiveness of a campaign, ideas need to be aimed at increasing funding opportunities for underdog candidates. For example, seed money for challengers might be provided through the public financing of congressional elections. Increasing spending early in campaigns may also provide voters with more information about unknown challengers.

Similarly, television stations can be mandated to provide a certain amount of free advertising for political candidates. Ensuring all candidates access to potential voters will increase citizens' familiarity and contact with candidates. In addition, if citizens are more knowledgeable of the ongoing contest, the news media may be encouraged to spend more time covering the campaign.

In addition, citizens and political elites can put pressure on the news media to improve their political reporting. Newspapers, for example, can institute a "campaign section" early in the electoral season to review and discuss campaign events. Examinations of the candidates' issue positions, "ad watches," documentation of voting records, and listings of campaign events should all be part of routine campaign coverage.

These ideas are meant to stimulate debate by party, media, and government elites. While campaigns provide a forum for political discourse, we know that the quality of the dialogue depends on the competitive nature of the contest. The discussions by the candidates, the media, and the citizens will be more detailed, more evenhanded, more inspired, more reflective, and more engaging when competition is high.

To be sure, competition is not a panacea for curing all the problems of U.S. campaigns. For example, there are inherent biases present in the media coverage that are not responsive to competition. Specifically, incumbents who spend more money receive more coverage and more prominent coverage for themselves and their opponents. Even more striking, newspapers provide the candidates whom they endorse with more favorable coverage while they print more critical commentary about those they don't. In fact, newspapers are more likely to print unattributed criticisms, those with no mention of a source, when writing about candidates who have failed to receive endorsements.

In conclusion, biases in media coverage and the dearth of policy discussion in noncompetitive elections produce campaign conversations that are inadequate in scope and detail and are potentially misleading. As democracies emerge throughout the world and incorporate campaigns as mechanisms to elect representatives, politicians and the media elite in the U.S. have an obligation to model how campaigns ensure electoral accountability and generate civic conversations among candidates, the press, and the voters. Recently, Amy Gutmann (1993: 141) explained why deliberations are an essential element of modern democracies:

Deliberative democracy articulates a compelling conception of people as self-governing, who reflect, evaluate, and decide issues on the basis of the broad range of relevant considerations that are available for their consideration in a society where every adult is treated as an autonomous person, and thereby granted political standing as an equal citizen. Accompanying this conception is an ideal of politics where people routinely relate to one another not merely by asserting their will or fighting for their predetermined interests, but by influencing each other through the publicly valued use of reasoned argument, evidence, evaluation, and persuasions that enlists reasons in its cause.

Election Day is one moment when every citizen in the republic has equal power. To allow citizens more influence over the course of their government, however, they need information emanating from thoughtful public deliberation during the weeks and months preceding Election Day. We maintain that campaigns can empower voters to make more informed decisions. As the twentieth century draws to a close, we need to enhance the quality of our representative government by increasing the quality and quantity of discussion in all elections, competitive or otherwise.

APPENDIXES

Appendix A ———————————————

INTERVIEW SCHEDULE FOR SUCCESSFUL INCUMBENTS

Hello, my name is ———————————. I am a research assistant at Arizona
State University and we are conducting a study of campaigns in the 1992 Senate
elections. We were wondering if you could answers a few questions we have.
The interview should only take about 15 or 20 minutes. Your answers will all
be confidential.

1. Date interview completed—Month
    11. November
    12. December
    1. January
    2. February
    3. March
2. Day interview completed—Day (Code actual day of month [01–31]):
3. Beginning time of interview:
4. Ending time of interview:
5. Length of interview (Code actual time in minutes):

   I'd like to start by asking you some questions about the themes that were
   stressed in [SENATOR'S NAME'S] 1988/1990/1992 campaign.

6. First, what were the main themes that you tried to stress in [SENATOR'S
   NAME] 1988/1990/1992 campaign for the Senate? Anything else?
7. Did you think you were effective in getting your position on these themes
   across to the voters?
   [If respondent only says YES or NO, ask respondent to explain.]
7a. On *which* themes were you *most* effective in reaching the voters?
7b. Did stressing these themes help you in the race?
    1. Yes
    2. No
    8. Don't know
8. Now thinking about [OPPONENT'S NAME], what were the main themes that
   [OPPONENT'S NAME] tried to stress in HIS/HER 1988/1990/1992 campaign for
   the Senate? Anything else?
9. Did you think that [OPPONENT'S NAME] was effective in getting these themes
   across to the voters?
   [If respondent only says YES or NO, ask respondent to explain]
9a. On *which* themes was [OPPONENT'S NAME] *most* effective in reaching the
    voters?
9b. Did stressing these themes help [OPPONENT'S NAME] in the race?
    1. Yes

  2. No

  8. Don't know

10. What policy positions did your campaign try to emphasize? Anything else?

11. What policy positions did [OPPONENT'S NAME] try to emphasize in HIS/HER campaign? Anything else?

12. Did you try to emphasize [SENATOR'S NAME]'s personal characteristics in the campaign?

  [If respondent says only YES, ask the respondent to explain.]

13. Did [OPPONENT'S NAME] emphasize HIS OWN/HER OWN personal characteristics in the campaign?

  [If respondent says only YES, ask the respondent to explain.]

14. We hear a lot of talk these days about liberals and conservatives. Think about a ruler for measuring political views that people might hold, from liberal to conservative. On this ruler, which goes from 1 to 7, a measurement of 1 means very liberal political views, and a measurement of 7 would be very conservative. Just like a regular ruler, it has points in between, at 2, 3, 4, 5, or 6.

Where would you place the following people on this scale where 1 means very liberal and 7 means very conservative?

SENATOR'S NAME

  1. Very liberal

  2.

  3.

  4. Middle of the road

  5.

  6.

  7. Very conservative

  8. Don't know

  9. Refused

  0. Haven't thought much about it

15. OPPONENT'S NAME

  1. Very liberal

  2.

  3.

  4. Middle of the road

  5.

  6.

  7. Very conservative

  8. Don't know

  9. Refused

  0. Haven't thought much about it

Now I'd like to ask you a few questions about the new media's coverage of the campaign.

16. What themes did the news media emphasize in their coverage of the campaign? Anything else?

17. What policy issues did the news media emphasize in their coverage of the the campaign?

18. Did the news media discuss [SENATOR'S NAME]'s personality traits in their coverage of the campaign?
[If respondent says only YES or NO, ask respondent to explain.]

19. Why do you think you won the election?

20. What reason did the news media give for your victory?
Anything else?

21. Would you describe the news coverage of your campaign as positive, negative, neutral, or mixed?
1. Positive
2. Negative
3. Neutral
4. Mixed
8. Don't know

Can you rate the effectiveness of the following mediums for communicating with potential voters?

22. How effective are televised political advertisements for communicating with potential voters? *Very effective, somewhat effective, somewhat ineffective, very ineffective*
1. Very effective
2. Somewhat effective
3. Somewhat ineffective
4. Very ineffective
8. Don't know

23. How effective is personal contact for communicating with potential voters?
1. Very effective
2. Somewhat effective
3. Somewhat ineffective
4. Very ineffective
8. Don't know

24. Was [SENATOR'S NAME] a *very effective* campaigner, a *somewhat effective* campaigner, a *somewhat ineffective* campaigner, or a *very ineffective* campaigner in the 1988/1990/1992 campaign?
1. Very effective
2. Somewhat effective
3. Somewhat ineffective
4. Very ineffective
8. Don't know

25. Was [OPPONENT'S NAME] a *very effective* campaigner, a *somewhat effective* campaigner, a *somewhat ineffective* campaigner, or a *very ineffective* campaigner in the 1988/1990/1992 campaign?
1. Very effective
2. Somewhat effective
3. Somewhat ineffective
4. Very ineffective

8. Don't know

That is the end of the survey. Thank you very much for your help. If you have any questions about this survey, you can contact the principal investigators, Professor Patrick Kenney and Professor Kim Kahn, at the Political Science Department at Arizona State University. Their address is: Department of Political Science, Arizona State University, Tempe, AZ 85287.
Thank you again for your help.

Ending time of interview:

Appendix B _____

POLITICAL ADVERTISING CODE SHEET

Variable Description	Code
Candidate Code (Campaign Manager Code)	___ ___ ___
Ad Number (Sequential)	___ ___ ___
Length of Ads (In Seconds)	___ ___

Type of Candidate

1 = Incumbent
2 = Challenger
3 = Open winner
4 = Open loser

Type of Ad

1 = Positive trait	9 = Negative ideology	___ ___
2 = Positive issue	10 = Endorsements	___ ___
3 = Negative trait	11 = Biography	___ ___
4 = Negative issue	12 = Comparison: combination	
5 = Positive combination	13 = Comparison:trait	
6 = Negative combination	14 = Comparison:issue	
7 = Elective experience (constituency/pork)	15 = Comparison:elective experience	
8 = Positive ideology	16 = Comparison:ideology	
	17 = Other _____	

Picture

1 = Picture of candidate
2 = Picture of opponent
3 = Picture of both

Partisanship (1 = Yes, 0 = No)

Endorsements

1 = President	5 = Celebrity	___
2 = National office holder—elective	6 = Newspaper	___
	7 = Interest group (Specify)	___
3 = National office holder—appointive	8 = Former office holder	
4 = State office holder	9 = Other _____	

Criticisms of Opponent   *Major Minor*

   1 = Candidate   ____ ____
   2 = Surrogates
   3 = Announcer

Candidate Ideology   ____

   1 = Liberal
   2 = Moderate
   3 = Conservative

Candidate Ideology   ____

   1 = Major
   2 = Minor

Opponent Ideology   ____

   1 = Liberal
   2 = Moderate
   3 = Conservative

Opponent Ideology   ____

   1 = Major
   2 = Minor

Traits of Candidate	Major	Minor	Traits of Opponent	Major	Minor
Honest	____	____	Dishonest	____	____
Trustworthy	____	____	Untrustworthy	____	____
Compassionate	____	____	Insensitive	____	____
Intelligent	____	____	Unintelligent	____	____
Effective	____	____	Ineffective	____	____
Knowledgeable	____	____	Uninformed	____	____
Hardworking	____	____	Lazy	____	____
Independent	____	____	Dependent	____	____
Strong leader	____	____	Weak leader	____	____
Moral	____	____	Immoral	____	____
Consistent, stable	____	____	Erratic	____	____
Aggressive	____	____	Passive	____	____
Experienced	____	____	Inexperienced	____	____
Ambitious	____	____	Power-hungry	____	____
Ties to state	____	____	No ties to state	____	____
War record	____	____	Lack of war record	____	____
Cares for state	____	____	No care for state	____	____
Pos. Wash. ties	____	____	Neg. Wash. ties	____	____
Voting record +	____	____	Voting record −	____	____
Special life exp.	____	____	(Un)common man	____	____
Seniority	____	____	Other _____	____	____
Common man	____	____	Other _____	____	____

Family	____	____	Other _____	____	____
Other _____	____	____			
Other _____	____	____			
Other _____	____	____			

Issues of Candidate   *Issues of Opponent*

	Major	Minor	Frame	Spend	Resp	Major	Minor	Frame	Spend	Resp
Defense issues	____	____	____	____	____	____	____	____	____	____
Foreign aid	____	____	____	____	____	____	____	____	____	____
Central America	____	____	____	____	____	____	____	____	____	____
Health	____	____	____	____	____	____	____	____	____	____
Elderly	____	____	____	____	____	____	____	____	____	____
Welfare	____	____	____	____	____	____	____	____	____	____
Education	____	____	____	____	____	____	____	____	____	____
Drugs	____	____	____	____	____	____	____	____	____	____
AIDS	____	____	____	____	____	____	____	____	____	____
Day care	____	____	____	____	____	____	____	____	____	____
Farm	____	____	____	____	____	____	____	____	____	____
S&L bailout	____	____	____	____	____	____	____	____	____	____
Big gov't	____	____	____	____	____	____	____	____	____	____
Crime	____	____	____	____	____	____	____	____	____	____
Taxes	____	____	____	____	____	____	____	____	____	____
Budget/spending	____	____	____	____	____	____	____	____	____	____

	Major	Minor	Frame	Reg	Resp	Major	Minor	Frame	Reg	Resp
Business	____	____	____	____	____	____	____	____	____	____
Energy/oil	____	____	____	____	____	____	____	____	____	____
Imports/trade	____	____	____	____	____	____	____	____	____	____
Environment	____	____	____	____	____	____	____	____	____	____

	Major	Minor	Frame	Plan	Resp	Major	Minor	Frame	Plan	Resp
Econ (general)	____	____	____	____	____	____	____	____	____	____
Inflation	____	____	____	____	____	____	____	____	____	____
Unemployment	____	____	____	____	____	____	____	____	____	____
Jobs	____	____	____	____	____	____	____	____	____	____

	Major	Minor	Frame	Social	Resp	Major	Minor	Frame	Social	Resp
Abortion	____	____	____	____	____	____	____	____	____	____
Civil Rts/race	____	____	____	____	____	____	____	____	____	____
Prayer in school	____	____	____	____	____	____	____	____	____	____
Family values	____	____	____	____	____	____	____	____	____	____
Apartheid	____	____	____	____	____	____	____	____	____	____
Gulf War	____	____	____	____	____	____	____	____	____	____
Panama	____	____	____	____	____	____	____	____	____	____
Israel	____	____	____	____	____	____	____	____	____	____
Yugoslavia	____	____	____	____	____	____	____	____	____	____
Death penalty	____	____	____	____	____	____	____	____	____	____
Gun control	____	____	____	____	____	____	____	____	____	____

Camp finance   ____ ____ ____ ____ ____   ____ ____ ____ ____ ____
Term limits   ____ ____ ____ ____ ____   ____ ____ ____ ____ ____
Other _____   ____ ____ ____ ____ ____   ____ ____ ____ ____ ____
Other _____   ____ ____ ____ ____ ____   ____ ____ ____ ____ ____
Other _____   ____ ____ ____ ____ ____   ____ ____ ____ ____ ____

Frame	*Responsibility*	*Spending*	*Regulation*	*Plans*	*Social*
1 = Societal (statistics)	1 = Credit	1 = Up	1 = Up	1 = Yes	1 = Pro
2 = Individual (case)	2 = Blame	2 = Same	2 = Same	2 = No	2 = Anti
3 = Combination		3 = Down	3 = Down		
4 = Other __		4 = Mixture	4 = Mixture		

Appendix C ————————————————————

SAMPLE OF NEWSPAPERS

State	Year(s) of U.S. Senate Race	Newspaper
AL	1990, 1992	*Birmingham News*
AK	1990, 1992	*Anchorage Daily News*
AZ	1988, 1992	*Arizona Republic*
AR	1992	*Arkansas Gazette*
CA	1988, 1992 (2)	*Los Angeles Times*
CO	1990, 1992	*Denver Rocky Mountain News*
CT	1988, 1992	*Hartford Courant*
DE	1988, 1990	*Wilmington News Journal*
FL	1988, 1992	*Miami Herald*
HI	1988, 1990, 1992	*Honolulu Advertiser*
GA	1992	*Atlanta Constitution*
ID	1990, 1992	*Idaho Statesman*
IL	1990, 1992	*Chicago Tribune*
IN	1988, 1990	*Indianapolis Star*
IA	1990, 1992	*Des Moines Register*
KS	1990, 1992	*Wichita Eagle-Beacon*
KY	1990, 1992	*Louisville Courier-Journal*
ME	1988, 1990	*Bangor Daily News*
MD	1988, 1992	*Baltimore Sun*
MA	1988, 1990	*Boston Globe*
MI	1988, 1990	*Detroit News*
MN	1988, 1990	*Minneapolis Star Tribune*
MS	1988	*Clarion-Ledger*
MO	1988, 1992	*St. Louis Post-Dispatch*
MT	1988, 1990	*Billings Gazette*
NE	1988, 1990	*Omaha World-Herald*
NV	1992	*Las Vegas Review Journal*
NH	1990, 1992	*Manchester Union-Leader*
NJ	1988, 1990	*Newark Star-Ledger*
NM	1988, 1990	*Albuquerque Journal*
NY	1988, 1992	*New York Daily News*
NC	1990, 1992	*Raleigh News & Observer*
ND	1988, 1992	*Forum Fargo-Moorehead*
OH	1988, 1992	*Cleveland Plain Dealer*
OK	1990, 1992	*Oklahoma City Daily Oklahoman*
OR	1990, 1992	*Portland Oregonian*
PA	1988, 1992	*Philadelphia Inquirer*

RI	1988, 1990	*Providence Journal*
SC	1990, 1992	*Columbia State*
SD	1990, 1992	*Argus Leader (Sioux Falls)*
TN	1988, 1990	*Memphis Commercial Appeal*
TX	1988, 1990	*Houston Chronicle*
UT	1988, 1992	*Salt Lake Tribune*
VT	1988, 1992	*Burlington Free Press*
VA	1988	*Norfolk Virginian-Pilot*
WA	1988, 1992	*Seattle Times*
WV	1988, 1990	*Daily Progress (Charlottesville)*
WI	1988, 1992	*Milwaukee Times*
WY	1988, 1990	*Casper Star-Tribune*

Appendix D _____

NEWSPAPER CONTENT ANALYSIS CODE SHEET

Variable Description   **Code**

Newspaper code   ___ ___ ___
Date (month/day/year)   ___ ___ ___ ___ ___ ___
Article number (sequential)   ___ ___ ___
Location of article (page number)   ___ ___ ___
Location of article (section)   ___ ___
Length of article (number of paragraphs)   ___ ___ ___

Type of Article

   1 = News story   4 = News analysis   ___
   2 = Column   5 = Other,
   3 = Editorial   specify ___

Type of Race   ___

   1 = Incumbent race   2 = Open race

Candidate Mentioned in Headline   ___

   1 = Only incumbent/only winner in open race
   2 = Only challenger/only loser in open race
   3 = Both candidates
   4 = Neither candidates

Number of Paragraphs

   About incumbent/winner in open race   ___ ___ ___
   About challenger/loser in open race   ___ ___ ___

Tone of Headline: Incumbent/Winner in Open Race

   1 = Positive   ___
   2 = Negative
   3 = Mixture
   4 = Indifferent/neutral
   0 = Not about candidate

Tone of Headline: Challenger/ Loser in Open Race

   1 = Positive   ___
   2 = Negative
   3 = Mixture
   4 = Indifferent/neutral

0 = Not about candidates

Tone of Article: Incumbent/Winner in Open Race

1 = Positive   _____
2 = Negative
3 = Mixture
4 = Indifferent/neutral
0 = Not about candidate

Tone of Article: Challenger/Loser in Open Race

1 = Positive   _____
2 = Negative
3 = Mixture
4 = Indifferent/neutral
0 = Not about candidate

Criticisms of Incumbent/Winner in Open Race   Source _____   Number _____ _____
1 = By Opponent   Source _____
2 = By Other Source   Source _____
3 = Unattributed
0 = Not Criticized

Criticisms of Challenger/Loser in Open Race   Source _____   Number _____ _____
1 = By opponent   Source _____
2 = By other source   Source _____
3 = Unattributed
0 = Not criticized

Horse Race Paragraphs about Incumbent/Winner in Open Race   _____ _____

If poll results are given, what is the percentage for incumbent/winner in open race?   _____ _____

Horse Race Content about Incumbent/Winner in Open Race   _____

5 = Sure winner
4 = Likely winner
3 = Competitive
2 = Likely loser
1 = Sure loser
0 = No mention of horse Race

Horse Race Paragraphs about Challenger/Loser in Open Race   _____ _____

If Poll Results Are Given, What Is the Percentage for Challenger/Loser in Open Race?   _____ _____

*Horse Race Content about Challenger/Loser
in Open Race*   ____

5 = Sure winner
4 = Likely winner
3 = Competitive
2 = Likely loser
1 = Sure loser
0 = No mention of horse race

Endorsement in Newspaper   ____

1 = Incumbent/winner in open race
2 = Challenger/loser in open race
0 = No endorsement

*Campaign Resources of Incumbent/Winner
in Open Race*   ____

1 = Positive resources mentioned
2 = Mixed resources mentioned
3 = Negative resources mentioned
0 = No resources mentioned

*Campaign Resources of Challenger/Loser in
Open Race*   ____

1 = Positive resources mentioned
2 = Mixed resources mentioned
3 = Negative resources mentioned
0 = No resources mentioned

Traits (Number of Mentions)

	Inc/Winner	Chall/Loser		Inc/Winner	Chall/Loser
Honest	____ ____	____ ____	Dishonest	____ ____	____ ____
Trustworthy	____ ____	____ ____	Untrustworthy	____ ____	____ ____
Compassionate	____ ____	____ ____	Insensitive	____ ____	____ ____
Intelligent	____ ____	____ ____	Unintelligent	____ ____	____ ____
Effective	____ ____	____ ____	Ineffective	____ ____	____ ____
Knowledgeable	____ ____	____ ____	Uninformed	____ ____	____ ____
Hardworking	____ ____	____ ____	Lazy	____ ____	____ ____
Independent	____ ____	____ ____	Dependent	____ ____	____ ____
Strong leader	____ ____	____ ____	Weak leader	____ ____	____ ____
Consistent, stable	____ ____	____ ____	Erratic (flip-flop)	____ ____	____ ____
Aggressive	____ ____	____ ____	Passive	____ ____	____ ____
Experienced	____ ____	____ ____	Inexperienced	____ ____	____ ____
Moral	____ ____	____ ____	Immoral	____ ____	____ ____
Ambitious	____ ____	____ ____	Power-hungry	____ ____	____ ____
Ties to the state	____ ____	____ ____	No ties to state	____ ____	____ ____
Elective experience	____ ____	____ ____	Lack of elective exp.	____ ____	____ ____
War record	____ ____	____ ____	Lack of war record	____ ____	____ ____

Cares for state ___ ___ ___ ___ No care for state ___ ___ ___ ___
Washington Ties + ___ ___ ___ ___ Washington ties − ___ ___ ___ ___
Special life exp. ___ ___ ___ ___ Other ___ ___ ___ ___ ___

Ideology of Incumbent/Winner in Open Race
Mentions ___   Content ___
  1 = Liberal   Content ___
  2 = Moderate   Content ___
  3 = Conservative
  0 = Not mentioned

Ideology of Challenger/Loser in Open Race
Mentions ___   Content ___
  1 = Liberal   Content ___
  2 = Moderate   Content ___
  3 = Conservative
  0 = Not mentioned

Debate Outcome for Incumbent/Winner in Open Race
Mentions ___   Content ___
  1 = Gained something
  2 = Mixtures of gains and losses
  3 = Lost something
  0 = Not mentioned

Debate Outcome for Challenger/Loser in Open Race
Mentions ___   Content ___
  1 = Gained something
  2 = Mixtures of gains and losses
  3 = Lost something
  0 = Not mentioned

Assessments of Ads of Incumbent/Winner in Open Race
Mentions ___   Content ___
  1 = Are ads portrayed as accurate by press?
  2 = Are ads described as accurate and
      inaccurate by press?
  3 = Are ads portrayed as inaccurate by
      press?

Assessments of Ads of Challenger/Loser in Open Race
Mentions ___   Content ___
  1 = Are ads portrayed as accurate by press?
  2 = Are ads described as accurate and
      inaccurate by press?
  3 = Are ads portrayed as inaccurate by
      press?

Issues

Responsibility (1 = Credit, 2 = Blame, 0 = No mention)
A. Spending (1 = Up, 2 = Same, 3 = Down, 0 = No mention)

B.   Regulation (1 = Up, 2 = Same, 3 = Down, 0 = No mention)
C.   Plans or programs (1 = Yes, 2 = No, 0 = No mention)
D.   Social issues (1 = Pro, 2 = Anti, 0 = No mention)

A.	Incumbent/Winner in Open Race			Challenger/Loser in Open Race		
	# Mentions	*Spending*	*Responsibility*	*# Mentions*	*Spending*	*Responsibility*
Defense	___ ___	___	___	___ ___	___	___
Foreign aid	___ ___	___	___	___ ___	___	___
Cent. America	___ ___	___	___	___ ___	___	___
Health	___ ___	___	___	___ ___	___	___
Elderly	___ ___	___	___	___ ___	___	___
Welfare	___ ___	___	___	___ ___	___	___
Education	___ ___	___	___	___ ___	___	___
Drugs	___ ___	___	___	___ ___	___	___
AIDS	___ ___	___	___	___ ___	___	___
Day care	___ ___	___	___	___ ___	___	___
Farm	___ ___	___	___	___ ___	___	___
S&L bailout	___ ___	___	___	___ ___	___	___
Big gov't	___ ___	___	___	___ ___	___	___
Other _____	___ ___	___	___	___ ___	___	___

B.	Incumbent/Winner in Open Race			Challenger/Loser in Open Race		
	# Mentions	*Regulate*	*Responsibility*	*# Mentions*	*Regulate*	*Responsibility*
Business	___ ___	___	___	___ ___	___	___
Oil prices	___ ___	___	___	___ ___	___	___
Trade	___ ___	___	___	___ ___	___	___
Environment	___ ___	___	___	___ ___	___	___
Other _____	___ ___	___	___	___ ___	___	___

C.	Incumbent/Winner in Open Race			Challenger/Loser in Open Race		
	# Mentions	*Plans*	*Responsibility*	*# Mentions*	*Plans*	*Responsibility*
Econ.–general	___ ___	___	___	___ ___	___	___
Inflation	___ ___	___	___	___ ___	___	___
Unemployment	___ ___	___	___	___ ___	___	___
Jobs	___ ___	___	___	___ ___	___	___
Taxes	___ ___	___	___	___ ___	___	___
Budget	___ ___	___	___	___ ___	___	___
Other _____	___ ___	___	___	___ ___	___	___

D.	Incumbent/Winner in Open Race			Challenger/Loser in Open Race		
	# Mentions	*Social*	*Responsibility*	*# Mentions*	*Social*	*Responsibility*
Abortion	___ ___	___	___	___ ___	___	___
Civil rights	___ ___	___	___	___ ___	___	___
Prayer Sch.	___ ___	___	___	___ ___	___	___
Fam. values	___ ___	___	___	___ ___	___	___
Apartheid	___ ___	___	___	___ ___	___	___
Gulf War	___ ___	___	___	___ ___	___	___
Panama	___ ___	___	___	___ ___	___	___

Israel	___ ___ ___	___	___ ___ ___	___
Yugoslavia	___ ___ ___	___	___ ___ ___	___
Death penalty	___ ___ ___	___	___ ___ ___	___
Other _____	___ ___ ___	___	___ ___ ___	___

Content of Article (Mainly About)

1 = Polls	3 = Scandal	5 = Ads	7 = Traits	9 = Mixture	___ ___
2 = Debates	4 = Visits by Leaders	6 = Issues	8 = Biography	10 = Other (Specify)	

_____

References ————————————————————————

Abramowitz, Alan I. 1980. "A Comparison of Voting for U.S. Senator and Representative." *American Political Science Review*, 74: 633–640.

Abramowitz, Alan I. 1988. "Explaining Senate Election Outcomes." *American Political Science Review*, 82: 385–403.

Abramowitz, Alan I., and Jeffrey A. Segal. 1990. "Beyond Willie Horton and the Pledge of Allegiance: National Issues in the 1988 Elections." *Legislative Studies Quarterly*, 15: 565–580.

Abramowitz, Alan I., and Jeffrey A. Segal. 1992. *Senate Elections*. Ann Arbor: University of Michigan Press.

Abramson, Paul R., John H. Aldrich, and David W. Rohde. 1995. *Change and Continuity in the 1992 Elections*. Washington, D.C.: Congressional Quarterly Press.

Aldrich, John H. 1980. *Before the Convention: Strategies and Choices in Presidential Nomination Campaigns*. Chicago: University of Chicago Press.

Alexander, Herbert E. 1992. *Financing Politics: Money, Elections, and Political Reform*. Washington, D.C.: Congressional Quarterly Press.

Alger, Dean. 1996. "Constructing Campaign Messages and Public Understanding: 1990 Wellstone-Boshwitz in Minnesota." In Ann Crigler, ed., *The Psychology of Political Communication*. Ann Arbor: University of Michigan Press.

Ansolabehere, Steven, Roy Behr, and Shanto Iyengar. 1993. *The Media Game: American Politics in the Television Age*. New York: Macmillan.

Ansolabehere, Steven, and Shanto Iyengar. 1995. *Going Negative*. New York: Free Press.

Ansolabehere, Steven, Shanto Iyengar, Adam Simon, and Nicholas Valentine. 1994. "Does Attack Advertising Demobilize the Electorate?" *American Political Science Review*, 88: 829–838.

Axelrod, Robert. 1972. "Where the Votes Come From: An Analysis of Electoral Coalitions." *American Political Science Review*, 66: 11–20.

Axelrod, Robert. 1982. "Communication." *American Political Science Review*, 76: 394–395.

Bagdikian, Ben H. 1990. *The Media Monopoly*. Boston: Beacon Press.

Bartels, Larry. 1986. "Issue Voting under Uncertainty: An Empirical Test." *American Journal of Political Science*, 25: 112–118.

Bartels, Larry M. 1988. *Presidential Primaries and the Dynamics of Public Choice*. Princeton, N.J.: Princeton University Press.

Bartels, Larry M. 1991. "Instrumental and 'Quasi-Instrumental' Variables." *American Journal of Political Science*, 35: 777–791.

Bartels, Larry M. 1993. "Messages Received: The Political Impact of Media Exposure." *American Political Science Review*, 87: 267–285.

Basil, Michael, Caroline Schooler, and Byron Reeves. 1991. "Positive and Negative Political Advertising: Effectiveness of Ads and Perceptions of Candidates." In

Frank Biocca, ed., *Television and Political Advertising, vol. 1: Psychological Processes*. Hillsdale, N.J.: Lawrence Erlbaum Associates.

Baumer, Donald C., and Howard J. Gold. 1995. "Party Images and the American Electorate." *American Politics Quarterly*, 23: 33–61.

Bennett, W. Lance. 1996. "An Introduction to Journalism Norms and Representations of Politics." *Political Communication*, 13: 373–384.

Berelson, Bernard, Paul Lazarsfeld, and William McPhee. 1954. *Voting: A Study of Opinion Formation in a Presidential Campaign*. Chicago: University of Chicago Press.

Biersack, Robert, Paul Herrnson, and Clyde Wilcox. 1993. "Seeds for Success: Early Money in Congressional Elections." *Legislative Studies Quarterly*, 18: 535–553.

Box-Steffensmeier, Janet M. 1996. "A Dynamic Analysis of the Role of War-Chests in Campaign Strategy." *American Journal of Political Science*, 40: 352–371.

Brady, Henry E., and Richard Johnston. 1987. "What's the Primary Message: Horserace or Issue Journalism." In Gary R. Orren and Nelson Polsby, eds., *Media and Momentum*. Chatham, N.J.: Chatham House.

Brians, Craig Leonard, and Martin P. Wattenberg. 1996. "Campaign Issue Knowledge and Salience: Comparing Reception from TV Commercials, TV News and Newspapers." *American Journal of Political Science*, 40: 172–193.

Buchanan, Bruce. 1991. *Electing a President*. Austin: University of Texas Press.

Caldeira, Gregory, Samuel C. Patterson, and Gregory Markko. 1985. "The Mobilization of Voters in Congressional Elections." *Journal of Politics*, 47: 490–509.

Calvert, Randall L., and John A. Ferejohn. 1983. "Coattail Voting in Recent Presidential Elections." *American Political Science Review*, 77: 407–419.

Campbell, Angus, Philip Converse, Warren Miller, and Donald Stokes. 1960. *The American Voter*. New York: Wiley.

Campbell, Angus, Philip Converse, and Willard L. Rogers. 1976. *The Quality of American Life*. New York: Russell Sage Foundation.

Campbell, James E., and Joe A. Sumners. 1990. "Presidential Coattails in Senate Elections." *American Political Science Review*, 84: 513–524.

Chomsky, Noam, and Edward Herman. 1989. *Manufacturing Consent*. New York: St. Martin's Press.

Clarke, Peter, and Susan Evans. 1983. *Covering Campaigns: Journalism in Congressional Elections*. Stanford, Calif.: Stanford University Press.

Clarke, Peter, and Eric Fredin. 1978. "Newspapers, Television, and Political Reasoning." *Public Opinion Quarterly*, 42: 143–160.

Congressional Quarterly. October 15, 1988, 2880–2954. Washington, D.C.: Congressional Quarterly, Inc.

Congressional Quarterly. October 13, 1990, 3280–3358. Washington, D.C.: Congressional Quarterly, Inc.

Congressional Quarterly. October 24, 1992, 3339–3355. Washington, D.C.: Congressional Quarterly, Inc.

Conover, Pamela J., and Stanley Feldman. 1989. "Candidate Perception in an Ambiguous World: Campaigns, Cues, and Inference Processes." *American Journal of Political Science*, 33: 912–940.

Converse, Jean, and Stanley Presser. 1986. *Survey Questions: Handcrafting the Standardized Questionnaire*. Beverly Hills, Calif.: Sage.

Converse, Philip E. 1962. "Information Flow and Stability of Partisan Attitudes." *Public Opinion Quarterly*, 26: 578–599.

Converse, Philip E. 1964. "Nature of Belief Systems in Mass Publics." In David Apter, ed., *Ideology and Discontent*. New York: Free Press.

Converse, Philip E. 1976. *Dynamics of Party Support*. Beverly Hills, Calif.: Sage Publications.

Converse, Philip E. 1990. "Popular Representation and the Distribution of Information." In John A. Ferejohn and James H. Kuklinski, eds., *Information and Democratic Processes*. Urbana: University of Illinois Press.

Converse, Philip E., and Gregory Markus. 1979. "Plus Change . . . The New CPS Panel Study." *American Political Science Review*, 73: 32–49.

Cook, Timothy. 1989. *Making Laws and Making News: Media Strategies in the U.S. House of Representatives*. Washington, D.C.: Brookings Institution.

Cook, Timothy. 1996. "Afterword: Political Values and Production Values." *Political Communication*, 3: 469–482.

Dahl, Robert. 1956. *A Preface to Democratic Theory*. Chicago: University of Chicago Press.

Dalager, Jon K. 1996. "Voters, Issues, and Elections: Are the Candidates' Messages Getting Through?" *Journal of Politics*, 58: 486–515.

Davis, Richard. 1996. *The Press and American Politics: The New Mediator*. Upper Saddle River, N.J.: Prentice Hall.

Delli Carpini, Michael X., and Scott Keeter. 1993. "Measuring Political Knowledge: Putting First Things First." *American Journal of Political Science*, 37: 1179–1206.

Delli Carpini, Michael X., and Scott Keeter. 1996. *What Americans Know About Politics and Why It Matters*. New Haven, Conn.: Yale University Press.

Diamond, Edwin, and Stephen Bates. 1984. *The Spot*. Cambridge, MA: MIT Press.

Downs, Anthony. 1957. *An Economic Theory of Democracy*. New York: Harper and Row.

Drew, Dan, and David Weaver. 1991. "Voter Learning in the 1988 Presidential Election: Did the Debates and the Media Matter?" *Journalism Quarterly*, 68: 27–37.

Edelman, Murray J. 1988. *Constructing the Political Spectacle*. Chicago: University of Chicago Press.

Enelow, James, and Melvin J. Hinich. 1981. "A New Approach to Voter Uncertainty in the Downsian Spatial Model." *American Journal of Political Science*, 25: 483–493.

Erbring, Lutz, Edie N. Goldenberg, and Arthur H. Miller. 1980. "Front-Page News and Real World Cues: A New Look at Agenda-Setting by the Media." *American Journal of Political Science*, 24: 16–49.

Erikson, Robert S., and Kent L. Tedin. 1995. *American Public Opinion: Its Origins, Content, and Impact*. Boston: Allyn and Bacon.

Feldman, Stanley, and Pamela J. Conover. 1983. "Candidates, Issues and Voters: The Role of Inference in Political Perception." *Journal of Politics*, 45: 811–839.

Fenno, Richard F. 1978. *Homestyle: House Members in Their Districts*. Boston: Little, Brown and Company.

Fenno, Richard F. 1996. *Senators on the Campaign Trail*. Norman: University of Oklahoma Press.

Ferejohn, John A., and Randall L. Calvert. 1984. "Presidential Coattails in Historical Perspective." *American Journal of Political Science*, 28: 127–146.

Filer, John E., Lawrence W. Kenny, and Rebecca B. Morton. 1993. "Redistribution, Income, and Voting." *American Journal of Political Science*, 37: 63–87.

Finkel, Steven. 1993. "The Impact of the Campaign in Recent Presidential Elections: Minimal Effects Revisited." *Journal of Politics*, 55:1–21

Finkel, Steven, and John Geer. 1997. "A Spot Check: Casting Doubt on the Demobilizing Effect of Attack Advertising." *American Journal of Political Science*, 42: 573–595.

Fiorina, Morris P. 1977. *Representatives, Roll Calls and Constituencies*. Lexington, Mass.: D. C. Heath and Company.

Fiorina, Morris P. 1981. *Retrospective Voting in American National Elections*. New Haven, Conn.: Yale University Press.

Fiorina, Morris P. 1996. *Divided Government*. Boston: Allyn and Bacon.

Fiske, Susan T., Richard R. Lau, and Richard A. Smith. 1990. "On the Varieties and Utilities of Political Expertise." *Social Cognition*, 8: 31–48.

Fowler, Linda. 1993. *Candidates, Congress, and the American Democracy*. Ann Arbor: University of Michigan Press.

Franklin, Charles H. 1991. "Eschewing Obfuscation? Campaigns and the Perceptions of U.S. Senate Incumbents." *American Political Science Review*, 85: 1193–1214.

Friedrich, Robert J. 1982. "In Defense of Multiplicative Terms in Multiple Regression Equations." *American Journal of Political Science*, 26: 797–833.

Gans, Herbert J. 1980. *Deciding What's News: A Study of CBS Evening News, NBC Nightly News, Newsweek, and Time*. New York: Vintage Books.

Garramone, Gina. 1984. "Voter Response to Negative Political Ads: Clarifying Sponsor Effects." *Journalism Quarterly*, 61: 250–259.

Geer, John G. 1992. "Searching for Differences: Campaigns, Competition, and Political Advertising." Paper presented at the Annual Meeting of the Southern Political Science Association, Atlanta, Georgia.

Goldenberg, Edie N., and Michael W. Traugott. 1984. *Campaigning for Congress*. Washington, D.C.: Congressional Quarterly Press.

Goldenberg, Edie N., and Michael W. Traugott. 1987. "Mass Media Effects in Recognizing and Rating Candidates in U.S. Senate Elections." In Jan Vermeer, ed., *Campaigns in the News: Mass Media and Congressional Elections*. New York: Greenwood Press.

Goldenberg, Edie N., Michael W. Traugott, and Kim F. Kahn. 1988. "Voter Assessments of Presidential and Senatorial Candidates." Paper presented at the Midwest Political Science Association Annual Meeting, Chicago.

Graber, Doris. 1989. *Mass Media and American Politics*. Washington, D.C.: Congressional Quarterly Press.

Graber, Doris. 1993. *Mass Media and American Politics*. Washington, D.C.: Congressional Quarterly Press.

Green, Donald Philip, and Jonathon S. Krasno. 1988. "Salvation for the Spendthrift Incumbent: Reestimating the Effects of Campaign Spending in House Elections." *American Journal of Political Science*, 32: 884–907.

Green, Donald Philip, and Jonathan S. Krasno. 1990. "Rebuttal to Jacobson's 'New Evidence for Old Arguments.'" *American Journal of Political Science*, 34: 363–372.

Gutmann, Amy. 1993. "The Disharmony of Democracy." In John W. Chapman and Ian Shapiro, eds., *Democratic Community*. New York: New York University Press.

Hallin, Daniel C. 1986. *The "Uncensored War": The Media and Vietnam.* New York: Oxford University Press.

Hamilton, D. L., and M. P. Zanna. 1974. "Context Effects in Impression Formation: Changes in Connotative Meaning. *Journal of Personality and Social Psychology,*29: 649–654.

Herrnson, Paul S. 1995. *Congressional Elections: Campaigning at Home and in Washington.* Washington, D.C.: Congressional Quarterly Press.

Hess, Stephen. 1996. *News and Newsmaking.* Washington, D.C. : Brookings Institution.

Hetherington, Marc J. 1996. "The Media's Role in Forming Voters' National Economic Evaluations in 1992." *American Journal of Political Science,* 40: 372–395.

Hibbing, John R., and John R. Alford. 1981. "The Electoral Impact of Economic Conditions: Who Is Held Responsible?" *American Journal of Political Science,* 25: 423–439.

Hibbing, John R., and John R. Alford. 1982. "Economic Conditions and the Forgotten Side of Congress: A Foray into U.S. Senate Elections." *British Journal of Political Science,* 27: 808–819.

Hibbing, John R., and Sara L. Brandes. 1983. "State Population and the Electoral Success of U.S. Senators." *American Journal of Political Science,* 27: 808–819.

Hinckley, Barbara. 1980. "House Reelections and Senate Defeats: The Role of the Challenger." *British Journal of Political Science,* 10: 441–460.

Holbrook, Thomas M. 1996. *Do Campaigns Matter?* Thousands Oaks, Calif.: Sage Publications.

Iyengar, Shanto. 1991. *Is Anyone Responsible? How the Media Frames Public Issues.* Chicago: University of Chicago Press.

Iyengar, Shanto, and Donald R. Kinder. 1987. *News That Matters.* Chicago: University of Chicago Press.

Iyengar, Shanto, Mark D. Peters, and Donald R Kinder. 1982. "Experimental Demonstrations of the 'Not So Minimal' Consequences of Television News Programs." *American Political Science Review,* 76: 848–858.

Jacobson, Gary C. 1980. *Money in Congressional Elections.* New Haven, Conn.: Yale University Press.

Jacobson, Gary C. 1987. *The Politics of Congressional Elections.* Boston: Little, Brown and Company.

Jacobson, Gary C. 1990. "The Effects of Campaign Spending in House Elections: New Evidence for Old Arguments. *American Journal of Political Science,* 34: 334–362.

Jacobson, Gary C. 1992. *The Politics of Congressional Elections.* New York: Harper Collins.

Jacobson, Gary C. 1997. *The Politics of Congressional Elections.* New York: Longman.

Jacobson, Gary C., and Samuel Kernell. 1983. *Strategy and Choice in Congressional Elections.* New Haven, Conn.: Yale University Press.

Jacobson, Gary C., and Raymond Wolfinger. 1989. "Information and Voting in California Senate Elections." *Legislative Studies Quarterly,* 14: 509–524.

Jamieson, Kathleen Hall. 1984. *Packaging the Presidency: A History and Criticism of Presidential Campaign Advertising.* Oxford: Oxford University Press.

Jamieson, Kathleen Hall. 1992. *Dirty Politics*. Oxford: Oxford University Press.

Johnson-Cartee, Karen S., and Gary Copeland. 1989. "Southern Voters' Reaction to Negative Political Ads in 1986 Election." *Journalism Quarterly*, 66: 188–193, 196.

Johnson-Cartee, Karen S., and Gary A. Copeland. 1991. *Negative Political Advertising: Coming of Age*. Hillsdale, N.J.: Lawrence Earlbaum Associates.

Johnston, J. 1972. *Econometric Methods*. 2d ed. New York: McGraw-Hill.

Joslyn, Richard. 1984. *Mass Media and Elections*. Boston: Addison-Wesley.

Judd, C. M., and M. A. Milburn. 1980. "The Structure of Attitude Systems in the General Public: Comparison of a Structural Equation Model." *American Sociological Review*, 45: 627–643.

Just, Marion R., Ann N. Crigler, Dean E. Alger, Timothy E. Cook, Montague Kern, and Darrell M. West. 1996. *Crosstalk: Citizens, Candidates and the Media in a Presidential Campaign*. Chicago: University of Chicago Press.

Kahn, Kim Fridkin. 1991. "Senate Elections in the News: An Examination of the Characteristics and Determinants of Campaign Coverage." *Legislative Studies Quarterly*, 16: 349–374.

Kahn, Kim Fridkin, and John G. Geer. 1994. "Creating Impressions: An Experimental Investigation of the Effectiveness of Television Advertising." *Political Behavior*, 16: 93–115.

Kahn, Kim Fridkin 1996. *The Political Consequences of Being a Woman: How Stereotypes Influence the Content and Impact of Statewide Campaigns*. New York: Columbia University Press.

Kahn, Kim Fridkin, and Patrick J. Kenney. 1997. "A Model of Candidate Evaluations in Senate Elections: The Impact of Campaign Intensity." *Journal of Politics*, 49: 1173–1205.

Kahneman, Daniel, and Amos Tversky. 1984. "Choices, Values, and Frames." *American Psychologist*, 39: 341–350.

Kaid, Lynda L., and Dorothy K. Davidson. 1986. "Elements of Videostyle: Candidate Presentations through Television Advertising." In L. L. Kaid, D. Nimmo, and K. R. Sanders, eds., *New Perspectives on Political Advertising*. Carbondale: Southern Illinois University Press.

Kenney, Patrick J., and Tom W. Rice. 1988. "Presidential Prenomination Preferences and Candidate Evaluations." *American Political Science Review*, 82: 1309–1320.

Kerbel, Matthew Robert. 1995. *Remote and Controlled: Media Politics in a Cynical Age*. Boulder, Colo.: Westview Press.

Kern, Montague. 1989. *30-Second Politics: Political Advertising in the 80's*. New York: Praeger.

Kernell, Samuel. 1977. "Presidential Popularity and Negative Voting: An Alternative Explanation of Midterm Congressional Decline of the President's Party." *American Political Science Review*, 71: 44–66.

Key, V. O., Jr. 1966. *Responsible Electorate*. Cambridge, Mass.: Harvard University Press.

Kinder, Donald R. 1983. "Diversity and Complexity in American Public Opinion." In *Political Science: The State of the Discipline*, ed. Ada W. Finifter. Washington, D.C.: American Political Science Association.

Kinder, Donald R. 1986. "Presidential Character Revisited." In Richard R. Lau and

David O. Sears, eds., *Political Cognition*. Hillsdale, N.J.: Lawrence Erlbaum Associates.

Kinder, Donald R., and Robert P. Abelson. 1981. "Appraising Presidential Candidates: Personality and Affect in the 1980 Campaign." Paper presented at the American Political Science Association Meeting, New York.

Kinder, Donald R., and Roderick D. Kiewiet. 1979. "Economic Discontent and Political Behavior: The role of Personal Greivances and Collective Economic Judgements in Congressional Voting." *American Journal of Political Science*, 23: 495–527.

Kinder, Donald R., and Lynn M. Sanders. 1990. "Mimicking Political Debate with Survey Questions: The Case of White Opinion on Affirmative Action for Blacks." *Social Cognition*, 8: 83–103.

Kinder, Donald R., and Lynn M. Sanders. 1996. *Divided By Color: Racial Politics and Democratic Ideals*. Chicago: University of Chicago Press.

Kinder, Donald R., and David O. Sears. 1985. "Public Opinion and Political Action." In Gardner Lindzey and Elliot Aronson, eds., *Handbook of Social Psychology*. New York: Random House.

King, Gary. 1989. *Unifying Political Methodology*. Cambridge: Cambridge University Press.

Kingdon, John W. 1968. *Candidates for Office: Beliefs and Strategies*. New York: Random House.

Knoke, David, and Peter J. Burke. 1980. *Log-Linear Models*. Quantative Applications in the Social Science Series. Newbury Park, Calif.: Sage Publications.

Kramer, Gerald H. 1971. "Short-Term Fluctuations in U.S. Voting Behavior, 1896–1964." *American Political Science Review*, 65: 131–143.

Kramer, Gerald H. 1983. "The Ecological Fallacy Revisited: Aggregate versus Individual Level Findings on Economics and Elections and Sociotropic Voting." *American Political Science Review*, 77: 92–111.

Krasno, Jonathan S. 1994. *Challengers, Competition, and Reelection: Comparing Senate and House Elections*. New Haven, Conn.: Yale University Press.

Krasno, Jonathan S., Donald Philip Green, and Jonathan A. Cowden. 1994. "The Dynamics of Fundraising in House Elections." *Journal of Politics*, 56: 459–474.

Krasno, Jonathan S., and Donald Philip Green. 1988. "Preempting Quality Challengers in U.S. House Elections." *Journal of Politics*, 50: 920–936.

Krosnick, Jon A. 1990. "Expertise and Political Psychology." *Social Cognition*, 8: 1–8.

Krosnick, Jon A., and Donald R. Kinder. 1990. "Altering the Foundations of Support for the President Through Priming." *American Political Science Review*, 84: 497–512.

Lang, Annie. 1991. "Emotion, Formal Features, and Memory for Televised Political Advertisements." In Frank Biocca, ed., *Television and Political Advertising, Volume 1: Psychological Processes*. Hillsdale, N.J.: Lawrence Erlbaum Associates.

Larson, Stephanie Greco. 1990. "Information and Learning in a Congressional district: Social Experiment." *American Journal of Political Science*, 34: 1102–1118.

Lau, Richard. 1985. "Two Explanations for Negativity Effects in Political Behavior." *American Journal of Political Science*, 29: 119–138.

Lazarsfeld, Paul, Bernard Berelson, and Hazel Gaudet. 1944. *The People's Choice*. New York: Columbia University Press.

Leary, Mary Ellen. 1977. *Phantom Politics: Campaigning in California.* Washington, D.C.: Public Affairs Press.

Lee, Frances B., and Bruce I. Oppenheimer. 1997. "Senate Apportionment: Competitiveness and Partisan Advantage." *Legislative Studies Quarterly*, 22: 3–24.

Lewis, Neil A. 1990. "Folksy and Sharp-Tongued, Simpson Makes National Splash." *Casper Star-Tribune*, A3.

Lewis-Beck, Michael. 1980. *Applied Regression.* Quantitative Applications in the Social Sciences. Newbury Park, Calif.: Sage Publications.

Lichter, S. Robert, Stanley Rothman, and Linda S. Lichter. 1986. *The Media Elites.* Bethesda, Md: Adler and Adler.

Lichter, S. Robert, Daniel Amundson, and Richard Noyes. 1988. *The Video Campaign: Network Coverage of the 1988 Primaries.* Washington, D.C.: American Enterprise Institute for Public Policy Research.

Lodge, Milton G., and Ruth Hamill. 1986. "Partisan Schema for Political Information Processing." *American Political Science Review*, 80: 505–519.

Luntz, Frank I. 1988. *Candidates Consultants and Campaigns: The Style and Substance of American Electioneering.* Oxford: Basil Blackwell.

Lupia, Arthur. 1994. "Shortcuts versus Encyclopedias: Information and Voting Behavior in California Insurance Reform Elections." *American Political Science Review*, 88: 63–76.

Lusk, Cynthia, and Charles M. Judd. 1988. "Political Expertise and the Structural Mediators of Candidate Evaluations." *Journal of Experimental Social Psychology*, 24: 105–126.

Luskin, Robert. 1987. "Measuring Political Sophistication." *American Journal of Political Science*, 31: 856–899.

MacKuen, Michael. 1981. "Social Communication and the Mass Policy Agenda." In *More Than News.* Beverly Hills, Calif.: Sage Publications.

MacKuen, Michael. 1983. "Political Drama, Economic Conditions, and the Dynamics of Presidential Popularity." *American Journal of Political Science*, 26: 165–192.

Madison, James. 1964. "Federalist #49." In *The Federalist Papers.* New York: Simon and Schuster.

Magleby, David B., and Candice J. Nelson. 1990. *The Money Chase: Congressional Campaign Finance Reform.* Washington, D.C.: Brookings Institution.

Mann, Thomas. 1978. *Unsafe at Any Margin.* Washington, D.C.: American Enterprise Institute.

Mann, Thomas, and Raymond Wolfinger. 1980. "Candidates and Parties in Congressional Elections." *American Political Science Review*, 74: 617–632.

Markus, Gregory B. 1979. *Analyzing Panel Data.* Beverly Hills, Calif.: Sage Publications.

Markus, Gregory B. 1982. "Political Attitudes during an Election Year: A Report on the 1980 NES Panel Study." *American Political Science Review*, 76: 538–560.

Markus, Gregory B., and Philip E. Converse. 1979. "A Dynamic Simultaneous Equation Model of Electoral Choice." *American Political Science Review*, 73: 1055–1070.

Mayer, William G. 1993. "Poll Trends: Trends in Media Usage." *Public Opinion Quarterly*, 57: 593–611.

Mayhew, David. 1974. *Congress: The Electoral Connection*. New Haven, Conn.: Yale University Press.

McGraw, Kathleen M., and Neil Pinney. 1990. "The Effects of General and Domain-Specific Expertise on Political Memory and Judgment." *Social Cognition*, 8: 9–30.

McGuire, William J. 1968. "The Nature of Attitudes and Attitude Change." In Gardner Lindzey and Elliot Aronson, eds., *The Handbook of Social Psychology*. Reading, Mass.: Addison-Wesley.

McLeod, Jack M., and Daniel McDonald. 1985. "Beyond Simple Exposure: Media Orientations and Their Impact on Political Processes." *Communication Research*, 12: 3–34.

Mill, John Stuart. [1859] 1951. "On Liberty." In *Three Essays*. Oxford: Oxford University Press.

Mill, John Stuart. [1861] 1991. "Considerations on Representative Government." In *On Liberty and Other Essays*. Oxford: Oxford University Press.

Miller, Arthur. 1990. "Public Judgments of Senate and House Candidates." *Legislative Studies Quarterly*, 15: 525–542.

Miller, Arthur, Martin Wattenburg, and Oksana Malanchuk. 1986. "Schematic Assessments of Presedential Candidates." *American Political Science Review*, 80: 521–540.

Miller, Warren E., and J. Merrill Shanks. 1996. *The New American Voter*. Cambridge, Mass.: Harvard University Press.

Mondak, Jeffrey J . 1995. *Nothing to Read: Newspapers and Elections in a Social Experiment*. Ann Arbor: University of Michigan Press.

Mutz, Diana C. 1995. "Effects of Horse-Race Coverage on Campaign Coffers: Strategic Contributing in Presidential Primaries." *Journal of Politics*, 57: 1015–1042.

Newhagen, John E., and Byron Reeves. 1991. "Emotion and Memory Responses for Negative Political Advertising: A Study of Television Commercials Used in the 1988 Presidential Election." In Frank Biocca, ed., *Television and Political Advertising, vol. 1: Psychological Processes*. Hillsdale, N.J.: Lawrence Erlbaum Associates.

Nie, Norman, Sidney Verba, and John R. Petrocik. 1976. *The Changing American Voter*. Cambridge, Mass.: Harvard University Press.

Otatti, Victor C., and Robert S. Wyer. 1990. "The Cognitive Mediators of Political Choice: Toward a Comprehensive Model of Political Information Processes." In John A. Ferejohn and James H. Kuklinski, eds., *Information and Democratic Processes*. Urbana: University of Illinois Press.

Page, Benjamin. 1978. *Choices and Echoes in Presidential Elections*. Chicago: University of Chicago Press.

Page, Benjamin I. 1996. *Who Deliberates*? Chicago: University of Chicago Press.

Page, Benjamin I., and Calvin Jones. 1979. "Reciprocal Effects of Policy Preferences, Party Loyalties and the Vote." *American Political Science Review*, 73: 1071–1089.

Page, Benjamin I., and Robert Y. Schapiro. 1987. "What Moves Public Opinion?" *American Political Science Review*, 80: 521–540.

Page, Benjamin, and Robert Y. Shapiro. 1992. *The Rational Public: Fifty Years of Trends in Americans' Policy Preferences*. Chicago: University of Chicago Press.

Paletz, David L., and Richard J. Vinegar. 1977. "Presidents on Television: The Effects of Instant Analysis." *Public Opinion Quarterly*, 41: 488–497.

Parenti, Michael. 1993. *Inventing Reality*. 2d ed. New York: St. Martin's Press.

Patterson, Thomas E. 1980. *The Mass Media Election*. New York: Praeger.

Patterson, Thomas E. 1993. *Out of Order*. New York: A. Knopf.

Pfau, Michael, and Henry C. Kenski. 1990. *Attack Politics: Strategy and Defense*. New York: Praeger.

Pitkin, Hanna Fenichel. 1967. *The Concept of Representation*. Berkeley: University of California Press.

Popkin, Samuel. 1991. *The Reasoning Voter*. Chicago: University of Chicago Press.

Rabinowitz, George, and Stuart Elaine MacDonald. 1989. "A Directional Theory of Issue Voting." *American Political Science Review*, 83: 93–122.

Ragsdale, Lyn, and Jerold G. Rusk. 1995. "Candidates, Issues, and Participation in Senate Election." *Legislative Studies Quarterly*, 20: 305–328.

Rahn, Wendy M. 1993. "The Role of Partisan Stereotypes in Information Processing about Political Candidates." *American Journal of Political Science*, 37: 472–496.

Rahn, Wendy M., Jon A. Krosnick, and Marjike Breuning. 1994. "Rationalization and Derivation Processes in Survey Studies of Political Candidate Evaluation." *American Journal of Political Science*, 38: 582–600.

Rapoport, Robert B. 1997. "Partisanship Change in a Candidate-Centered Race." *Journal of Politics*, 59: 185–199.

Rapoport, Robert B., Kelly L. Metcalf, and Jon A. Hartman. 1989. "Candidate Traits and Voter Inferences: An Experimental Study." *Journal of Politics*, 51: 917–932.

Reyes, Robert M., William C. Thompson, and Gordon H. Bower. 1980. "Judgmental Biases Resulting from Differing Availability of Arguments." *Journal of Personality and Social Psychology*, 39: 2–12.

Rivers, Douglas. 1988. "Heterogeneity in Models of Electoral Choice." *American Journal of Political Science*, 32: 737–757.

Robinson, Michael J. 1976. "Public Affairs Television and the Growth of Political Malaise: The Case of 'The Selling of the Pentagon.'" *American Political Science Review*, 70: 409–432.

Robinson, Michael J., and Dennis K. Davis. 1990. "Television News and the Informed Public." *Journal of Communication*, 40: 106–119.

Robinson, Michael J., and Margaret Sheehan. 1983. *Over the Wire and on TV: CBS and UPI in Campaign '80*. New York: Russell Sage Foundation.

Rosenstone, Steven J., and John Mark Hansen. 1993. *Mobilization, Participation, and Democracy in America*. New York: Macmillan.

Sabato, Larry. 1989. *Paying for Elections: The Campaign Finance Thicket*. New York: Priority Press.

Shepsle, Kenneth A. 1972. "The Strategy of Ambiguity: Uncertainty and Electoral Competition." *American Political Science Review*, 66: 555–568.

Sigal, Leon V. 1973. *Reporters and Officials: The Organization and Politics of Newsmaking*. Lexington, Mass.: D. C. Heath.

Smith, Eliot R., and Frederick D. Miller. 1979. "Salience and the Cognitive Mediation of Attribution." *Journal of Personality and Social Psychology*, 37: 2240–2252.

Smith, Eric R.A.N., and Peverill Squire. 1991. "Voter Sophistication and Evaluation of Senate Challengers." Paper presented at the American Political Science Association Annual Meeting, Washington, D.C.

Sniderman, Paul M., James M. Glaser, and Robert Griffin. 1990. "Information and Electoral Choice." In John A. Ferejohn and James H. Kuklinski, eds., *Information and the Democratic Processes*. Urbana: University of Illinois Press.

Squire, Peverill. 1989. "Challengers in U.S. Senate Elections." *Legislative Studies Quarterly*, 14: 531–547.

Squire, Peverill. 1992. "Challenger Quality and Voting Behavior in U.S. Senate Elections." *Legislative Studies Quarterly*, 17: 247–264.

Squire, Peverill, and Eric R.A.N. Smith. 1996. "A Further Examination of Challenger Quality in Senate Elections." *Legislative Studies Quarterly*, 21: 235–248.

Steeper, Fred T. 1978. "Public Response to Gerald Ford's Statements on Eastern Europe in the Second Debate." In George F. Bishop, Robert Meadow, and Marilyn Jackson-Beeck, eds., *Presidential Debates: Media, Electoral and Policy Perspectives*. New York: Praeger Publishing.

Stein, Robert M. 1990. "Economic Voting for Governor and U.S. Senator: The Electoral Consequences of Federalism." *Journal of Politics*, 52: 29–53.

Stewart, Charles. 1989. "A Sequential Model of U.S. Senate Elections." *Legislative Studies Quarterly*, 14: 567–601.

Stokes, Donald E., and Warren E. Miller. 1966. "Party Government and the Saliency of Congress." In Angus Campbell, Philip E. Converse, Warren E. Miller, and Donald E. Stokes, eds., *Elections and the Political Order*. New York: Wiley.

Taylor, Shelly E., and Susan T. Fiske. 1978. "Salience, Attention, and Attribution: Top of the Head Phenomena." In L. Berkowitz, ed., *Advances in Experimental Social Psychology*. New York: Academic Press.

Trish, Barbara. 1997. "Journalistic Decision-Making: The Decision to Cover." Paper presented at the Annual Meeting of the American Political Science Association, Washington, D.C.

Tufte, Edward R. 1975. "Determinants of the Outcomes of Midterm Congressional Elections." *American Political Science Review*, 69: 812–826.

Tversky, Amos, and Daniel Kahneman. 1981. "The Framing of Decisions and the Psychology of Choice." *Science*, 211: 453–458.

Wattenberg, Martin. 1991. *The Rise of Candidate-Centered Politics*. Cambridge, Mass.: Harvard University Press.

Weaver, David H., and G. Cleveland Wilhoit. 1986. *The American Journalist: A Portrait of U.S. News People and Their Work*. Bloomington: Indiana University Press.

Weaver, David H., Doris A. Graber, Maxwell Mccombs, and Chaim H. Eyal. 1981. *Media Agenda-Setting in a Presidential Election*. New York: Praeger.

Welch, Susan, and John Hibbing. 1997. "The Effects of Charges of Corruption on Voting Behavior in Congressional Elections: 1982–1990." *Journal of Politics*, 59: 226–239.

West, Darrell M. 1993. *Air Wars: Television Advertising in Election Campaigns, 1952–1992*. Washington, D.C.: Congressional Quarterly Press.

Westlye, Mark C. 1991. *Senate Elections and Campaign Intensity*. Baltimore: Johns Hopkins University Press.

Whitby, Kenny J., and Timothy Bledsoe. 1986. "The Impact of Policy Voting and the Electoral Fortunes of Senate Incumbents." *Western Political Quarterly*, 39: 690–700.

Winters, Matt. 1988. "Vinich Charges Wallop Lies about His Record, Running for 3rd Senate Term." *Casper Star-Tribune*, 1, 24.

Wright, Gerald C., Jr., and Mark B. Berkman. 1986. "Candidates and Policy in U.S. Senate Elections." *American Political Science Review*, 80: 567–590.

Wright, Gerald C., Robert S. Erikson, and John P. McIver. 1985. "Measuring State Partisanship and Ideology with Survey Data." *Journal of Politics*, 47: 479–489.

Wyer, Robert S., Jr. 1974. *Cognitive Organization and Change: An Information Processing Approach*. Hillsdale, N.J.: Lawrence Erlbaum Associates.

Zaller, John R. 1990. "Political Awareness, Elite Opinion Leadership, and the Mass Survey Response." *Social Cognition*, 8: 125–153.

Zaller, John R. 1992. *Nature and Origins of Mass Opinion*. Cambridge, U.K.: Cambridge University Press.

Zaller, John R. 1997. "The Political Economy of Election News: How the Interests of Politicians, Journalists, and Voters Shape Coverage of Presidential Campaigns." Paper presented at the Annual Meeting of the American Political Science Association, Washington, D.C.

Zaller, John R., and Stanley Feldman. 1992. "A Simple Theory of the Survey Response: Answering Questions versus Revealing Preferences." *American Journal of Political Science*, 36: 579–616.

Zhao, Xinshu, and Steven H. Chaffee. 1995. "Campaign Advertisements versus Television News as Sources of Political Issue Information." *Public Opinion Quarterly*, 59: 41–65.

Index